Romans

Romans

An Exposition of Chapters 3.20-4.25
Atonement and Justification

D. M. Lloyd-Jones

ZONDERVAN
PUBLISHING HOUSE
OF THE ZONDERVAN CORPORATION
GRAND RAPIDS, MICHIGAN 49506

ROMANS — ATONEMENT AND JUSTIFICATION
© D. M. Lloyd-Jones 1970

First published in the U.S.A. 1971
Second printing 1974
Third printing 1975
Fourth printing 1976

Set in 11 on 13 pt Monotype Garamond

Printed in the United States of America

To the faithful and enthusiastic Friday-nighters at
Westminster Chapel 1955-68

Contents

Contents

Contents

Preface

This is the first of what I hope will be several volumes of sermons on the greatest of the Pauline Epistles. They will consist of sermons preached regularly week by week at Westminster Chapel, London, on Friday evenings. These weekly meetings were held yearly from the beginning of October until the end of May, apart from brief breaks at Christmas and Easter. The Romans series, commencing at chapter 1, ran from October 1955 until March 1968, when we had reached chapter 14.17.

There are certain matters to which I should like to call attention and also explain.

This series of volumes begins in the third chapter at verse 20, and some may ask, Why start here and not at chapter 1? The answer is that I am anxious to proceed at once to what may be called the 'heart' of the Epistle. That does not mean that I regard the rest as being unimportant and that I may not publish my expositions of chapters 1.1 to 3.20 later. Indeed I have tried to show in chapter 1 of this book that the opening section of the Epistle to the Romans is essential to an understanding of the doctrine of justification by faith. But there is a sense in which the crucial matters – and also the difficulties – arise at the point where this volume begins. I have therefore summarized the argument of the first two and a half chapters at the beginning of this volume in order that we might move directly to a consideration of the great doctrines of justification by faith and the atonement.

The sermons in this volume, apart from the first, were delivered during the Friday nights of the period February to October, 1957.

[xi]

That leads me to say a word about the form. These are expository sermons which apart from minor corrections and adjustments were delivered as printed here. They are not lectures nor a running commentary on verses or passages. They are expositions which take the form of a sermon.

It has always been my view that this is how Scripture should be handled. Commentaries are of great value in arriving at an accurate understanding of the text, yet at their best they are only of value as scaffolding in the erection of a building. Moreover, it is vital that we should understand that an epistle such as this is only a summary of what the Apostle Paul preached. He explains that in chapter 1 verses 11–15. He wrote the Epistle because he was not able to visit them in Rome. Had he been with them he would not merely have given them what he says in this Letter, for this is but a synopsis. He would have preached an endless series of sermons as he did daily in the school of Tyrannus (Acts 19. 9) and probably have often gone on until midnight (Acts 20.7). The business of the preacher and teacher is to open out and expand what is given here by the Apostle in summary form.

Not only that, we must ever remember that the Truth of God while meant primarily for the mind is also meant to grip and to influence the entire personality. Truth must always be applied, and to handle a portion of Scripture as one might handle a play of Shakespeare in a purely intellectual and analytical manner is to abuse it. People have often complained that commentaries are 'as dry as dust'. There is surely something seriously wrong if that is the case. Any kind of exposition of 'the glorious gospel of the blessed God' should never produce such an impression. It is my opinion that we have had far too many brief commentaries on and studies in the Scriptures. The greatest need today is a return to expository preaching. That is what happened in the time of the Reformation and the Puritan Revival and the Evangelical Awakening of the 18th Century. It is only as we return to this that we shall be able to show people the grandeur, glory and majesty of the Scriptures and their message.

This of course will involve much repetition. The Apostle

himself, as I have emphasized in many of these sermons, repeated himself frequently; indeed he delighted in doing so. He was so moved by the various aspects of the Truth that he states them again and again. It follows therefore that there is something lacking in the condition of a Christian who says, 'Oh yes, I know that, I have come across that before', and who wants to pass on impatiently to something new. That was the mentality of the Athenians (Acts 17. 21), and, alas, there is much of that today.

I have tried to follow the apostolic method and manner, and nothing gave me greater joy and encouragement while delivering these sermons than the fact that from 1,000 to 1,200 people attended regularly to hear them though each one took some forty-five minutes in delivery.

My hope is that this volume and those that are to follow, God willing, will not only help Christian people to understand more clearly the great central doctrines of our Faith, but that they will also fill them with a joy 'unspeakable and full of glory' and bring them into a condition in which they will be 'Lost in wonder, love, and praise.'

That these sermons can now be printed is mainly due to the untiring and sacrificial labour of Mrs. E. Burney who throughout the years has transcribed from tape-recordings what I have delivered extemporaneously from notes. I avail myself of this opportunity of thanking her.

Mr. S. M. Houghton has saved me endless trouble in helping with the preparation of the MS for publication. My own work on the original typescripts was done mainly in Cincinnati, Ohio, USA during the summer of 1969 while my wife and I enjoyed the fellowship and the most generous hospitality of Mr. and Mrs. A. M. Kinney, who are so widely known throughout the USA for their zeal in God's work. As ever, the greatest help and encouragement has come from 'my best critic'.

July 1970   D. M. LLOYD-JONES

Romans

1 Laying the Foundation

*

Now we know that what things soever the law saith, it saith to them who are under the law: that every mouth may be stopped, and all the world may become guilty before God.
Therefore by the deeds of the law there shall no flesh be justified in his sight: for by the law is the knowledge of sin. Romans 3:19, 20

No book or section of Scripture has played a more important part in the history of the Church and some of its most notable leaders than Paul's Epistle to the Romans. It was through reading some verses at the end of its thirteenth chapter that the great Saint Augustine was converted. His majestic figure towers over the story of the Church from the fifth century onwards. It was through being enlightened as to the real meaning of the seventeenth verse of the first chapter, with its teaching on justification by faith only, that Martin Luther was delivered from his bondage and became the leader of the Protestant Reformation. The same doctrine, as expounded by Luther, led to the conversion of John Bunyan, the 'Immortal Tinker of Bedford', and so gave us *The Pilgrim's Progress* and *Grace Abounding*. Similarly it was as he listened to a man reading from the Preface of Luther's Commentary on this Epistle that John Wesley's heart was 'strangely warmed' on the evening of 24 May 1738. The same has been the testimony of countless other less well-known Christians. Surely no further reasons are necessary for a most careful study of the contents of this Epistle.

What is the theme of the *Epistle to the Romans*? It is made quite clear by the Apostle in verses 16 and 17 of the first chapter. It is the good news of God's way of salvation in the Lord Jesus Christ. That, of course, is the grand theme of the entire Bible,

[1]

but nowhere is it set forth more clearly, and argued out in a more masterly manner, than in this Epistle. Here we have the most extended treatment found in the entire range of Scripture of the crucial and vital doctrine of 'justification by faith'. That is the theme which we shall find the Apostle working out in detail in the section from chapter 3 verse 19 to chapter 5, verse 11.

What is the teaching? What does justification by faith mean? As we proceed with our detailed exposition the answer will become progressively clearer; but we must start with a brief definition. This is the doctrine which tells us that God has contrived a way whereby men and women can be saved and reconciled unto Himself. It is all of His doing. It tells us that God, on the basis of what He has done in His Son, our blessed Lord and Saviour, freely forgives, and absolves from all their sin, all who believe the Gospel. But it does not stop at that; they are furthermore 'clothed with the righteousness of Jesus Christ' and declared to be just and righteous in God's sight. It is not only negative, there is this positive aspect also. We are clothed with the righteousness of Christ which is 'imputed' to us, 'put to our account', and so we stand accepted in the sight of God. As Romans 5 verse 19 puts it, we are 'constituted' righteous people in the presence of this holy and righteous God.

Now that is the essence of the doctrine of justification by faith; and having stated it, let me show that it is derived solely from the Scriptures. Anyone therefore who does not agree with this doctrine, with this teaching, is disagreeing with the Scriptures. This is not a theory or an idea of men, it is not like any human philosophy; this is something which men have 'found' in the Scriptures. This is important for this reason, that there are doctrines taught by sections of the Christian Church – we will grant them the name for the time being – which cannot be found in the Scriptures. They say that they have derived them from tradition, from further revelations that have been given to them; but our position as Protestants is that we test every teaching and every doctrine by the Word. That is why it is essential that we should be doing so now.

But this of course immediately raises another point. If you do not like the doctrine of justification by faith only, and disagree with it, you are not disagreeing merely with the teaching of the Church, you are disagreeing with the Scriptures themselves. That is the position of all who reject this doctrine. There are many who do so; for instead of being guided by the Scripture and submitting themselves to it, they are governed by the teaching of philosophy, that is, by the thinking and the ideas of men. That is the position of the vast majority at the present time, even, unfortunately, within what is called the Christian Church. Their ultimate sanction is not the Scriptures, it is philosophy, it is men's ideas of God and of truth rather than that which has been revealed.

Let me deal also with another preliminary objection. There are people who have rejected this doctrine because they say that it is only the doctrine of Paul, Paul the typical Pharisee. This they say therefore is typical rabbinical teaching. There is not quite so much heard of this objection now as there was in the early part of this century when the popular idea was to contrast the teaching of 'the Jesus of history' with the teaching and the theology of the Apostle Paul. But there are many who unconsciously still subscribe to this point of view. They believe, they say, in the simple 'Gospel of Jesus', the Gospel of Love, and they think that it was a great calamity that this legalistic Jew, Paul – this man with an obviously legalistic mind – should have come along and foisted his legalistic ideas and opinions upon that delightfully simple Gospel. They say that Paul modified the essence of the Christian message and changed it into something different.

The simple answer to all that is that this message concerning justification is found from the beginning to the end of the Scriptures. The Apostle himself makes that perfectly plain in this very third chapter where he says in verse 21; 'But now the righteousness of God without the law is manifested, being witnessed by the law and the prophets.' In other words he claims that this was something which had been adumbrated, something that was to be found in suggestion and embryo, throughout the Old Testament. It is indeed the consistent message of the whole of the Bible, and those who are familiar with the Old

Testament will agree with Augustine when he said that, 'The New Testament is hidden in the Old, and the Old Testament is made open and explicit in the New', or 'The New Testament is latent in the Old, and the Old is patent in the New'. That is, of course, a simple statement of fact.

The same point is found in the teaching of our Lord Himself. Why had He come into the world? His own answer is: 'The Son of man is come to seek and to save that which was lost' [*Luke* 19: 10]. That is why He came. His teaching in the parable concerning the Pharisee and the publican who went up to the temple to pray [*Luke* 18: 9–14] deals with this very subject, as so many of His parables and so much of His teaching did. But it is especially clear when He comes to talk about His death: 'Even as the Son of man came not to be ministered unto, but to minister, and to give his life a ransom for many' [*Matthew* 20: 28].

The idea, therefore, that this doctrine is something peculiar to this rabbinical, this legalistic Jew, the Apostle Paul, is just an idle fancy; it does not stand up to the test of facts. You have the same teaching again in the Epistle to the Hebrews, you have it also in the First Epistle of John, and, indeed, in the Gospel of John in so many places, and in the Book of Revelation. It is a message that is common to the whole Bible. Although, for the reasons explained in the Introduction, we are not now going to consider in detail the great statement that begins in chapter 1 verse 16 and ends in chapter 3 verse 20, it is essential that we should grasp and understand its argument. In it the Apostle is preparing us for the 'But now' of verse 21 and the glorious things that follow.

Here then is a summary of the Apostle's argument. He starts with the bold and ringing asseveration, 'I am not ashamed of the gospel of Christ'. By that he means, of course, that he is very proud of it. He uses litotes, the figure of speech in which, in order to give emphasis to what you are saying, you put it negatively. It is a very good way of bringing out an emphasis. It is particularly an English way of doing so. 'I am not ashamed of the gospel of Christ.' What he means is, 'I glory in it', 'I exult in it', 'I thrill with pride whenever I think of it'. He is ready to go to Rome to preach to the Emperor or to the slaves – to anybody. 'I am a debtor both to the Greeks, and to the Barbarians; both to the wise and to the unwise' [1: 14]. Why does he feel thus? Because 'the gospel is the power of God unto salvation to every one that believeth; to the Jew first and also to the Greek. For therein is the righteousness of God revealed from faith to faith: as it is written, The just shall live by faith.'

That is the theme of this whole Epistle, but it is especially the theme of this section which expounds at length the doctrine of justification by faith only. He is proud of the Gospel – Why? Because 'it is the power of God'; it is certain, it cannot fail. It is not of man, it is of God.

I am always interested in the technique of the Apostle. I am fascinated by his method of approach. The construction of his Epistles is invariably fascinating. I never read these Epistles without thinking of a musical composition, for example, a great symphony. You generally have an introduction, an overture in which the 'leit motifs' are thrown out just in suggestion. Then the composer takes them up one by one, works out the first, then takes up the next and works it out, and so on; and then after he has worked them all out, he gathers them up into one almighty conclusion and climax.

Now that is what he does here. In these two verses he throws out this hint by telling us why he is so proud of the Gospel and why he is so ready to preach in Rome. It is because the Gospel is the power of God. He is not a philosopher who is anxious to come to Rome to put up yet another theory, or another blueprint for Utopia. His message is not from man, it is of God. And it is for all, and comprehensive – '. . . every one that believeth; to the Jew first, and also to the Greek' [1: 17]. But, still more, it is because this, and this alone, is the way of salvation, and it is a certain and sure way of salvation.

But that drives Paul at once to take up this question: Why is any such thing necessary at all? That is the question to ask. And he gives the answer in the eighteenth verse: 'Because the wrath of God is revealed from heaven against all ungodliness and unrighteousness of men, who hold the truth in unrighteousness.'

There we have the theme that he is going to work out from that point until the twentieth verse in the third chapter. There is a twofold problem in connection with the salvation of men, he says, and it is because this Gospel, and it alone, is the answer to the twofold problem that he is so proud of it and so thrilled by it. The first part is, 'the wrath of God against all ungodliness and unrighteousness of men'. The second is the actual ungodly and unrighteous condition of man.

I want to emphasize the order in which the Apostle puts these two things, for not only is this order not observed today, it is being violated and that deliberately. You notice that the Apostle puts 'ungodliness' first, and that in his thinking 'unrighteousness' only follows ungodliness. To him the big thing, the important thing, is 'ungodliness'.

This is particularly important today, for the modern approach in the Church, and obviously in the world, is to say that the real problem is that of unrighteouness and that alone. Ungodliness is not mentioned. The great problem, we are told, is the problem of man, and particularly the problem of man in society. We are told that the great need today is to reconcile man to man, and that this is the task of the Church. The world is torn and divided over race issues, colour issues, political issues; it is a world of various kinds of curtains – iron, bamboo and others – and the great need, we are told, is to reconcile man to man. That, they say, is the great task of the Church. That is where they begin, and that is where they end. Someone has summed it up by saying that man's great need is to find 'a gracious neighbour', that this is the task before us. And in addition to this, and to that end, we are told that what we need is to be cured of our ills and weaknesses. Sin is regarded as sickness, a disease, of which we need to be cured. But all the time, you notice, it is in terms of man, and man's relationship to man. It does not mention what the Apostle puts first – ungodliness, man in his relationship to God.

That is the essence of this modern attitude. I came across a notable example of it a year or two ago. A religious conference was being held in the City of Glasgow in Scotland; and as they will do, for some extraordinary reason, when they have a religious conference they invited the Lord Provost of the City to attend the inaugural meeting. You must always have these civic dignitaries present whether they are Christians or not! So this man, the Lord Provost of Glasgow, was asked to address the conference and in doing so he made a typical statement. He said: 'Now all you men are very learned theologians, I am not. I am just a plain man. I am a man of affairs and I do not understand your theology and all these things. Indeed I am not interested in your theology, and I believe you people are wasting a lot of your time over theology.' He went on, 'What I want to know is this, How can I love my neighbour? That is what we want to know from you. We are not interested in your great theology. I want to know, and the common man wants to know, How can I love my neighbour?' He thereby revealed his total ignorance of the whole doctrine of salvation as taught by our Lord Himself and by the Apostle as he puts it here. Man's first need is the need of knowing God, of discovering, as Luther put it, 'a gracious God', not a gracious neighbour.

This is man's primary need. 'Ungodliness' comes before 'unrighteousness', for unrighteousness is but a consequence of ungodliness. Failure to realize this is the whole tragedy of the modern world. The world is medicating symptoms and forgetting the disease. It is dealing with particular manifestations of the trouble instead of with the radical root trouble itself. That is why the world wastes so much time and so much energy. With all its political and social and educational activities it is not facing the real essential trouble. As our Lord Himself replied when asked by a lawyer which was the first commandment of all, 'Thou shalt love the Lord thy God with all thy heart, and with all thy soul, and with all thy mind, and with all thy strength; this is the first commandment.' 'And the second' (which the Lord Provost of Glasgow put first) is, 'Thou shalt love thy neighbour as thyself' [*Mark* 12: 28–31]. But no man will ever 'love his neighbour as himself' until he first loves God. He does not know the truth about himself. You cannot love your neighbour as yourself if you do not know the truth about yourself. For every reason,

[7]

therefore, the utter neglect by the world of the fact of 'ungodliness' results in a complete and utter fallacy.

We must start where the Apostle starts. What is the first great problem? It is the problem of 'the wrath of God'. That is the starting point. This cannot be stated too often. Evangelism does not start even with the Lord Jesus Christ; it starts with God. There is no meaning to evangelism apart from God, and the wrath of God. There is no sense or meaning in anything else. We must not invite people to 'come to Jesus' as a friend, or as a healer of the body, or as one who gives a bit of comfort, and so on. No, He is 'the Saviour'. He has 'come to seek and to save that which was lost'. But why do we need salvation? The answer is, because of 'the wrath of God upon all ungodliness and unrighteousness of men', and the Apostle tells us that it has been revealed already. It is in the light of that revealed fact that he rejoices in this Gospel which he has come to believe, and now has the privilege of declaring.

But this is a doctrine that is utterly abhorrent to the modern man. He heartily dislikes the whole notion of the wrath of God. Indeed he dislikes the whole notion of justice and righteousness. He does not like discipline, he does not like law, and that is why our world is as it is. This is, I say again, the tragedy of modern man. He has departed from these basic principles and so is confused; and he objects to the one thing that can put him right.

He objects to the idea of justice, and righteousness, and retribution; and then he is surprised that there is lawlessness in his own home, and in the schools and colleges and universities, and on the streets and in the different strata of society. It is entirely due to the fact that he has abandoned the whole notion of law, and that he hates it and detests it. But our business is to preach this; and it is an essential part of our message.

Of course we do not mean by 'the wrath of God' capriciousness or some uncontrolled emotion, or arbitrary anger, and loss of self-control. What it means is God's utter detestation of sin and evil.

This is something that is revealed everywhere in Scripture.

What is the meaning of the Ten Commandments if it is not this? They are a revelation of the holy character of God. God says to His people 'Be ye holy; for I am holy'. The reason for being holy is not that sin does us harm, or that sin is wrong in and of itself; it is because it is offensive to God, and an offence against God; and because He hates it. God cannot but hate sin. God would not be God if He did not hate sin. 'He is of such a pure countenance', says Habakkuk, 'that he cannot even look upon sin.' 'God is light, and in him is no darkness at all.' God is holy and so are all the attributes of God.

Is not this precisely the point at which the Church has gone astray – even at times the evangelical section of the Church? God is forgotten. That is the tragedy of the situation. They pray to 'Jesus'; they start with 'Jesus', they end with 'Jesus'. They never mention God the Father, the holy God with whom we are concerned, God in His utter righteousness and absolute holiness, the God who revealed Himself and His holy character to the Children of Israel. That is the great message that runs through the whole of the Old Testament.

You find the same emphasis in the teaching of our blessed Lord Himself. He taught men to pray. They asked Him, 'Lord, teach us to pray as John (the Baptist) also taught his disciples?' Very well, He said, I will teach you how to pray. When you pray say, 'Our Father'. Then, lest somebody might begin referring to God as 'Dad' or 'Dear Dad', He says, 'Our Father which art in heaven'. He is utterly different from every father we have ever known: 'which art in heaven'. The easy familiarity with God that seems to be creeping in is foreign to our Lord's own teaching. God is altogether Other. He is to be addressed as 'Our Father which art in heaven, Hallowed be Thy Name'. That is how He taught men to pray. And when He Himself engaged in prayer – He, the eternal Son of God – His way of addressing God is: 'Holy Father'. This, then, is the teaching of the Lord Jesus Christ, who is the love of God incarnate, the very expression of the love of God. He addressed God in that way and in that manner.

Now the Apostle's whole case is this. He is proud of this Gospel that he preached, because it, and it alone, can deal with this question of the wrath of God 'against all ungodliness and unrighteousness of men'. If it cannot do this it is no Gospel and there is no message of good news. This is its primary objective and purpose; not primarily to do something to us subjectively, but to put us into the right relationship with God.

Paul goes on to say that this wrath of God has been 'revealed against all ungodliness and unrighteousness of men'. Where has it been revealed? In the Old Testament. The Old Testament is full of it. It was revealed in the Garden of Eden. Here is man created perfect, given a helpmeet equally perfect; and here they are, enjoying a life of communion with God. Man is the acme, the highest point of God's perfect creation, and He puts the man and the woman in Paradise. But they disobeyed Him, rebelled against Him, and listened to the Tempter. Then God came down and spoke to them in His wrath against sin, and turned them out of the Garden and told them of the consequences that they were going to reap.

That is the most amazing demonstration of the wrath of God that has ever been known. It begins there, and from there it goes on. Read the Old Testament; look at those men who appear to be 'favourites', as it were, with God and observe how, when they sinned, God punished them. Look at a man like Moses. What a wonderful man God made of Moses. Yet because of Moses' disobedience he was never allowed to enter into the land of promise. That is a manifestation of the wrath of God.

God's wrath has been 'revealed'. He has said that 'The soul that sinneth it shall die'. He has made it perfectly plain and explicit. We are without any excuse whatsoever. There is no excuse for ignorance. God has said that if man sins he must bear the consequences, and he must be punished.

We must get this clear, and especially at the present time, because such a scholar as Professor C. H. Dodd in his Commentary on the Epistle to the Romans denies this altogether. He does not believe in the wrath of God against sin. He teaches that what this really means is that sin always brings its own punishment. If you put your finger into the fire you will have pain, you will burn yourself. He does not believe that God, in addition to the immediate consequences, metes out punishment in a 'wrath to come'. But God says that He is going to do so, and in some cases He has done so already. That is the wrath of God, and it has been manifested.

But then the Apostle in this section of his Epistle gives us a particular statement of the way in which the wrath of God has been revealed. It starts at verse 24 in the first chapter: 'Wherefore God also gave them up to uncleanness through the lusts of their own hearts, to dishonour their own bodies between themselves: who changed the truth of God into a lie, and worshipped and served the creature more than the Creator, who is blessed for ever. Amen. For this cause God gave them up unto vile affections: for even their women did change the natural use into that which is against nature: And likewise the men, leaving the natural use of the woman, burned in their lust one toward another; men with men working that which is unseemly, and receiving in themselves that recompence of their error which was meet. And even as they did not like to retain God in their knowledge, God gave them over to a reprobate mind, to do those things which are not convenient.' Then comes that terrible list of the sins they were committing. But we must be careful to note what exactly the Apostle is saying. 'That', he says, 'is a manifestation, a revelation, of the wrath of God against all ungodliness and unrighteousness of men.'

Is this only ancient history? No, it is modern history as well. Here is the sole explanation of your modern world. Had you realized that? People often ask us as Christians, 'How do you explain the twentieth century with its two terrible world wars? What about all the immorality and vice and a-morality that is so rampant today? What about the sex perversions, and the horrors that are being committed?' The explanation of this twentieth century and of life today is that it is but another instance of God giving mankind over to a reprobate mind. This is how God acts, and the Apostle says that it had been happening in history, it had happened before his time. Take a true view of history, he says, and this is what you find. When people refuse to listen to God and reject His laws and say that they can manage life without Him,

[11]

God first appeals to them. God sends His messengers to them to try to restrain them; but if they persist in their evil ways, and in their rebellion, a time comes, says the Apostle, when He just lets them go, He 'hands them over' as it were to themselves. 'Very well,' He says in effect, 'if you think and say that you can live without Me, do so, and see what you will make of it.'

That is what is happening today. The explanation of the moral condition of the world is simply this. For a hundred years and more mankind in its cleverness and sophistication has been turning its back upon God, it has been guilty of 'ungodliness'. Even those who say they believe in God do not believe in the God of the Scriptures who has revealed Himself. They have constructed a god of their own that suits their own little ideas. They are primarily guilty of ungodliness, and the unrighteousness has followed. God has abandoned them to it. It is the sole explanation of the state of the world today. This is a manifestation of the wrath of God. He has taken His restraints away, He has handed them over.

The biblical teaching is that when man fell into sin God put certain bounds upon it, He restrained it. If God had not restrained sin by means of governments and other institutions the world would have festered to nothing long ago. But God has put His restraints upon sin, He keeps it within bounds. But, periodically, says Paul, to manifest His wrath against it all, His hatred and detestation of it all, He withdraws His restraints and man is abandoned to his own devices. Then you have man without God, and you see the result.

Now this is the Apostle's way of introducing this doctrine of justification by faith only. God hands man over to this 'reprobate mind' in order that he may hit his head against the wall, as it were, and smash himself and realize his folly, and so be humbled. That is the Apostle's great argument. This is what we may call the condition of man.

I have already emphasized, and I do so again, the order of these two things – 'ungodliness' comes before 'unrighteousness'. Let us never forget this. As the Shorter Catechism in its first question and answer puts it: 'What is the chief end of man?'

'Man's chief end is to glorify God, and to enjoy Him for ever.'

Man then has turned his back upon God; as the Apostle says here, he prefers the creature to the Creator. He puts man before God. That is what men are doing now. They are worshipping science and technology, the creation of man the creature, 'more than the Creator, who is blessed for ever'. So they have been handed over to a reprobate mind. These are but symptoms of that original disease which is still continuing.

Paul then works this out in detail. He tells us all about the Gentiles and their failure, and the deplorable depths to which they had sunk. And the ultimate condemnation of these Gentiles is made clear. Certainly, they were not all guilty of all those sins; there were good men among them. Certain Greek philosophers were trying to improve matters, to uplift humanity with their teaching. So someone may say, 'Surely the wrath of God is not against that?' The answer is that the wrath of God is against it, unless its aim is to bring man back into the position of submission and obedience to God.

In other words, as Paul puts it in the fourth verse of the second chapter: 'Despisest thou the riches of his goodness and forbearance and long-suffering; not knowing that the goodness of God leadeth thee to repentance?' So it does not matter how moral a man may be, or how idealistic he may be, or how philanthropic he may be; if he has not repented in the sense of turning back to God and acknowledging his rebellion and his sin and his folly, it is all useless, it does not count at all. He is abusing God's goodness and kindness, turning it to his own end instead of allowing it to lead him to see the goodness of God. We must not stay with these detailed arguments, but even in the first chapter the Apostle has said that the very marks of God in Nature should have brought man back to God. God has left His marks, His imprint there. 'The invisible things of him from the creation of the world are clearly seen, being understood by the things that are made, even his eternal power and Godhead; so that they are without excuse.' So whatever man may discover, however much he may advance, however much he may introduce social amelioration and mitigate injustices and wrongs, all is of no value in the sight of God unless it has brought man to repentance and an acknowledgement of his folly in turning away from God.

Having dealt in that way with the Gentiles, Paul turns to the Jews. This is the main theme of the second chapter; because, after all, the Jew was in a special position. The Jew knew this; his tragedy was that he relied upon it. The Jew felt that all was well with him because he had the Law in this explicit external form, as given by God to Moses, through the disposition of angels. Then, over and above that, he had the sign of circumcision. The whole trouble with the Jews was that they thought that these things put them right with God. So the Apostle has to take this up and to show them that the mere possession of the Law does not put them right at all. But that was the whole tragedy of the Jews. They thought that because they had been circumcised they were of necessity the children of God and had nothing to worry about. Paul shows them in chapter 2 verse 25 the folly of that position, 'For circumcision verily profiteth, if thou keep the law: but if thou be a breaker of the law, thy circumcision is made uncircumcision. Therefore if the uncircumcision keep the righteousness of the law, shall not his uncircumcision be counted for circumcision?' In other words, circumcision is not the main thing; it is the keeping of the Law that is the main thing. 'And shall not uncircumcision which is by nature, if it fulfil the law, judge thee, who by the letter and circumcision dost transgress the law?' And then, explicitly, 'For he is not a Jew, which is one outwardly; neither is that circumcision, which is outward in the flesh.' This is one of Paul's leading ideas. He continues, 'But he is a Jew, which is one inwardly; and circumcision is that of the heart, in the spirit, and not in the letter; whose praise is not of men, but of God.'

In that way Paul has demolished the whole case of the Jew who relied on his circumcision. At the same time he has demolished the position of all who think that, because they were born in Great Britain or in America, they are Christians, whereas if they had been born in countries such as Japan or India they would be pagan. All that is demolished in terms of the argument about circumcision. The same applies to the case of the man who

Romans 3 : 19, 20

says, 'My parents were Christians, therefore I am a Christian'. All such reliance upon nationality or some human association is entirely excluded by this argument about circumcision.

But what about the Law? He takes this up also. The crucial statement is in the thirteenth verse of the second chapter: 'For not the hearers of the law are just before God, but the doers of the law shall be justified.'

Paul comes back to this again in the tenth chapter, verse 5. He says, 'For Moses describeth the righteousness which is of the law' like this, 'That the man which doeth those things shall live by them'. That means that when the Law was given through Moses God said, 'If you can keep this it will save you; the man who does these things shall live by them'. So it is not a question merely of possessing the Law, or of hearing the Law, or of being acquainted with the Law. The Jew was hiding behind that façade. He said: 'Of course, those Gentiles know nothing about the Law, the Law was not given to them; they are lawless, they are dogs, they are without God, outside the Covenants, they are nobody, they are hopeless; but we, we have the Law, we are familiar with the Law.' This was, in their thinking, the thing that saved them. The Apostle proves to them here that it does not. 'Behold, thou art called a Jew', he says in the seventeenth verse, 'and restest in the law, and makest thy boast of God, and knowest his will, and approvest the things that are more excellent, being instructed out of the law; and art confident that thou thyself art a guide of the blind, a light of them which are in darkness, an instructor of the foolish, a teacher of babes, which hast the form of knowledge and of the truth in the law.'

That was how the Jews thought of themselves. That is also the position of all men today who rely on their own morality and are not Christians: that is precisely what they say for themselves. They see no need of Christ and His blood; they object to that and ridicule it. Why? Because they say, we are doing all the good we can and trying to get others to do the same. These are good people, these are noble people, these are teachers of others. But listen to the Apostle's questions. 'Thou therefore which teachest another, teachest thou not thyself? thou that preachest a man should not steal, dost thou steal? Thou that sayest a man should not commit adultery, dost thou commit adultery? thou that abhorrest idols, dost thou commit sacrilege? Thou that makest thy boast of the law, through breaking the law dishonourest thou God? For the name of God is blasphemed among the Gentiles through you, as it is written' – and so on.

What does all that mean? Let me summarize it in this way. What was the trouble with the Jews, and particularly with their leaders, their religious leaders, the Pharisees? They thought, as the Apostle himself thought before his conversion, that they were experts in the Law; and yet their real trouble was that they were ignorant of the Law. In what respects? Here are some of them. They thought that the mere possession of the Law saved them; but it does not. You may know the Law of your State or district, but if you break it, the fact that you know it will not help you in the Court. They were relying on their possession of the Law and their knowledge of it. They did not realize that the Law has to be carried out and to be put into practice.

Secondly, they were under the impression that as long as they kept the majority of the laws, the main part of the Law, all was well with them. James puts them right at this point in the words, 'Whosoever shall keep the whole law, and yet offend in one point, he is guilty of all' [*James* 2: 10]. It is no use saying that you have kept ninety-nine per cent of it; if you have failed in one per cent you have broken the whole Law, and you are a transgressor of the Law. They were not aware of that.

But still more serious, they were experts only, and correct only, in regard to the letter of the Law, not the spirit. This, of course, is the point that our Lord brings out so clearly in the Sermon on the Mount. The proud Pharisee would stand up and say, 'I have never been guilty of murder'. 'Wait a minute,' says our Lord – and this is the real exposition of those questions put by Paul in Romans 2 – 'You say that you have never committed murder, but I say unto you, That whosoever is angry with his brother without a cause shall be in danger of the judgment: and whosoever shall say to his brother, "Raca" shall be in danger of the council: but whosoever shall say, Thou fool, shall be in danger of hell fire.' If you call your brother a fool, you have murdered him in your heart, you are guilty of murder in the sight of the Law.

He says the same thing with regard to adultery. Many of these people were claiming that they were innocent of these particular charges. But our Lord puts the same searchlight on to this again and says, 'Ye have heard that it was said by them of old time, Thou shalt not commit adultery'. The Pharisee said 'I have never committed adultery' because he was only thinking of the letter and the external act. 'But I say unto you', says our Lord, 'that whosoever looketh on a woman to lust after her hath committed adultery already in his heart.' 'Yes', says Paul, 'thou that teachest another, teachest thou not thyself? thou that sayest a man should not commit adultery, dost thou commit adultery?' It is the difference between the letter and the spirit; and if you are guilty of the offence in the spirit you are guilty of adultery in the sight of God. The Pharisee had not realized this; this was the whole trouble with the Jews as Paul shows them here.

Then another most important point which he brings out later is this – the terrible business of 'coveting'. This is dealt with at length as we shall find in chapter 7. What was the trouble? Neither Paul nor the Pharisees had ever realized the meaning of coveting. 'I had not known lust except the law had said, Thou shalt not covet.' The tragedy of the Jew was that he thought that as long as he had not committed the deed he was innocent. But as the Lord had shown, and as Paul had come to see, in this realm to covet is as reprehensible as to commit, and a desire is as damnable as a deed. The Jew had never realized the real meaning of the Law; and that is why he thought that he was justified before God because he was a possessor of the Law.

Then at the beginning of chapter 3 Paul imagines someone saying, 'Are you telling us then that there is no advantage whatsoever in being a Jew, and that there is no profit in circumcision?' 'Oh no,' says Paul, 'I am saying nothing of the sort. "Much every way; because that unto them (the Jews) were committed the oracles of God" '. The Jew has been put in a special position, and he should have profited from that fact; he, in contradistinction to the Gentiles, had been given this explicit statement of the Law. He has already said in the fourteenth verse of the second chapter: 'For when the Gentiles, which have not the law, do by nature the things contained in the law, these, having not the law, are a law unto themselves: which shew the work of the law written in their hearts, their conscience also bearing witness, and their thoughts the meanwhile accusing or else excusing one another.' The Gentiles had not recieved the explicit statement of the Law, but it was in their hearts as men.

In other words the position is this: the whole of mankind is aware of the Law of God; it is in the heart of the whole of the human race. The advantage the Jews had is that God had given it to them externally, over and above this, explicitly, had given it to them in this written form. That was a great advantage. But had this advantage helped them? The remainder of the third chapter up to verse 20 is to prove that because of their innate depravity it had not helped them at all.

So we come to the tremendous conclusion and summary in verses 19 and 20 of this third chapter, and to the essential introduction to the doctrine of justification by faith. In this context these are incomparably the most important verses of all. 'Now we know that what things soever the law saith, it saith to them who are under the law: that every mouth may be stopped, and the whole world become guilty before God. Therefore by the deeds of the law there shall no flesh be justified in his sight: for by the law is the knowledge of sin.'

What does that mean? It is the great summary of the whole argument; Paul is winding up what he started saying in chapter 1. 16. He is proud of the Gospel. Why? 'Because it is the power of God unto salvation to every one that believeth; to the Jew first, and also to the Greek.' He started by saying that it is all-inclusive, and he winds up on the same point – 'the whole world'. He has been showing that the whole world is under this Law of God. There is just that difference between the Gentile and the Jew, that it was only in the heart of the former but had been stated explicitly to the latter. In many respects this is a great and an important difference, but it does not make any ultimate differ-

ence at all. The Jews thought that they understood it all and
boasted of their knowledge. But Paul now points out to them
that when you realize what the Law is truly saying to you the
result is that 'every mouth shall be stopped'. You are rendered
speechless. You are not a Christian unless you have been made
speechless! How do you know whether you are a Christian or
not? It is that you 'stop talking'. The trouble with the non-
Christian is that he goes on talking. He says 'I do not see this, I
do not see that. After all I am doing this and I am doing that.' He
is still talking.

How do you know whether a man is a Christian? The answer
is that his mouth is 'shut'. I like this forthrightness of the Gospel.
People need to have their mouths shut, 'stopped'. They are for
ever talking about God, and criticizing God, and pontificating
about what God should or should not do, and asking 'Why does
God allow this and that?' You do not begin to be a Christian
until your mouth is shut, is stopped, and you are speechless
and have nothing to say. You put up your arguments, and produce all your righteousness; then the Law speaks and it all withers
to nothing – becomes 'filthy rags' and 'dung', and you have nothing to say. That is what the Law does: That 'every mouth may be
stopped and all the world become guilty before God.' Paul
repeats this later on. He says, 'All have sinned' – without a single
exception – 'and come short of the glory of God'. Your self-
righteous Pharisee, your modern moral man who does not see
the need of the Atonement steps forward and tells us what he
has done and what he has not done; but the Law puts this question to him: Have you arrived at the glory of God? He has not;
no one has. 'All have sinned and come short of the glory of God.'
'The whole world lieth guilty before God.' You must estimate
these things, not primarily in terms of actions, but in terms of
your total attitude to God, and your relationship to God, and
your position under the wrath of God.

In other words this is the conclusion. The whole trouble
arises because of the mistake with regard to the function and
purpose of the Law. Why did God ever give this Law? I mean
the law that is written in our hearts, and the explicit Law given

through Moses. The first answer to that question is that the Law was never given in order to save us. That was the fallacious supposition of the Jew, as it is also the case with so many today. People think that God gave the Law to the people and said: 'Now all you have got to do is to keep the Law and you will be saved in my sight.' The Law was not given for that reason, because man in sin could not possibly keep it. The Apostle tells us why he could not in the third verse of chapter 8: 'For what the law could not do, in that it was weak through the flesh, God sending his own Son in the likeness of sinful flesh, and for sin, condemned sin in the flesh.' There is the perfect statement of the doctrine. God knew that the Law could not save us, because of the weakness of our flesh. He never gave it in order to save.

Another fallacy, and a popular one in evangelical circles, is that God, first of all, in this matter of salvation, tried the Law, and finding that the Law did not work, He then had an afterthought and introduced the whole notion of the Cross. The Cross as an afterthought! What an un-biblical conception! It is characteristic of the type of teaching that divides up the Bible into numerous sections or dispensations and fails to see the essential unity of all its parts.

No, the Apostle tells us here once and for ever why the Law was given. Here it is: 'Therefore by the deeds of the law there shall no flesh be justified in his sight: for by the law is the knowledge of sin.' That is why the Law was given through Moses, to give to us 'the knowledge of sin'. Not to deliver us from sin, but to give us the knowledge of its terrible character.

The Apostle comes back to this in many places. One of the clearest statements is in chapter 5, verse 20: 'Moreover the law entered' – 'came in by the side' as it were. That is the very phrase he uses. Why did it come in? 'That the offence might abound.' The Law did not come in to deal with the offence, but to make it 'abound'. But he adds, Thank God that 'where sin abounded grace did much more abound'. Or again you get it in chapter 7, verse 7 and following. 'What shall we say then? Is the law sin?' He has been saying in verse 5 that the main effect of the Law was to make him sin all the more, 'When we were in the flesh, the motions of sin, which were by the law' – which means 'which were energized by the law' – 'did work in our members to bring forth fruit unto death'. Paul says we are in such a terrible state, that the very Law that has been given to us to warn us against sin makes us sin all the more. So he says in verse 7: 'Is the law sin? God forbid. I had not known sin but by the law, for I had not known lust except the law had said, Thou shalt not covet.' That is the function of the Law. 'But sin, taking occasion by the commandment, wrought in me all manner of concupiscence. For without the law sin was dead. For I was alive without the law once: but when the commandment came, sin revived, and I died' – and so on. In other words, the whole function of the Law is to define sin, to reveal its nature; and that is why we are without any excuse at all. The law is in our hearts; but that is not clear enough, so God made it explicit. He has defined it, He has underlined it, He has shown it plainly in the written Law given to the Jews.

But there is yet another function of the Law. This is one of the greatest statements of all – verse 13 in chapter 7: 'Was then that which is good made death unto me? God forbid. But sin, that it might appear sin, working death in me by that which is good; that sin by the commandment might become exceeding sinful.' That is what the Law has done. The Law was given to pinpoint sin, to define it, to bring it out of its hiding-place and to show its exceeding sinful character. Sin in man is as deep as this, that the very Law of God which should have helped him makes him worse, drives him into sin, turns it into a means of death. Nothing so shows the exceeding sinfulness of sin as the Law itself does; and once a man has seen the real meaning of the Law he sees the foulness, the vileness of his own nature. He sees that he has 'an evil heart of unbelief', a heart that covets, a heart that is vile and foul – 'Vile and full of sin I am'. Nothing brings a man to see that but the Law.

So that, finally, we can put it like this. The Law was never given to save man, but it was given as a 'school-master' to bring him to the Saviour. The whole object and purpose of the Law is to show man that he can never save himself. Once he has understood the Law and its spiritual meaning and content he knows that he cannot keep it. He is undone. Our Lord has shown us that the teaching of the Law is not just that you must not drink or that you must not smoke or that you must not commit adultery or this or that. What is the summary of the Law? It is: 'Thou shalt love the Lord thy God with all thy heart, and all thy soul, and all thy mind, and all thy strength; and thou shalt love thy neighbour as thyself.' Has anyone done that and so kept the Law? No, 'All have sinned and come short of the glory of God'. That is what the Law says. It shows us our utter helplessness and hopelessness, and thereby it becomes 'our schoolmaster to lead us to Christ', the only One Who by the grace of God can save us, and deliver us, and reconcile us to God, and make us safe for all eternity. Paul glories in the Gospel which proclaims that 'the just shall live by faith', because 'by the deeds of the law shall no flesh be justified in his sight, because by the law is the knowledge of sin'.

2 The Great Turning Point – "But Now"

*

But now the righteousness of God without the law is manifested, being witnessed by the law and the prophets;
Even the righteousness of God which is by faith of Jesus Christ unto all and upon all them that believe: for there is no difference:
For all have sinned, and come short of the glory of God;
Being justified freely by his grace through the redemption that is in Christ Jesus:
Whom God hath set forth to be a propitiation through faith in his blood, to declare his righteousness for the remission of sins that are past, through the forbearance of God;
To declare, I say, at this time his righteousness: that he might be just, and the justifier of him which believeth in Jesus.
Where is boasting then? It is excluded. By what law? of works? Nay: but by the law of faith.
Therefore we conclude that a man is justified by faith without the deeds of the law.
Is he the God of the Jews only? is He not also of the Gentiles? Yes, of the Gentiles also:
Seeing it is one God, which shall justify the circumcision by faith, and uncircumcision through faith.
Do we then make void the law through faith? God forbid: yea, we establish the law.   Romans 3:21–31

We turn now to look at this most important section of the third chapter of this Epistle which begins at verse 21 and goes on to the end of the chapter. It starts with the words: 'But now the righteousness of God without the law is manifested, being witnessed by the law and the prophets; even the righteousness of God which is by faith of Jesus Christ unto all and upon all them that believe: for there is no difference; for all have sinned and come short of the glory of God.'

The Great Turning Point

This marks the beginning of a new section of this great Epistle and a new section in the third chapter. This chapter can obviously be divided conveniently into three sections. The first section runs from the first verse to the end of the eighth verse; then there follows the section of quotations beginning at verse 9 and going on to the end of verse 20; and then we come to the third section which begins at verse 21. This twenty-first verse is the start of a new section in two senses. One is that it is a new section of the third chapter: but still more important, and indeed altogether more important, it is the beginning of one of the major sections of the whole Epistle.

Verse 20 ended a section which began right away back in the first chapter – in the eighteenth verse of the first chapter, or indeed you can almost say the sixteenth verse of the first chapter. But perhaps it is wiser to regard verses 16 and 17 in the first chapter as a statement of the Gospel, and the reason why the Apostle was so glad and proud of it and glad to preach it. Then, starting at verse 18 in that first chapter is this tremendous statement about the wrath of God which has been revealed against all ungodliness and unrighteousness of men. Then the Apostle goes on in the remainder of that chapter, and in chapter 2 and the early part of chapter 3, to prove that this is as applicable to the Jews as it is to the Gentiles. He has worked that out in detail, considering all opposing arguments, and he ends at verse 20 in the third chapter by saying: 'Therefore by the deeds of the law shall no flesh be justified in his sight; for by the law is the knowledge of sin.' He has established beyond any question or doubt or cavil that no man ever has been or ever will be able to justify himself in the presence of God. No man ever has provided or ever will provide a righteousness that will satisfy God and the demands of His most holy Law. That is clear, that is definite; he has proved it from every conceivable angle.

Having established that, he now goes on to show that there is only one way of salvation. But thank God there is one. As we are left at the end of the twentieth verse in this third chapter we see ourselves in a completely hopeless position. That we should so see ourselves is always vital and essential. No man can be a

Christian without realizing his utter hopelessness. It is of no use to talk about 'coming to Christ' if you do not see your hopelessness and your helplessness. You cannot just come to Him for help or something else; there is but one reason for going to Christ, and that is that you realize that no flesh can possibly be justified by the Law in the sight of God. 'Every mouth has been stopped and the whole world lieth guilty before God.'

Having come to that point the question we obviously ask is, 'Well, is there no hope for us? Can nothing be done for us? Are we irretrievably doomed?' The Apostle now goes on to answer that question. He does so, you notice, in two words, two little words – 'But now'. There are no more wonderful words in the whole of the Scripture than just these two words 'But now'. What vital words these are! These are the words with which the Apostle always introduces the Gospel. He first paints his dark and hopeless picture – and this is not only true of this Apostle but also of the others; but it is especially true of the Apostle Paul and of his particular style. He first of all paints his black and his sombre and his hopeless picture. Then, having done that he says, 'But now'.

It was because they had understood this teaching and manner that the Puritans, and many of their successors until comparatively recently, always taught that in true evangelism you must always start with a 'law work'. They said that there should always be a law work before you introduce the Gospel. Read the lives of some of the greatest evangelists that the world has ever known and you will find they all did that; not only the Puritans but the men of the eighteenth century who leaned so much upon the Puritans, and who were so familiar with their work. They always began with conviction of sin. This is as true of John Wesley as it is of George Whitefield; it is true of Jonathan Edwards, it is true also of Robert Murray McCheyne and other nineteenth-century men. These men always said that you must start with law work.

Until this point the Apostle has been doing precisely that, and it is only after he has done that that he says, 'But now'. Having followed him through all that in detail, and having considered every statement that he makes about man under sin and in sin, and having seen ourselves as we are by nature and as descendants of Adam, can there be two words which are more blessed and more wonderful for us than just these two words, 'But now'? To me they provide a very subtle and thorough-going test of our whole position as Christians. Would you like to know for certain at this moment whether you are a Christian or not? I suggest that this is one of the best tests. As I repeat these two words, 'But now', is there something within you that makes you say, 'Thank God!' Is there a 'But now' in your experience? All this is brought out strikingly in Matson's well-known hymn:

> *Lord, I was blind: I could not see*
> *In Thy marred visage any grace;*
> *But now the beauty of Thy face*
> *In radiant vision dawns on me.*

> *Lord, I was deaf: I could not hear*
> *The thrilling music of Thy voice;*
> *But now I hear Thee and rejoice,*
> *And all Thine uttered words are dear.*

> *Lord, I was dumb: I could not speak*
> *The grace and glory of Thy name;*
> *But now, as touched with living flame,*
> *My lips Thine eager praises wake.*

> *Lord, I was dead: I could not stir*
> *My lifeless soul to come to Thee;*
> *But now, since Thou hast quickened me,*
> *I rise from sin's dark sepulchre.*

> *Lord, Thou hast made the blind to see,*
> *The deaf to hear, the dumb to speak,*
> *The dead to live; and lo, I break*
> *The chains of my captivity.*

because it keeps on bringing in that point – did you notice it? Notice that in the third line of all the verses except the last you have this 'But now'. He keeps on saying it. He 'could not stir his lifeless soul to come . . .' 'But now . . .' Everything is changed – why? Well, because the Gospel has come to him. He was 'dead', he was 'blind', he was 'dumb', BUT NOW he is no longer like that.

These words come to us in a two fold manner. They come as the introduction of the Gospel, but at the same time they come as words that test us. This, to me, is so important that I cannot leave it. Let us examine our experiences.

When the devil attacks you and suggests to you that you are not a Christian, and that you have never been a Christian because of what is still in your heart, or because of what you are still doing, or because of something you once did – when he comes and thus accuses you, what do you say to him? Do you agree with him? Or do you say to him: 'Yes, that was true, but now . . .' Do you hold up these words against him? Or when, perhaps, you feel condemned as you read the Scripture, as you read the Law in the Old Testament, as you read the Sermon on the Mount, and as you feel that you are undone, do you remain lying on the ground in hopelessness, or do you lift up your head and say, 'But now'? This is the essence of the Christian position; this is how faith answers the accusations of the Law, the accusations of conscience, and everything else that would condemn and depress us. These are indeed very wonderful words, and it is most important that we should lay hold of them and realize their tremendous importance and their real significance.

There is an aspect of faith of which it is true to say this, that faith is a kind of protest. All things seem to be against us. Very well, are you a man of faith, or not? That is the vital question, and your answer to it proclaims what you are. Having listened to all that can be said against you, and in the most grievous circumstances, do you then say, 'But now'? That is a part of the fight of faith. Do not imagine that as a Christian you are going to be immune to the assaults of Satan or to attacks of doubt. They will certainly come. But the whole secret of faith is the ability to stand up with these two words against it all – 'we walk by faith and not by sight'. There is a sense in which what Brown-

[27]

ing said about faith is true. It is not the whole statement about
faith, but there is this aspect to it. 'With me', he said, 'faith
means perpetual unbelief kept quiet, like the snake 'neath
Michael's foot.' He paints the picture of Michael standing there
with his foot on the head of a snake. The snake is wriggling and
is trying to get at him in order to bite him; but as long as Michael
keeps his pressure firm upon the neck of the snake it cannot
harm him. On top of all the wriggling of doubt and unbelief
and denial, and all these accusations, faith keeps its foot firmly
down and says, 'But now'.

I am putting in that way the kind of thing that Martin Luther
never stopped saying from the moment he really saw this truth of
'justification by faith only'. That is really a kind of synopsis of
the whole of his great preaching and teaching. That is exactly
what faith does; it is this protest, it is this standing up in spite
of everything that may be said against us on earth or in hell.
We say, 'No, no one can finally convict me because of my new
position in Christ Jesus. "But now" I am no longer in condemnation; I was once there but I am no longer there.'

I leave this by asking a question just once more. Do you see
that you stand by faith? It would be useless for us to go on if
you are still holding on to any sort of idea that you can ever
make yourself a Christian, that by living a better life, or by
doing this or that or the other, you are going to improve your
position in the sight of God. Has it become clear that it does not
matter if you were to live to be as old as Methuselah, or even a
million years, you would never put yourself right before God?
Time will not help you, nothing can help you. We are all of us
under condemnation, we are all under the wrath of God. We
can never produce a righteousness that can stand up to God's
searching glance and examination and investigation. We are
altogether hopeless. Are you clear about that? If you are, you
are ready to rejoice in these two words, 'But now'.

What then is their meaning and import? They do two main
things. First and foremost they provide us with a contrast to
all that the Apostle has been saying before, a contrast to all the
old Law position, to our being under the Law in any shape or

form. But in addition to that, of course, the 'but now' brings in the time factor. What he is really saying is this: 'But now the righteousness of God without the law is manifested' – it has only just been manifested. Paul was preaching and writing within a comparatively short time after all the events associated with the Name of the Lord Jesus Christ had taken place – His incarnation, His life, His death, His resurrection, everything. What he is saying is, 'NOW' this thing that has happened has changed everything. And he goes on to tell them about it. Something had happened, he reminds these Romans, which is absolutely new, and which is the most amazing good news that has ever come to a sinful race of men. That is why back in the first chapter, he said: 'I am not ashamed of the Gospel of Christ, for it is the power of God unto salvation to every one that believeth . . . For therein a righteousness of God is revealed from faith to faith: as it is written, The just by faith shall live' (verses 16 and 17). The Apostle cannot think of these things without being thrilled to the very marrow of his being. He is longing to be in Rome to tell them more about it and to enjoy it with them again. His whole life, now, is controlled by this – this tremendous thing that has happened. It took him a long time to see it and to believe it. He had to pass through that experience on the road to Damascus; he had to see the Risen Lord. But once he had seen Him, and once he had understood the truth concerning Him, everything else had become nothing. All his 'righteousness' was dung and refuse, everything recedes into insignificance – this is the one thing that matters.

Let us look, then, at this wonderful thing which he is now about to unfold to these Romans, this wonderful good news. He gives us a great summary of it, as I say, in this section from verse 21 to verse 31. Let us start with a general analysis of this great statement before we come to look at its particular elements. It is such a great passage that we must not just read through it and say, 'Well it sounds very wonderful, but I am not quite sure what it is saying and what its exact meaning is'. There are a number of possible analyses, but let me suggest the analysis which commends itself best to me. I would divide the section into two main portions, two main statements. I suggest that from verse 21 to the end of verse 24 he describes the way of salvation; and then from verse 25 to the end he tells us about the characteristics of that way of salvation. Both these aspects are very important.

Let me divide it up further in this way. The first section, verses 21–24, is a description of the way of salvation. What does he say? The first thing is this: God has provided a righteousness, and has now revealed it. He had promised it before, but He has now made it manifest, He has provided it. The second thing is this: this righteousness becomes ours, not as the result of our actions or our conformity to any kind of law, but solely and entirely through faith. The third thing is, that it is open to all – 'for all have sinned and come short of the glory of God'. It is as open to the Gentiles as to the Jews. You see, the Apostle, all along carries this great argument that he has just finished in his mind. Until this point he has been dealing with it negatively; he is now dealing with it positively. It is the same for all. It is open to all, Jews and Gentiles – there is no difference. The next point he makes, the fourth point, is: that it is entirely of God's grace. It is a free gift of God. Then the last point, and the most important in many ways, is this: it has been made possible and available through the redeeming work of the Lord Jesus Christ. There is our first section. What a tremendous statement it is! There is the essence of the Gospel. There it is stated very generally, and you need not add anything to that, it is all there. We will come back to it again in detail.

However, let us go on to an analysis of the second sub-section – the characteristics of this great salvation. These are described from verse 25 to verse 31. The first point is that this is a way of salvation which is consistent with God's character. That is in verses 25 and 26. It is, secondly, a way that gives all the glory to God and none to man. That is in verses 27 and 28. All the glory belongs to God and none to man. Thirdly, it is a way that shows that God is the God of the whole world and not only of a section of mankind. He is not the God of the Jews only but of the Gentiles also. He is the God of the whole world, so the righteousness that He has provided is in the same way open to the whole world. That is in verses 29 and 30. Then the last thing he tells us about it is, that it is a way that honours and confirms the Law. This is one of the most amazing statements that even this great Apostle ever made. You notice that all along he is still thinking of the section which ends at verse 20. There it was negative; here it is positive. This way of salvation does not deride or dismiss the Law of God, it establishes it, pays it the greatest compliment, in a sense. All along he safeguards his statements and shows their consistency.

There is the general analysis of the section. It is no exaggeration to say of this section that it is one of the greatest and most important sections in the whole of Scripture. It follows, therefore, that our ideas of salvation must always be true to this section, and must be tested by it. In the same way, we must never state the way of salvation in any way that denies any of these tests, or that fails to satisfy, and to give due weight to, any one of them.

You notice that I am emphasizing these things, and I do so because of the situation in which we find ourselves today. It seems to me that we are in far too great a hurry to rush people anyhow, somehow, to Christ. We are so anxious to get results. But we are to be governed in our methods as well as in our message by this Word of God. This is the statement of God's way of salvation, and it must be ours. We must leave nothing out, and everything we say must come up to these tests. We must not say less, we must not say more: but we must say this. Here then is the great standard especially for all evangelists; our message must be conformable to this. 'Ah but', you say, 'that will not appeal to people today, they are not interested in theology.' The answer is that they must become interested in theology if they are to become Christians; they must hear the truth and must believe it. Men have never been interested in theology, and never will be, until the Holy Spirit deals with them. So our business is to preach the truth to them, trusting to the Holy Spirit to open their eyes and their understanding, and to apply it to them with power. Here then, I say, is one of these crucial passages which indeed governs the whole of our preaching. It must always be within the bounds of this tremendous statement which we have here.

Now let us begin to look at it in detail. Take the first section: the way of salvation. I do not know whether you feel as I do as you read the Apostle Paul. His mind and his way of doing things fascinates me more and more, and I am tremendously interested in the way in which he introduces this great section, this great statement. His way of doing so is to repeat almost word for word what he said at the very beginning of his Epistle. Go back to verses 1 and 2 of the first chapter: 'Paul, a servant of Jesus Christ, called to be an apostle, separated unto the Gospel of God, which he had promised afore by his prophets in the Holy Scriptures, concerning his Son Jesus Christ our Lord, which was made of the seed of David according to the flesh', etc. It is almost an exact repetition of that. And in the same way, of course, he is virtually going back and saying once more what he says in verses 16 and 17 also of that first chapter.

There are always lessons to be learned as you watch a master like this, and one of the lessons which we must of necessity learn at this point is that we should always have a scheme in our presentation of the truth. This man does not write at random, he does not say the next thing that comes into his mind. No! He is establishing a case. He has a general introduction, then he announces his Gospel, then he shows the absolute necessity for it. Having done that, he comes back to it, and proceeds to deal with it in greater detail.

What are the cardinal points that he stresses? Here is the first. The Gospel is entirely God's. 'But now the righteousness of God without the law is manifested.' The term 'the righteousness of God', already used in 1:17, means a righteousness provided by God, a righteousness prepared by God, a righteousness that is made available by God. Therefore the Gospel is entirely God's. You notice that he actually used that phrase in the first verse of the Epistle: 'Paul, a servant of Jesus Christ, called to be an apostle, separated unto the Gospel of God.' You would perhaps have expected that there he would have said, 'the Gospel of the Lord Jesus Christ', but Paul says 'the Gospel of God'. This kind of thing is not accidental; it is something that the Apostle always says and always stresses.

I am calling attention to this because of the tendency today, which is so evident, almost to leave out God altogether and to speak only about, and in terms of, the Lord Jesus Christ. In our evangelical zeal we so concentrate on the Son, the second Person, as almost to ignore the Father! People even seem to pray to the Lord Jesus Christ always, and it is about Him they always speak; and so God the Father seems to be forgotten, neglected and ignored. Surely this is a very terrible and a very serious thing.

But here we are reminded by the Apostle that the Gospel is God's Gospel; God is the planner of this Gospel, God is the initiator of this Gospel. Indeed everything about the Gospel should always be in terms of God primarily, for this reason, that sin after all is rebellion against God. Sin is not just something that means that you and I have failed, and have let down ourselves and our standard; sin is not just something that makes us miserable and unhappy. The essence of sin is rebellion against God leading to estrangement from God; and if we do not conceive of sin always in reference to God and our relationship to him, we have an inadequate conception of sin. This, then, is the starting point of evangelism, this is the starting point of the Gospel. Man is a rebel against God, and estranged from God; and our central need, therefore, is to be reconciled to God. We do not merely come to the Lord Jesus Christ, our object is to come to God. That is what we need. As our sin is separation from Him, salvation is reconciliation to Him.

The next thing that is made so plain and clear is that it is God Himself who provides this way of salvation, it is God who provides everything that is in the Lord Jesus Christ. It is God who sent Him, it is God who gave Him His task. The entire action is from God. It is God who 'so loved the world that he gave his only begotten Son' – and yet there is this tendency to forget that, and to leave it out, and to be so Christo-centric

[33]

that we are guilty of forgetting and ignoring God the Father, the first Person in the blessed Holy Trinity. As we are reminded in the First Epistle of Peter, the whole object and intent of the work of the Lord Jesus Christ is to bring us to God [1 *Peter* 3:18]. We believe in God by Him, says Peter, and all He did was in order to bring us to God, not to glorify Himself but to glorify the Father and to bring men to the Father. The Lord Jesus Christ does not tell us to stop at Himself; He takes us to the Father and reconciles us to the Father. 'God was in Christ reconciling the world unto himself.' It is God's salvation from beginning to end. The Apostle reminds us of that here at the beginning: it is a God-provided righteousness that is now available for us.

Then the next thing is this: that it is something that has been planned in eternity before the very foundation of the world. He puts that in verse 21, when he says: 'But now the righteousness of God without the law is manifested, being witnessed by the law and the prophets.' The gospel of Jesus Christ is not an afterthought; it is not something that God thought of when the Law had failed to redeem men. How often that is taught! But verse 20 has already shown clearly that the Law was never meant to save anybody – 'by the law is the knowledge of sin'. It is complete error to say that the Law was first given an opportunity to save men, and that when it failed God thought of the Gospel. That is entirely wrong. The Gospel was planned before the foundation of the world, and it was because God had planned it before the foundation of the world that He was able to reveal it in 'the law' and in 'the prophets'. That is why you have in the Old Testament all these prophecies of the Gospel and what it was going to do. You have it in the Law, you have it in the Prophets – 'witnessed to', says the Apostle, 'by the law and prophets'.

What does he mean? In the term 'the law', he is obviously referring to the Five Books of Moses, the first five books of the Old Testament. I am not going to consider the entire evidence; it would take too long. Here is some of it. You get it in Genesis 3:15 with the promise about the seed of the woman that was to bruise the serpent's head. There it is, 'witnessed to by the law'. Some say they find it in the story of Cain and Abel – especially in the acceptance of the latter's offering. It is certainly found in the call of Abraham. Our Lord Himself said, 'Abraham rejoiced to see my day'. What happened to Abraham, as recorded in Genesis, chapter 17, is a kind of adumbration of the Gospel and of the work of the Lord Jesus Christ; his very offering of Isaac may be a dim suggestion of it. It is especially plain in the promise that through him and his seed all nations should be blessed. Again, it is found in all the ceremonial law, which you find beginning in the Book of Exodus and elaborated so extensively in the Book of Leviticus. What is all this? What is all this about burnt offerings and sacrifices, meat offerings and sweet offerings and peace offerings? What does it all mean? It is nothing but a foreshadowing of the Lord Jesus Christ and all that He has done; it is the Law witnessing to this thing that God has done once and for ever in the Person of His only begotten Son.

Then go on from the Law to the Prophets. This includes the Book of Psalms, because there are many prophecies in the Book of Psalms. The twenty-second Psalm is a perfect description of our Lord's crucifixion and death. And there are many other so-called Messianic psalms. Turn then to the great prophecies. You remember the prophecy about a virgin bearing a Son in Isaiah, chapter 7. You remember the prophecies in chapter 9 and chapter 11 of Isaiah. You remember the great fortieth chapter: 'Comfort ye, comfort ye, my people, saith your God': – God is about to do this great thing, and there is the prophecy of John the Baptist preparing the way for this great Personage who is coming; and also the results of His coming. It is all looking forward to Him – 'witnessed to by the prophets'. In Jeremiah 23 : 6 you read, 'This is the name whereby he shall be called, the Lord our righteousness' – 'the righteousness of God by faith in Jesus Christ'. The prophets were witnessing to it, fore-telling it.

Then think of Daniel with his prophecies, especially chapter 9. He tells us the exact time of His coming, he tells us that this Messiah is going to be 'cut off but not for himself'. It is nothing but a foretelling, it is a witnessing to all this which has happened. You get it in the prophecy of Zechariah – indeed you have it everywhere.

Let me remind you of how we are told in the twenty-fourth chapter of Luke's Gospel that the Lord Himself, after His resurrection, took the incredulous Apostles through the Books of Moses and the Psalms and the Prophets and showed them there all the things pertaining unto Himself. It had all been foreseen and foretold in the Old Testament – His death, His resurrection; it is all there. Peter puts it likewise in the first chapter of his First Epistle. He says that the prophets did not fully understand what they were writing about – these things that were going to happen – they did not know when these things were going to take place. What did they write about? He says they prophesied concerning 'the sufferings of Christ and the glory that should follow' (verses 10–12). The point is that all that happened to our Lord had been predicted in the Old Testament. This reminds us of the importance of always taking the two sections of the Bible together, the importance of studying the two Testaments. Do you see how the two Testaments are absolutely vital even for Christians? I have known Christian people who have rather taken the view that they, of course, need not now bother about the Old Testament. So they just carry a New Testament in their pockets. They think that they do not need the Old Testament. What a tragic error that is! You need the whole Bible. If you really want to understand the truth in its fullness, see how vital it is to have the Old as well as the New. There is no doubt but that it was the Holy Spirit who led the Early Church, which at that time had become mainly Gentile, to hold on to the Old Testament, the Scriptures of the Jews, and to incorporate them in one Book with their new literature, their Gospels, their Acts and their Epistles. That was the leading of the Holy Ghost. If they had been left to themselves, like many of us, they would doubtless have said, 'Well we do not need to know all that any more. Christ has come and we know the Gospel.' But oh! what a truncated Gospel you have if you think like that, and how incomplete is your understanding!

This is very important for this reason: any way of explaining salvation that does not show that the New Testament Gospel is a fulfilment of the Old Testament prophecy is seriously defective – and there is a great deal of that today. Men deny and criticize much of the Old Testament. 'Ah', they say, 'we are only interested in the Gospel.' Here, the Apostle lays it down very plainly and clearly, and you find it in other places in the New Testament, that unless our explanation of the way of salvation is clearly a fulfilment of the Old Testament prophecy it is not a true statement of the way of salvation. Or, to put that in another way, a way of stating the Gospel that puts it as a complete contrast to the Old Testament is entirely wrong. There are many who do that. 'Ah,' they say, 'that Old Testament had a very inadequate notion of God and of His love. That is why you have all that sacrificial teaching and all that talk about blood – that is legalism, that is Judaism. We are not interested in all that.' They deny that, they reject that, and they put the Gospel as a complete contrast to it. That is because they do not like preaching about the blood of Christ; that is because they do not like the doctrine of the wrath of God. If you deny the doctrines of the wrath of God and the blood of Christ you have got to reject the Old Testament, and that is why they do so. They are perfectly consistent with themselves. Yes, but they deny the teaching of the Apostle, who says that this righteousness of God which has been manifested was 'witnessed unto' by the Law and the Prophets. 'It is latent in the Old, it is patent in the New', as Augustine put it. It is there in the Old if you have eyes to see it. The tragedy of the Jews was that they could not see it, though it was there the whole time. But now it has been revealed and manifested in a much greater and fuller and a much more glorious manner.

This section is authoritative for all preaching and presentation of the Gospel. A man very quickly betrays what his view of the Gospel is when he tells you his view of the Old Testament. If they wipe out all the sacrificial law and the idea of appeasing God, and the teaching concerning 'propitiation' – the term we shall come to in verse 25 – if they hate that teaching and refuse to accept it, saying it is an inadequate and unworthy view of God, though they do not realize it, they are also denying the New Testament at the same time. For the New Testament is the fulfilment of the Old. What was prophesied there has actually now come to pass, and is fully open before us. You cannot drive a wedge between the New Testament and the Old Testament. It was the Holy Ghost who led the Early Church to incorporate the Old with their new literature. If we remember nothing else, therefore, let us remember that. 'The law is our school-master to bring us to Christ.' The Law at one and the same time shows us our desperate need and points forward to His coming. What a perfect schoolmaster the Law is! It does the two things that were essential; it convicts of sin, it points to the way of salvation; and any notion of salvation that leaves out the law work is seriously defective, because it was to save us from the condemnation of the Law and the wrath of God that the Son of God came and did all He did on our behalf.

3 More Than Forgiveness

*

But now the righteousness of God without the law is manifested, being witnessed by the law and the prophets;

Even the righteousness of God which is by faith of Jesus Christ unto all and upon all them that believe: for there is no difference:

For all have sinned, and come short of the glory of God;

Being justified freely by his grace through the redemption that is in Christ Jesus:

Whom God hath set forth to be a propitiation through faith in his blood, to declare his righteousness for the remission of sins that are past, through the forbearance of God;

To declare, I say, at this time his righteousness: that he might be just, and the justifier of him which believeth in Jesus.

Where is boasting then? It is excluded. By what law? of works? Nay: but by the law of faith.

Therefore we conclude that a man is justified by faith without the deeds of the law.

Is he the God of the Jews only? is he not also of the Gentiles? Yes, of the Gentiles also:

Seeing it is one God, which shall justify the circumcision by faith, and uncircumcision through faith.

Do we then make void the law through faith? God forbid: yea, we establish the law.   Romans 3:21-31

The next thing we must emphasize is that the Apostle is moved by the fact that this salvation is now manifested. That is what he is really saying – 'But now the righteousness of God without the law is manifested'. That is the thing he emphasizes. It has been revealed, it is made clear now. It was only suggested before – hinted at, put in types and shadows – but now the revelation has come, the full manifestation has taken place. Anyone familiar with this Epistle will have noticed that this is a very important word in the Apostle's thinking and in all his reasoning and arguing. Away back in the first chapter he says he is not ashamed of the Gospel 'for therein is the righteousness of God *revealed* from faith to faith; as it is written, The just shall live by faith' (chapter 1, verses 16–17). Then he goes on to say that he has a further reason for rejoicing in it, 'For', he says in verse 18, 'the wrath of God is, or has been, *revealed* from heaven against all ungodliness and unrighteousness of men.' Here we have exactly the same term. He is repeating what he said in chapter 1, that it is because the wrath of God has already been revealed that he now rejoices in the fact that God's way of righteousness has also been revealed.

We must emphasize the word 'now', and we do so for this reason. It is not merely brought in here as a kind of grammatical connection. It is not that the Apostle is just saying, Well, we have been seeing how no attempt to justify oneself by means of the law can possibly succeed, 'but now' by way of contrast there is this other way. It includes that. But I believe that the word 'now' is used by the Apostle in order that he might emphasize also the historical aspect of this matter. What he is saying is that something has recently happened which has opened up a new possibility for us – 'now'. We have seen how things had been throughout the centuries, what the position was under the Law and under the Prophets; but it is no longer like that. Something new has happened – 'now'. The great turning point in all history had just taken place: that was the coming of the Son of God into the world. So that we are living in a new age – the 'now'. It is no longer the old, it is the new age. It has arrived. We are living in the 'ends of the earth', as he puts it elsewhere. This is a most important word to watch, therefore, as you read the New Testament; there is this contrast between what once was and what is now. The Old Testament was looking forward to this age; but this age has come now, and we are living in it. The 'now' emphasizes the historical aspect.

Or to put the matter in another way: The Christian faith is not a philosophy, it is not merely a teaching. It is based on a series of historical events. The teaching derives from and is grounded in the historical events. That can never be too much emphasized, because this is the point at which our faith differs from every so-called religion. All religions are teachings; this is event and historical happening before it is a teaching; it is an announcement of events, of actions and of facts. This word 'now' reminds us of that. I am now in the position, says the Apostle in effect, of being able to tell you that God has revealed this, and He has done so in the historical events connected with the life and work and ministry, the death and resurrection and ascension of the Son of God, and with the descent of the Holy Ghost on the Day of Pentecost.

This is a fundamental principle of which we must never lose sight. It is particularly important at this present time. Those who have any kind of theological interest will know exactly what I have in mind. There is a school of thought, a theological school, which is having great vogue on the Continent of Europe at the present time, and to a lesser extent in this country. There have been talks about it on the Third Programme of the radio and books and articles are written about it. It teaches that really nothing matters in the New Testament but the teaching, that the facts do not matter at all.

This is the teaching of Bultmann in Germany. He talks about the need of 'demythologizing' the Gospel. He says that the modern man is educated, and especially in a scientific manner, and that therefore you cannot expect him to believe in miracles and manifestations of the supernatural. He cannot possibly believe in the Virgin Birth and in the miracles. You cannot ask him to believe in anything like the substitutionary idea of the Atonement, and a literal physical resurrection. According to that teaching all such matters are but unfortunate first-century accretions and additions. It is the truth that matters, it is the idea of God's forgiveness and of salvation that really counts, so we must throw the facts overboard and no longer trouble people with them. They are an offence and a hindrance to the modern man and stand between him and the message. You see the danger! Such teaching is not only an utter contradiction of this little word 'now', it is a contradiction of the whole of the New Testament teaching. 'If Christ be not risen from the dead, then is our preaching vain, and you are yet in your sins,' says the Apostle in 1 Corinthians 15. It is as vital as that.

No, we must never lose sight of the facts or let them go. The 'now' is the declaration of these events, these facts, that have taken place – the coming of the Son of God into the world and all that is recorded in the four Gospels. What the Apostle is saying here is this, that the Lord Jesus Christ did not come into the world merely to tell us that 'God is love' and that God is prepared to forgive. That was known in the Old Testament. He came in order to make this way of salvation that enables us to be justified by faith. It is the facts that matter. We shall see that the Apostle continues to emphasize this right through the whole of this section until we come to the end of the chapter. He has introduced it all by the word 'now'. We must hold on to the facts and never let them go.

Having emphasized that, I want to repeat something we have seen already, namely, that salvation does not merely consist in our receiving forgiveness of sins. The thing the Apostle stresses is that we are given a positive righteousness. 'But now', he says, 'the righteousness of God.' What man had been trying to produce, and especially the Jews, was a righteousness that would satisfy God. The Jews thought they were doing it through the Law; others thought they were doing it with their morality and their philosophy. Paul has proved that it was all vain. 'But now', he says, there is an entirely new position – a righteousness from God is available. That is the big thing in salvation; not merely that our sins are forgiven. That could never be enough; to have our sins forgiven does not of itself admit us to heaven. Before we can be admitted to heaven we must be clothed with righteousness. If we are not we shall find ourselves in the position of the man whom our Lord depicts in one of His parables, who went in to the king's wedding feast without a wedding garment. That man was thrown out [*Matthew* 22:1–14] and that is the position of all who think that forgiveness alone means salvation. We need a positive righteousness; and this great doctrine of justification by faith teaches us that God not only forgives us but also puts to our account the righteousness of Jesus Christ. He clothes us with it. A righteousness of God, or from God, is now available because of what Christ did when He came into the world and what He has completed by going back again to the Father. That is how this righteousness becomes ours.

We must now go on to the second matter which the Apostle considers in this first sub-section. I can best put this perhaps in the form of a question: How does this righteousness become ours? If this righteousness is available, how can I receive it, how can I become clothed with it? The Apostle answers the question. Nothing is more vital than this. The Authorised Version reads like this: 'But now the righteousness of God without the law is manifested.' But what the Apostle actually wrote is this: 'But now without the law a righteousness of God is manifested.' He put 'without the law' before the 'righteousness of God'; and he did that, of course, because he was anxious to emphasize that that is the big thing. He says this way of righteousness that God is now offering is something apart from the Law, without the Law.

What does he mean by saying 'without the law', 'apart from the law?' It is a very important point because sometimes it has been misunderstood and misinterpreted. There are those who say it means that God has done away with His Law altogether, that the Law has gone entirely out of existence, that God has abrogated the Law, and that since the coming of Jesus Christ into this world the Law has ceased to have any significance or any importance, and does not apply to anyone. They say that until Christ came and did His work the Law was preached to men and they were judged according to their conformity or lack of conformity to the Law, but that that is no longer the case. What judges men now is not the Law of God but their response to the Lord Jesus Christ. The Law does not come in any longer, they say, it has been done away – 'without the law'. It is now just a question of 'Do you believe in the Lord Jesus Christ or do you not?' Indeed the people that hold this view go so far as to say.that because mankind failed to keep the Law of God, God, as it were, brought in something simpler and something easier. It is just a question now, they say, of believing in the Lord Jesus Christ – nothing else but just believing. The Law has no application to us.

Now that, I want to show, is a very serious misinterpretation. Anyone who has ever read the thirty-first verse (the last verse) of this chapter should never have fallen into that particular trap and error, because there we read: 'Do we then make void the law through faith? God forbid: Yea, we establish the law.' So whatever your interpretation of 'without law' means you must never say that the Law has disappeared, vanished, or been cast away for ever out of God's sight. That is not the case. It does not mean that.

What then does it mean? It means that our attempting to keep the Law perfectly ourselves as the means of salvation has been entirely set aside, not because the Law no longer applies, but because Another has rendered this perfect obedience to the Law on our behalf. In other words, the Apostle is saying that no longer must anyone think of saving himself, or finding or achieving salvation, in terms of his own life and living and activity and morality. This way that God is now holding before us does not leave it to us to satisfy the Law, because 'by the deeds of the law shall no flesh be justified in his sight; for by the law is the knowledge of sin'. We shall see later how important it is to realize that the Lord Jesus Christ saves us by keeping and honouring the Law for us. The Law has not been removed; God has not done away with the Law. The Lord Jesus Christ has satisfied it and kept it, and we are given the fruit and the results of what He has done.

You may think that that is a distinction without a difference; but you will discover, the more you examine it, that it is far from being that. The Law of God is still there, and it is still the means of judgement; and there is no conceivable standing in the presence of God without a righteousness which answers the demands of the Law and satisfies it, and conforms to it. Our view of salvation must never be one that dismisses the Law; it must be one which 'establishes' the Law. What the Apostle is saying is that the Jew and the Gentile must no longer think that anything that they can do is ever going to satisfy God, because that is to put yourself back under the Law, that is putting yourself back under condemnation.

How then does God's righteousness come to me? Paul answers by saying in verse 22 that it comes to me, 'By faith of Jesus Christ unto all and upon all them that believe'. A better way of translating that would be, 'Through faith in Jesus Christ and belief in Him'. Now all these words are important. What does 'faith' mean? Faith includes these three aspects, or three elements. It means a knowledge of truth, it means assent to truth, it means a trust in the truth. There are always those three elements in faith, in true faith – an awareness of the truth, an assent to it, and a committal of oneself to it. We must never think of faith in terms that leave out any one of those elements. Faith, in other words, is not merely an intellectual awareness of the truth, or even an intellectual acceptance of the truth. You can have that and still be without faith. Faith means a real trusting in Him and what He has done on our behalf and for our salvation. That, according to the Apostle, is the way of obtaining this righteousness.

We can put it in this way: the man who has faith is the man who is no longer looking at himself, and no longer looking to himself. He no longer looks at anything he once was. He does not look at what he is now. He does not look at what he hopes to be as the result of his own efforts. He looks entirely to the Lord Jesus Christ and His finished work, and he rests on that alone. He has ceased to say, 'Ah yes, I have committed terrible sins but I have done this and that . . .' He stops saying that. If he goes on saying that, he has not got faith. Or if he says, 'Ah, there is still terrible blackness within me, and I find sin within myself still, how can I say that I am saved?' he is still wrong. He must not speak like that because he is still looking to himself. Faith speaks in an entirely different manner and makes a man say, 'Yes, I have sinned grievously, I have lived a life of sin. I was a blasphemer, I was injurious, I was vile; there is scarcely a sin I have not committed, and I am aware of sin within me still, yet

[45]

I know that I am a child of God because I am not resting on any righteousness of my own; my righteousness is in Jesus Christ, and God has put that to my account.' He does not look to himself at all; he looks only, utterly, exclusively to the Lord Jesus Christ.

Do you see the importance of this? Some people think that it is a mark of great spirituality to condemn oneself and to point to one's sins. I know what they mean, in a sense; but in another sense it is a denial of faith. If in any way you have not got assurance because of anything in yourself, it means that you are not exercising faith. Faith rests entirely and exclusively upon the Lord Jesus Christ and what He has done.

> *I rest my faith on Him and Him alone*
> *Who died for my transgressions to atone.*

We should never be in trouble concerning this. That is where the Old Testament is of such great value. Go back to the Book of Leviticus and read the instructions that are given there about the various offerings and sacrifices. You will find something like this, that the priests had to put their hands upon a beast, the animal, that was to be sacrificed for them. Why did they do that? Well, that was their symbolic way of laying their sins upon this animal that was going to be sacrificed in their stead. So what faith says is this:

> *I lay my sins on Jesus,*
> *The spotless Lamb of God.*

Take your sins, face them, recognize them, acknowledge them all with shame; but do not stop at that. Go on and say, 'I lay them on Him'. That is the word of faith. Whatever may be true of you does not matter. We are all sinners, and we will all remain as we are in that sense; but what enables us to know that we are forgiven, and justified, and stand righteous in the sight of God, is that the righteousness of Jesus Christ is given to us. That is what it means. Faith means seeing this truth, assenting to it, casting yourself upon it exactly as you are:

Just as I am without one plea
But that Thy blood was shed for me,
And that Thou bidd'st me come to Thee,
 O Lamb of God, I come.

That is it! Just as you are!

Just as I am, and waiting not
To rid my soul of one dark blot,
To Thee whose blood can cleanse each spot,
 O Lamb of God I come.

'All the fitness He requireth, Is to see your need of Him'. 'Not the righteous; sinners Jesus came to save'. What a tragedy that anyone should be held in the bondage of legalism, that anyone should be robbed by the devil of the joy of salvation through looking at himself or herself in any sense! Faith is that which looks only unto Him.

The next comment I would make about the place of faith is this. We must never say that it is our faith that saves us. Many people want to say that, and believe that. They say: Under the Old Dispensation it was works of the Law that saved. It is not that now; the Law has been abrogated; it is believing on Christ that saves us now. It is not! It is not our faith that saves us. Look at the words again: 'But now the righteousness of God without the law is manifested, being witnessed by the law and the prophets; even the righteousness of God which is by faith of Jesus Christ, unto all and upon all them that believe.' Does that mean that it is my belief that saves me? It does not. It is the Lord Jesus Christ who saves you. If you say that your faith saves you, your faith has become a work, and you have something to boast of. You can say, 'I have believed, the other man has not, and I therefore deserve salvation and he does not'. You are saving yourself. That is the very thing the Apostle is denouncing. Faith does not save us; it is through faith we are saved. Faith is only the instrument, it is not the cause of my justification. The cause of my justification is the Lord Jesus Christ and all He has done, and I must never put anything, not even my faith, there.

That is His position and His alone. If I do not do that, you see, I cannot face the twenty-seventh verse of this chapter, where I read: 'Where is boasting then? It is excluded.' There is no boasting in the Christian life; but if you say that your faith has saved you, you are boasting of your faith. Many say that, do they not? They say, in effect, 'Ah yes, the Gospel is preached to all; I chose to believe, the other man did not, and it is therefore my believing that saves me'. But that cannot be right because, if that were the case, it is something in them that was not in the other man that saves, and they would have something to boast of. But there is no boasting here at all. So we must never refer to faith as the cause of our salvation, or of our righteousness. It is merely the instrument by which we receive it.

I do not go into the question here, because it does not arise in this context, as to the origin of our faith. I am simply concerned to emphasize this, that it is not our faith that saves; it is only the channel through which the righteousness becomes mine.

So the Apostle declares that the way that God has now provided is this marvellous and wonderful way. It is all in Jesus Christ. 'He of God is made unto us wisdom, and righteousness, and sanctification, and redemption' [1 *Corinthians* 1:30]. He is 'the all and in all', 'the beginning and the end', and 'we are complete in him'. It is all in Him, and His must be the glory altogether. The Apostle will repeat that, and we shall do so, when we come to the twenty-fourth verse: 'Being justified by his grace through the redemption that is in Jesus Christ.'

Having seen that this is how the righteousness becomes mine, I must go on to ask the next question. To whom then is this open, this salvation, this righteousness of Jesus Christ which comes to us by faith? To whom does it come? The Apostle answers by saying it comes to all who believe – 'unto all and upon all them that believe'. There is a little difficulty about this expression 'upon all'. It is not in some of the most ancient and reliable manuscripts. It does not really matter. What the Apostle is saying is that it comes to all who believe; and obviously what he is thinking of once more is the point he has been arguing at such great length in the second half of the first chapter, and the whole of the second chapter, and the first half (indeed more than the first half) of chapter 3. He is still thinking of, and has still got in his mind, this distinction that the Jews were drawing between themselves and the Gentiles. So he answers them at once by saying, 'There is no difference, for all have sinned and have come short of the glory of God'. As I say, he has already said that at great length. That was the climax to his tremendous argument in the first part of this third chapter, where he proved that 'every mouth is stopped and the whole world is guilty before God' – that there is no difference between the Jew and the Gentile because all are in the same position. 'We have before proved, both Jews and Gentiles, that they are all under sin.' And yet he puts it here in this twenty-third verse in a most remarkable and astonishing manner, indeed in a most glorious manner. He states it here much more wonderfully than he has done anywhere else hitherto in this Epistle. Do you notice how he does so? There is no difference, he says, we are all in exactly the same condition, we are all in an identical position. What is it? Well, he describes it in a double manner. 'All,' he says, 'have sinned and come short of the glory of God.'

Look at these two ways of describing the condition of man by nature as the result of the Fall. All, he says, have sinned. Here he describes sin in and of itself and in its active character. This is what the Fall of man has done to the human race. It means that we have all sinned. What does sin mean? Let me give you some definitions of sin. It means 'missing a mark'; instead of hitting the mark, you are on one side or the other. It means that – failure to hit or to come up to the divine standard. Secondly, it means 'lawlessness'. Thirdly, it means 'unrighteousness' – a failure to be right, to be straight, to be upright, to be true. Fourthly, it means 'a trespass'. These are terms which you will find scattered about the Bible to bring out the meaning of sin. A trespass means that you follow your will instead of the will of God. Sin also means 'iniquity'; and iniquity means anything that is wrong in and of itself, something that is patently, inherently and essentially wrong. And then lastly, sixthly, sin, as John reminds us in his First Epistle, is 'the transgression of the law', a breaking

[49]

of the law [1 *John* 3:4]. Now the Apostle says that we all of us are guilty of all that. He has explained it at great length in verses 10–18. He sums it up in this one word 'sin'.

But there is another interesting point about the way he puts it here. The Apostle deliberately used the aorist tense of this verb 'to sin', which means 'something done once and for ever'. We should therefore translate this verse like this: 'For all sinned and are coming short of the glory of God.' He has used two different tenses, first the aorist, something complete, once and for all; then, secondly, something which is continuing in the present. What does he suggest by that? He says, 'all sinned'. When did all sin? The answer he will give us later in the fifth chapter is 'in Adam'. You will find it in the twelfth verse of the fifth chapter. I just mention it now; but we shall come to it again in greater detail. But he teaches here, as he teaches in chapter 5 and elsewhere, that we all sinned in Adam. We all died in Adam as the result of his sin. Adam was the federal head of humanity, and when he sinned we all sinned. He represented us. We were all in him. 'All sinned' – once and for all. So that in addition to the sins, the individual sins, that you and I have committed, we have all sinned in Adam. That is why 'death reigned from Adam to Moses', that is why death has come in at all and everybody dies. Even a new-born babe may die. It is the result of the sin in which we have all participated in Adam – 'all sinned'.

But I want to emphasize especially this other statement that he makes here. 'All sinned' and 'are coming short', or 'are falling short of the glory of God'. This is a remarkable statement. What does he mean by it? He means that we all lack, we all have a need of the glory of God. The word he uses here for 'falling short' or 'coming short' is exactly the same word that our blessed Lord used in the parable of the Prodigal Son, when He says about that young man in the far country that he began to 'be in want'. He no longer had any money, he was not having enough food, he 'began to be in want'. This is what we are told here; we are 'in want' of the glory of God, we have fallen short of it, we lack it.

What does he mean by this? It is surely one of the most amazing things. The way to answer the question is to look at other statements of the same thing. In the second chapter in verses 7 and 10 you have it. There we read that, 'To them who by patient continuance in well doing seek for glory and honour and immortality, eternal life'; and in the same way we find in the tenth verse that 'Glory and honour and peace (are given) to every man that worketh good, to the Jew first, and also to the Gentile'. Then there is another reference to it in the first and second verses of the fifth chapter, where we read, 'Therefore being justified by faith, we have peace with God through our Lord Jesus Christ: By whom also we have access by faith into this grace wherein we stand, and rejoice in hope of the glory of God.' Then go on into the eighth chapter and you will find it several times. Take the eighteenth verse: 'For I reckon that the sufferings of this present time are not worthy to be compared with the glory that shall be revealed in us.' Again in the twenty-first verse: 'Because the creature itself also shall be delivered from the bondage of corruption into the glorious liberty of the children of God.' Go on to verses 29 and 30: 'For whom he did foreknow he also did predestinate to be conformed to the image of his Son, that he might be the first-born among many brethren. Moreover whom he did predestinate, them he also called; and whom he called, them he also justified; and whom he justified, them he also glorified.'

What does he mean? What does he mean in 2 Corinthians 3:18, 'But we all, with open face beholding as in a glass the glory of the Lord, are changed into the same image from glory to glory, even as by the Spirit of the Lord'? What does he mean in 2 Corinthians 4:6 when he says, 'God, who commanded the light to shine out of darkness, hath shined in our hearts, to give the light of the knowledge of the glory of God in the face of Jesus Christ'? What does he mean in 2 Corinthians 4:17 when he says, 'Our light affliction, which is but for a moment, worketh for us a far more exceeding and eternal weight of glory'? What did the Lord Jesus Christ mean in John 17:22 when He said this: 'And the glory which thou gavest me I have given them'?

What does this mean, 'All have sinned and have come short of the glory of God'? This is the only adequate interpretation of all those great verses; it means, to behold the glory of God and to rejoice in it! 'God, who commanded the light to shine out of darkness, hath shined in our hearts.' What for? 'To give, reveal, the light of the knowledge of the glory of God.' The unbeliever does not know about the glory. He is a God-hater, he turns his back on God. Why? Because he has never seen, he does not know 'the glory'. But the Christian is a man to whom the glory has been revealed; he knows something about the glory of God, and he rejoices in it. It is everything to him. It is the most glorious thing of all.

Ah, but it is not only to know about the glory of God; some of the verses I have quoted tell us that as Christians we not only know about it but that we also share in it. We partake of it. 'We all with open face beholding as in a glass the glory of the Lord.' You remember how Moses was on a mountain with God, receiving the Law. He came down and was going to speak to the people, but when they saw him they stood back alarmed. What was it? The glory of God shining from the face of Moses! Something like that happens to everybody who is truly a Christian. It is not true of the unbeliever. They fall short of the glory of God; they do not see it; they do not partake of it. But to the Christian this is a glorious fact.

Never has the Apostle exposed the ravages of sin and the Fall in a more wonderful manner than in this twenty-third verse of the third chapter of the Epistle to the Romans. Sin not only makes a man unrighteous, it robs him of the glory of God. And if you understand that, you will realize how futile it is ever to think that you, by your works or activities, can ever be fit to stand in the presence of God. Before we can truly know Him, and have communion with Him, let alone stand before the glory of His presence, we must have something of His glory. However good we may be, and however moral, we never shall and never can develop a Divine glory. But without it we can never see God and never stand in His presence. But the Christian, as the Apostle Peter reminds us in the first chapter of his Second Epistle, is 'made a partaker of the Divine nature'. Is that true of me as a Christian? It is! It does not mean that it is visible and evident to everybody. Even the glory in the Lord Jesus Christ was not visible to everybody when He was here in the flesh. They crucified Him; they said, 'Who is this fellow? He is an impostor'. The glory was veiled by the flesh, and yet the eye of faith could see it, because as John says in the Prologue of his Gospel, 'And we beheld his glory, the glory as of the only begotten of the Father, full of grace and truth'. The glory is in us in a measure if we are Christians, though it is not always visible. A verse of a hymn puts it well:

> *Concealed as yet this honour lies,*
> *By this dark world unknown;*
> *A world that knew not when he came,*
> *E'en God's eternal Son.*

They do not see it. And, alas, we do not see it ourselves at times, and we do not see it in one another; but if we are in Christ it is true of us – 'Whom he justified, them he also glorified'. There is a new man in me, as a Christian, that is glorious, and he will go on 'being changed from glory to glory'. Still more wonderful, there is a day coming when even my body shall be made glorious. 'We look for the coming of the Son of God from heaven,' says Paul to the Philippians, 'who shall change this our vile body that it may be fashioned like unto his glorious body' [Philippians 3:20]. Then I shall be completely glorified! Glorious in spirit, glorious in body – entirely glorified.

What a terrible thing sin is! It robs us not only of righteousness, it robs us of 'the glory of God'. What a wonderful salvation this is! It not only gives me pardon and righteousness, it gives me glory: 'Whom he justified, them he also glorified.' Whatever we were before, if we have this faith in the Lord Jesus Christ and His perfect work, we are clothed with his righteousness, and something of the glory of God is implanted within us. We are 'made partakers of the divine nature' [2 *Peter* 1:4].

4 By Free Grace Alone

*

Being justified freely by his grace through the redemption that is in Christ Jesus.   Romans 3:24

In this most important verse which we are now going to consider, the Apostle continues his general outline of the way of salvation. I would remind you that he has been describing its general characteristics in verses 21 and the first part of 22. Then in the second half of verse 22 and verse 23 he digressed in order to emphasize the inclusiveness of this Gospel as regards Jew and Gentile; but here he returns again to the general theme and he states it in a most wonderful manner. This is undoubtedly one of the great verses of the Bible. It is a statement that can be compared with John 3: 16. It is a perfect synopsis of the Christian faith, and it is important, therefore, that we should understand it clearly.

But in addition to its intrinsic importance it is of particular importance that we should understand that it is a vital statement in connection with the whole of this Epistle. There is a sense, therefore, in which it is true to say that unless we grasp the meaning of this verse there is no purpose in proceeding any further. In any case an understanding of this verse is indispensable if we are to enjoy the liberty that is offered us in the Gospel. It is one of those essential statements of the Christian faith, and every word is of great importance.

The verse and its statement can be divided under three main headings: first, a description or a definition of what salvation is; second, how salvation becomes ours; and third, how it has ever been possible for God to provide such a salvation for us.

[54]

First, we come to consider the question – What is salvation? The Apostle tells us that it is 'being justified'. As this is one of those great crucial statements we must be clear as to its meaning. We shall go into this in greater detail later, but we must state immediately that it is primarily a declaration by God. It means that we are declared righteous by God. It is a legal or a forensic act. It does not mean that we are made righteous, but rather that God regards us as righteous and declares us to be righteous.

This has often been a difficulty to many people. They say that because they are conscious of sin within they cannot be in a justified state; but anyone who speaks like that shows immediately that he has no understanding of this great and crucial doctrine of justification. Justification makes no actual change in us; it is a declaration by God concerning us. It is not something that results from what we do but rather something that is done to us. We have only been made righteous in the sense that God regards us as righteous, and pronounces us to be righteous.

Then we must notice that the Apostle used the word 'being'. This is in the present tense. Here again is something wonderful which we must grasp clearly. The Day of Judgement is coming, and in that day we shall be declared righteous before God. But that is not what the Apostle is saying here. He is asserting that now, in the present, we are declared righteous the moment we exercise faith. At that very moment we are declared righteous by God. From the moment we believe, this becomes true of us. This is what we are exhorted to believe, and it is a great source of rejoicing to all truly Christian people.

We shall find in the first verse of the fifth chapter that the Apostle says, 'Being justified', but the meaning there is different, for there he uses the past tense, and that verse should really be translated, 'Having been justified'. There the Apostle is looking back at something that has already happened, but here his whole point is to tell us that it is something that can happen immediately in the present.

The great importance of this emphasis on the present comes out clearly in the story of Martin Luther. He had been brought up as a Roman Catholic and had been taught that there is no such thing as an assurance of salvation in this life. You had to depend upon the Church and her various activities. But when that great light broke in upon Luther and he was given to understand this doctrine of justification by faith, he awoke to the realization that this is something which is possible now in the immediate present. As a result he was filled with a spirit of rejoicing, and had an assurance of his salvation. In many ways, therefore, we see that this verse is one of the great statements which led to and explains the Protestant Reformation.

We now turn to the second matter: how can this salvation become ours? The Apostle is so much concerned that we should understand this that he states it twice over in two words – 'freely' and 'grace'. He has been saying this already earlier in the Epistle. He had already said in chapter 1, verse 16, that it was God's way of salvation. He repeats himself here but goes further; he tells us that it comes to us freely and by the grace of God. He is anxious to emphasize that it is a gift, something which is entirely gratuitous. Salvation is a gift from God. It is something that comes to us freely. In this word he emphasizes the manner of how it comes to us, and declares that we have done nothing whatsoever to deserve it. The point can be brought out by remembering that there is a statement of our Lord's in John's Gospel [15: 25] in which He says, 'They hated me without a cause.' The word translated 'without a cause' is the very word that the Apostle uses here. It stresses the fact that there is nothing in us to deserve this gift of salvation; there is no cause for it as far as we are concerned. It is something that we receive quite freely.

It is important therefore that we should ask ourselves certain questions at this point: Are we relying on anything in ourselves or in our family or in our church or in our nationality? All that is excluded. Salvation is a gift that comes to us freely from God without our deserving it in any respect whatsoever.

Another fact that emerges from this element of gratuitousness is that clearly it has nothing to do with the Law. This salvation, as the Apostle has already indicated in verse 21, is 'without the law' or 'apart from the law'. The Law makes demands upon us which have to be met, but there is nothing like this in salvation; it is entirely free.

Then the Apostle goes on to emphasize this still more by the use of the word 'grace'. The free gift is the result of the grace of God. This word 'grace' is one of the great words of the New Testament. It is not surprising that Philip Doddridge in the eighteenth century should write as follows:

> Grace! 'tis a charming sound,
> Harmonious to the ear:
> Heaven with the echo shall resound
> And all the earth shall hear.

> Grace first contrived the way
> To save rebellious man,
> And all the steps that grace display
> Which drew the wondrous plan.

There is no more wonderful word than 'grace'. It means unmerited favour, or kindness shown to one who is utterly undeserving. Here again the purely gratuitous character of our salvation is brought out. It is something that results from the sole exercise of the spontaneous love of God. It is not merely a free gift, but a free gift to those who deserve the exact opposite, and it is given to us while we are 'without hope and without God in the world'.

One of the best ways of understanding this great doctrine of grace is to contrast it with the Law. This is done in John's Gospel, chapter 1, verse 17: 'For the law was given by Moses, but grace and truth came by Jesus Christ.' The whole purpose of chapter 4 of this Epistle is, as we shall see, to bring out this same contrast; and indeed, it is found also in chapters 5 and 6.

The meaning of grace, and especially as it is contrasted with Law, is vital to a true understanding of the argument of the Epistle, and indeed to an understanding of any of the Gospels. What characterizes the new dispensation is that it is one of grace and not of Law. This does not mean that there was no grace in Law, but the broad distinction is made constantly in the New

Testament. The essential difference is that the Law revealed sin but had no power to remove it. As the Apostle will say in chapter 8: 3: 'What the law could not do, in that it was weak through the flesh. . . .' He has already reminded us in the twentieth verse of chapter 3 that 'by the law is the knowledge of sin' – that it had no pardon to give us. The most the Law could do was to say, 'An eye for an eye, and a tooth for a tooth'; that no more was to be taken by way of recompense than 'one for one'; but it could go no further. It was mainly regulative and its object was to bring out our sinfulness. This we shall see in great detail in chapters 5, 6 and 7. For the moment, the important point is that there is nothing free or gracious about the Law. 'But now' – as the Apostle says in those great words of jubilation in verse 21 – there is something entirely new, something which the Law could not give, though it foreshadowed it and prepared us for it. Grace in this sense is the exact opposite of law. It is the expression of the great love of God, the great love in His heart. Grace arises solely from the love of God without anything whatsoever in us to produce it; indeed it is entirely in spite of us.

What is your reaction to this word? In many ways this is the acid test of any profession of the Christian faith. The Christian is one who reacts in the same way as Philip Doddridge in the lines that I have just quoted. The same thought is also expressed by Charles Wesley:

> *His only righteousness I show,*
> *His saving grace proclaim.*

Do you feel that this word 'grace' opens the very gates of heaven to you? That is really what it means to be a Christian.

We must also notice that the Apostle says 'His grace' – 'We are justified freely by his grace'. This word refers, of course, to God the Father. It is God Himself who declares us to be justified. It is the righteousness of God that is revealed in the whole way of salvation. This is what makes the Gospel something that surpasses human understanding and comprehension. It is God Himself, and He alone, who provides it, the One whom we have defied, disobeyed and provoked, against whom we have rebelled and sinned. It is His grace that reconciles us to Him, and this, clearly and obviously, is the only way of salvation.

Having looked at the description of the way of salvation, and having seen how it actually comes to us, we must now proceed to consider the third great matter that is dealt with here. What is it that makes all this possible? With reverence we ask the question, On what grounds does God do this? The Apostle's answer is given immediately and directly by the word 'through' – '. . . through the redemption that is in Christ Jesus'. This is a most vital word. It means 'by means of', or 'in connection with'. It is important to grasp that, though salvation is given to us as a free gift, this does not happen merely as the result of a statement made by God, or a word uttered by Him. This is where our salvation differs so entirely from creation. In the matter of creation God merely had to make a statement, to utter a fiat. He said, 'Let there be light: and there was light'. But salvation is not possible in that way. Something further was necessary, and later we shall see at length what that was.

This is a most important, indeed a vital point, for many, especially in this century, have held the view that because God is love He has merely to say that He forgives. But the very essence of the New Testament Gospel is to show that this is not so, but that because of God's eternal justice and righteousness something else had to happen before our forgiveness could become possible. It is entirely wrong to think that our Lord came into this world merely to tell us that God is love, and that in His love He forgives us all our sins. Indeed there are those who would say that God has already done this, that our main trouble is that we are not aware of this, and that the business of preaching therefore is simply to proclaim to the whole of mankind that God in His love has already forgiven all our sins and trespasses. Here we find how completely wrong such ideas are. The word 'through' indicates in an unmistakable manner that it is only by means of all that has happened in and through our Lord – His life of perfect obedience and His sacrificial death and resurrection; all that God has done in Christ – that salvation is possible. We must be quite clear, therefore, about this, that even God could not justify the ungodly by simply uttering a word of forgiveness. This will become yet clearer to us as we look at verses 25 and 26.

The Church and the Word of God are certainly instrumental in God's way of salvation, but the vital point is that the Lord Jesus Christ did not come into the world merely to announce the way of salvation. He came to make the way of salvation. In other words, we see clearly at this point that the whole Gospel hangs upon the word 'through'; and it cannot be emphasized too much.

The next important word in this statement is the word 'redemption'. This is again one of the great New Testament words. It is a special word. It is used ten times in the New Testament, seven times in the Epistles of the Apostle Paul, twice in the Epistle to the Hebrews, and once in Luke's Gospel. There has been great controversy over this word during the past hundred years, and many have tried to take away its full meaning. We must therefore examine this word most carefully.

The root word as used by the Greeks had reference to the loosing of clothing or of armour, but later it began to be used for setting an animal loose, and also for the loosing of the bands and bonds of a prisoner. Later still it was used for the loosing or releasing of the bonds of a prisoner or slave by the payment of a ransom. In classical Greek literature it is always used in this sense. You will find that in the Old Testament the parallel word also is used in this sense. Take for instance Numbers 18: 15, 'Every thing that openeth the matrix in all flesh, which they bring unto the Lord, whether it be of men or beasts, shall be thine: nevertheless the firstborn of man shalt thou surely redeem, and the firstling of unclean beasts shalt thou redeem.' Occasionally, however, this Greek word was used to mean to 'buy' or to 'purchase' – for instance, fields or food.

Now if we combine these two meanings the word can be defined as 'the purchase of a release by means of the payment of a ransom price'. Redemption carries in it the meaning of 'ransom', and it is this idea of ransom or payment or substitution which many during the past century have tried to replace by the notion of deliverance only.

By now, however, we can claim that scholars are agreed as to the meaning, which is the one I have given. Such scholars are not all evangelical. For instance, Dr James Moffat in his well-known translation – and no one would charge him with being an evangelical – translates the verse in this way: 'They are justified for nothing by his grace through the ransom provided in Christ Jesus.' The Greek word used by the Apostle is prefixed by a word which means 'away'; we can translate therefore by the expression 'ransomed away'. I am not concerned to argue that the word does not mean 'delivered', because it does mean that. The point is that it does not only mean that, but that it is a much stronger and more powerful word. This word 'redemption', however, takes us yet further. If we need to be ransomed away from something, what is this? And the biblical answer is that it is from slavery and captivity. Man as the result of sin not only has become guilty before God, he has also become the slave of sin and of the devil. In this condition he is entirely helpless, he is a complete slave.

Now redemption means, as we have seen, release as the result of the payment of a price. This is an essential part of the meaning of the word and it must never be omitted. The truth about us all is that we are not able to pay the adequate price, but, thank God, Another has come and paid the price for us. Here we have the great idea of substitution. The Lord Jesus Christ came to ransom us, to deliver us; He has paid the price, and so the prison in which we were held captive by the devil has been opened, and we who were slaves have been made free. This is the doctrine which is taught here so plainly by the Apostle. The Apostle is so deeply concerned that we should be clear about this that he describes it as 'the redemption that is in Christ Jesus'. All the glory must go to Christ. It is He who by His work has purchased us and set us at liberty. We are forgiven and delivered from the power of Satan by Him alone.

Thus we see once more the full content of the expression 'But now' in verse 21. It is the coming of the Lord Jesus Christ that has made all the difference – His perfect obedience to the Law, His paying the price of the ransom. It is He who makes the redemption possible. That is why we were at such pains earlier to emphasize the word 'through'. The Lord Jesus Christ did not come only to tell us about the love of God. Of course He does that, but it is His actual coming and living and dying and rising again that provides the payment of the price which was essential to our deliverance. It was the only way. It is in Jesus Christ and His cross – 'Jesus Christ and him crucified' – that we have the deliverance. There is no Christianity apart from Him, but even His coming and His teaching alone could not have saved us. We had to be ransomed, and He ransomed us on the cross on Calvary's hill.

The point I want to emphasize is that the word 'redemption' is a bigger word than the word 'deliverance', which tends to be substituted for it by many at the present time.

Before we leave this great statement there is one other matter to which we must refer. There are those who say, in effect, 'I agree that this is the meaning here, but after all, is this not just Paul's way of looking at the subject? He, as an ex-Pharisee, had a legalistic outlook; is this not an example of the way in which he tends to foist his legalistic ideas upon the simple Gospel of Jesus?' There is no difficulty about answering this objection; we have but to look at statements made by our Lord Himself and by other New Testament writers to see the utter falsity of this suggestion. Take, for instance, the words of our Lord in Matthew 20, verse 28, and the corresponding statement in Mark 10, verse 45. Our Lord says, 'Even as the Son of man came not to be ministered unto, but to minister, and to give his life a ransom for many.' There you have exactly the same Greek word used (without the prefix), and in each case it is translated 'ransom'. The writers of the Gospel are recording the words of our Lord Jesus Christ Himself. At that time the Apostles and other followers could not grasp the meaning of His words, but afterwards, when He expounded it to them after the resurrection (see Luke 24, verses 25, 26, etc.) and as their minds were enlightened by the Holy Spirit after Pentecost, they came to see exactly what He meant.

You have precisely the same teaching in the Epistle to the

Hebrews, chapter 9, verses 11 and 12: 'But Christ being come an high priest of good things to come, by a greater and more perfect tabernacle, not made with hands, that is to say, not of this building; neither by the blood of goats and calves, but by his own blood he entered in once into the holy place, having obtained eternal redemption for us.' Once more it is exactly the same word. And again we have it in 1 Peter 1, verses 18 and 19: 'Forasmuch as ye know that ye were not redeemed with corruptible things, as silver and gold, from your vain conversation received by tradition from your fathers; but with the precious blood of Christ, as of a lamb without blemish and without spot.' He goes on to say, 'Who verily was foreordained before the foundation of the world but was manifest in these last times for you'.

In all of these cases it is exactly the same word that is used. Thus there is no basis whatsoever for saying that this is merely a Pauline idea. It belongs to the universal preaching of all the Apostles. It was what was believed by the early Christians. Nothing is more important for us than to be clear about the meaning of this great verse. Are we clear about it? Do we see that it is in this way only that anyone can be saved? Are you quite clear about the fact that you cannot save yourself? Do you see clearly that all has been done for you in Christ Jesus? Do you see that salvation is something that we obtain freely by the grace of God? Unless we are clear about this matter we are missing the very essence of the Christian Gospel which is stated by the Apostle in the words 'For by grace are ye saved through faith, and that not of yourselves, it is the gift of God' [*Ephesians* 2: 8]. All we need is to be found in the Lord Jesus Christ, and in Him alone. When we look at ourselves we see nothing but sin, its condemnation and its slavery; but when we look to Him and see what He has done on our behalf, we see that everything necessary for our reconciliation to God and deliverance from the thraldom of sin and Satan has already been accomplished and accepted. The Christian is one who looks to Him and says:

> *My hope is built on nothing less,*
> *Than Jesu's blood and righteousness.*

[63]

And with another we say:

> *Praise, my soul, the King of heaven;*
> *To His feet thy tribute bring;*
> *Ransomed, healed, restored, forgiven,*
> *Who like thee His praise should sing?*
> *Praise Him! Praise Him!*
> *Praise the everlasting King!*

Paul tells us in the Epistle to the Philippians [3 : 3] that, 'We are the circumcision, who worship God in the spirit, and rejoice in Christ Jesus, and have no confidence in the flesh'. We see our utter nothingness and worthlessness, and in the words of the Apostle in 1 Corinthians 1, verses 30 and 31, we glory only in the Lord because He 'of God is made unto us wisdom, and righteousness, and sanctification, and redemption'. 'Being justified freely by his grace through the redemption that is in Christ Jesus.'

5 Propitiation

*

Whom God hath set forth to be a propitiation through faith in his blood, to declare his righteousness for the remission of sins that are past, through the forbearance of God.   Romans 3:25

In this verse we come to the beginning of a new sub-section of the great statement that runs from the twenty-first verse to the end of this chapter. I have suggested that in verses 21 to 24 the Apostle announces the way of salvation, but that from verse 25 onwards he deals with some of the great characteristics of this salvation. There is a sense in which this division which I am making is not an absolute one. The two parts are obviously very closely connected; for here, at once, you notice that the Apostle continues a statement that he has already begun in the twenty-fourth verse. There, he tells us that we are 'justified freely by God's grace through the redemption that is in Christ Jesus'. Then, here, 'Whom God set forth'. So that while this is, from the ultimate standpoint, the beginning of a new sub-section, nevertheless it is vital for us to realize that the connection with the previous one is very close and intimate.

In other words the Apostle now begins to describe this redemption which he has already told us the Gospel announces and declares in Christ Jesus. He begins to explain how we are redeemed in this way by the Lord Jesus Christ, and, furthermore, why it had to happen in this way. We are looking here at one of the most important verses in the whole of Scripture; there is no doubt about that. Somebody has described this as 'the acropolis of the Bible and of the Christian faith'. The whole section we are dealing with, from verse 21 to verse 31 in this chapter, is absolutely crucial for a true understanding of Christian doctrine and the way of salvation. We therefore cannot examine it too closely or too carefully. Now because it is so important, it is a passage – and this verse in particular – which has led to a great deal of disputation and argument. There has possibly been more discussion and debating and argument in the Christian Church throughout her long history concerning the way of salvation, and especially concerning the death of our Lord and the Atonement, than concerning any other single subject. That should not surprise us. As it is the crucial, the key and the central doctrine it is not a bit surprising that the enemy, the devil, should have done his utmost to confuse people with respect to it, and that therefore there should have been all this discussion and debating instead of worship and adoration.

It would be very easy to spend many chapters in just giving an historical account of the ways in which people have argued and debated about this, and what they have said concerning it. Let me give just one illustration to show what I mean. The various translations show this very point which I am trying to make. Take for instance the American Revised Standard Version which has become so popular in these last few years. That translation puts it like this: 'Whom God hath put forward as an expiation by his blood.' You notice it is no longer 'propitiation' but 'expiation'. Now that is just one example of these tendencies to which I am referring and to which I shall refer in greater detail. It is an example of a translation that has already become exposition. It has put a word which has a different meaning in place of the word used by the Apostle. I could easily adduce many other examples of the same thing. So, obviously, as we come to look at this great verse we have to be unusually wary.

What, then, is the statement? The first thing is fairly clear. It is this, 'Whom God hath set forth'. Now the actual word which is translated 'set forth' can carry the meaning of nothing more than 'proposed', or, as it is translated in the first chapter of this Epistle, 'purposed' – 'I would not have you ignorant, brethren, that oftentimes I purposed to come unto you' [1: 13]. It is the same word. But that is not the only meaning of this word; and there is very little doubt that the translators of the Authorized Version were quite right in translating it as 'set forth'. The whole context demands that. You remember that in verse 21 the Apostle says, 'But now' – this 'something new' has happened, namely that 'The righteousness of God without the law is manifested'. 'Set forth' again, you see; made plain, revealed, manifested. That is his emphasis. Indeed he more or less says the same thing in verse 26: 'To declare, I say, at this time his righteousness' – something has been 'declared'. This AV translation is right, and we take it as 'Whom God hath set forth – publicly set forth.

That is the Apostle's way of describing the Cross, the death of our Lord on Calvary's hill. God was there 'setting forth' in public, He was making a public declaration, a public exposition. He was publishing something. It is interesting to observe that in writing to the Galatians the Apostle again conveys this same idea with another very interesting word. In the first verse of the third chapter of that Epistle he writes: 'O foolish Galatians, who hath bewitched you that ye should not obey the truth, before whose eyes Jesus Christ hath been evidently set forth.' Now the real meaning of that expression is 'placarded'. I 'placarded' Him, says the Apostle. That is the way he describes his preaching, that he 'set forth' in public, placarded, the death of Christ upon the Cross. And what he says here is that God has made a public declaration by what happened on the Cross.

But here is the vital question. What exactly was it that did happen on Calvary's hill? What is the meaning of the death of the Lord Jesus Christ upon the Cross? The answer is given in this great verse, and it is found in two words which are absolutely crucial. The first is the word 'propitiation'; the second is the word 'blood' – propitiation and blood. Let us look at them together. Take this word 'propitiation'. It is not only found here. We have it in the First Epistle of John, second chapter, second verse; and also in the same Epistle in the fourth chapter and the tenth verse. But we must be careful about the usage of this word 'propitiation' in the Authorized translation. The word which the Apostle used and which is translated 'propitiation' in the AV is not the same word as was used by John in the two examples I have just given. It is the same root word. It belongs to the same family, but it is not the identical word. That has introduced a certain amount of difficulty with regard to the verse we are looking at.

The word which Paul used and which is translated 'propitiation' is exactly the same word which you find in Hebrews chapter 9 verse 5: 'And over it the cherubims of glory shadowing the mercy-seat.' The author of the Epistle to the Hebrews is there describing the old tabernacle of worship. He says, 'There was a tabernacle made, the first, wherein was the candlestick and the table and the shewbread; which is called the sanctuary. And after the second veil, the tabernacle which is called the Holiest of all; which had the golden censer, and the ark of the covenant overlaid round about with gold, wherein was the golden pot that had manna, and Aaron's rod that budded, and the tables of the covenant; and over it the cherubims of glory shadowing the mercy-seat; of which we cannot now speak particularly.' The word translated 'propitiation' here is the exact word that was used there by that author, and which is rightly translated there as the 'mercy-seat'. It is also the same Greek word which the translation of the Old Testament known as the Septuagint uses to translate this word 'mercy-seat'. There are those, therefore, who say that it should have been translated as 'mercy-seat' here. What would that tell us? It involves the meaning and significance and purpose of the mercy-seat. There it was, in the Holiest of all, the innermost sanctum of the tabernacle, separated by a veil from the holy place, which was in turn separated from the outer court, and so on.

Now this is the significant fact – only one man was allowed to go into that Holiest of all, and he only once a year, and that was the High Priest. The High Priest used to go into the Holiest of all on the great Day of Atonement. He took blood that had been obtained from the sacrifice of animals, and he sprinkled it on the mercy-seat and before it. What was the object? It was the way of making atonement for the sins of the people. He went in bearing the sins of the nation, and carrying this blood. The animal had been sacrificed. He was taking the blood of the sacrificed animal and offering it thus to God; and God accepted it. Then he went out and the people knew that their sins had been atoned for, and covered for another year.

There are those who argue that that is what the Apostle is saying here, that he is saying that the Lord Jesus Christ is the mercy-seat appointed by God where He meets man and tells him that He has pardoned him and forgiven him. You remember that the mercy-seat was a slab of gold on top of the ark which contained the golden pot with the manna, and Aaron's rod that budded, and the tables of the Covenant. Now the top of this box, this ark, was that sheet of gold, with a cherub made of beaten gold at each end of it – the cherubim facing each other and over-shadowing the mercy-seat and representing the presence of God. The two cherubim were looking upon the mercy-seat. Under the mercy-seat was the Law, God's Law to man, which man has to keep. There it is – the mercy-seat with the Law underneath, and God as it were looking down upon it. When the High Priest came in and sprinkled the blood, God announced that He was satisfied, that the Law had been honoured, and that the people were forgiven.

There are many who have held therefore that that is exactly what is being taught here – that the Lord Jesus Christ is God's new mercy-seat, where He meets all of us who believe in Christ, and says to us in this way that the Law has been honoured, that our sins are forgiven. Jesus Christ as the mercy-seat.

But it seems to me that we really must agree once more with those AV translators, and with the vast majority of commentators throughout the centuries – and especially the vast majority of evangelical commentators – who have said that it is better to translate this word in verse 25 as 'propitiation' or 'propitiatory sacrifice'. Why? For the reason that it would be a very odd thing for the Apostle suddenly to introduce a technical term like 'mercy-seat' without giving any explanation at all. He does not make use of any of the Levitical ceremonial in this Epistle, and it would be an odd thing for him suddenly to introduce it without saying anything at all about it or explaining it. So there is very little doubt that the real meaning is better conveyed by this idea of propitiation or propitiatory sacrifice. Of course, in the end, it comes to very much the same thing. The propitiatory sacrifice, the blood of the propitiatory sacrifice, is sprinkled on the place of propitiation, which is the mercy-seat. But there is no single place in the whole of Scripture where the Lord Jesus Christ is referred to as the mercy-seat. There are many places in which He is referred to as the propitiation or the Atonement, and so on, but not a single instance of where He is described as the mercy-seat. It seems to me, therefore, that that is sufficient ground for us to accept this translation and to call it the 'means of propitiation' or 'propitiatory sacrifice'.

What, then, does propitiation mean? What is it to propitiate? It means to appease, to placate, to avert wrath. That great Puritan divine, Dr John Owen, said that there are four things which are essential elements in any propitiation, and here they are:

1 An offence to be taken away,
2 A person offended who needs to be pacified,
3 An offending person; a person guilty of the offence,
4 A sacrifice or some other means of making atonement for the offence.

Those four points are most important and have been generally accepted. The whole notion of propitiation implies these four things. What the Apostle is teaching here is that what our Lord did by His death upon the cross was to appease God's wrath. This is a statement to the effect that God's wrath has been appeased and that God has been placated as the result of the work which our Lord did there by dying upon the Cross.

I am giving a positive exposition. I must, however, go on to say that this is an exposition which is hotly disputed today, and has been so disputed for some time. Someone may say, 'Well, why do you bother to deal with that; why not be content with just giving us a positive exposition; why do you trouble to tell us about the people who disagree with this?' Let me tell you why I feel compelled to do so. I have already said that there are certain translations of the Bible which reject the exposition I have just given. Many evangelical people use such translations and imagine that they are more accurate. Because they are easier to read they think they must be better. But what should be a translation sometimes becomes an interpretation which is determined by the theological opinions of the translator. The mere fact that a translation seems to read easily does not mean, of necessity, that it is good or a true translation. The translator's prejudices may come in, his interpretation comes in. And that is undoubtedly the case with the modern translations at this point. We have got to deal with this matter for that reason.

Not only that; I have a further reason. I was reading in a well-known evangelical periodical recently a review of books for reading during Lent, and there I saw that one book was praised very much. The reviewer said that he 'warmly recommended' this for devotional reading. I must confess I was surprised, because I knew something about the standpoint of the author of the book. It was a book on the Cross. The next step was that I saw a review of the same book in a paper that is not only not evangelical, but opposes evangelical doctrine, and is frankly and avowedly liberal in its theology. That also gave the book great praise. Then, almost by accident, the book came into my hands, and I read it and found that that book, which had been warmly recommended by the evangelical periodical, not only does not believe in propitiation but attacks the notion, and, indeed, attacks the generally accepted evangelical view of our Lord's work upon the Cross. So I feel constrained to deal with this matter in detail. People, unfortunately, still tend to believe anything they read in a paper or a journal; and if they see anything in supposedly evangelical journals they assume that it must be right.

Then, and still more interesting in a way, I discovered only last week an article on this very subject in another paper which is not evangelical. This is what it said: 'To propitiate is usually taken to mean placating or pacifying an angry person, doing something to appease someone who has been offended. A great many people have supposed that this sort of reasoning can be applied to our relationship with God. He is offended by our sins and something must be done to avert the anger. And since man cannot accomplish this on his own, Christ, it is said, has appeased

God's wrath against sin through the death on the Cross. It is quite in this sense that many understand the texts, "Whom God set forth to be a propitiation through faith in his blood" [*Romans* 3:25], and "He is the propitiation for our sins" [1 *John* 2:2].' The author goes on to say: 'I cannot think that this is a satisfactory explanation of what those texts mean'; indeed he suggests that the explanation is almost blasphemous.

We are living in times when it is not enough just to accept an interpretation that is put before us. We must know why we accept it. We must be able to defend it, we must be able to comprehend it and to grasp it. On what grounds is it that people reject this term 'propitiation' and want to substitute for it that other word 'expiation'? The man in the article I have quoted does that very thing. He says we ought to get rid of the word 'propitiation' and put 'expiation' in place of it. Why do they say that? These are their two main reasons. They say, first of all, that they have reasons from language, philological reasons, linguistic reasons. They grant that the word as used by non-biblical and pagan authors certainly did convey always that suggestion of placating and appeasing an angry deity; but they say that when you come to the Greek translation of the Old Testament, the Septuagint, it no longer carries that meaning. And as the Apostle generally quotes the Septuagint Version it is obvious that he likewise did not mean it to have that particular connotation. That is their first reason.

Their second reason is this – and this is the more important one – that this whole notion of the wrath of God is not only wrong and must be utterly rejected, but that it is almost blasphemous. They do not hesitate to say that. They say that it turns God into some sort of monster or ogre, that it is a totally unworthy idea. Some dismiss it as being but the Jews' conception of God in the Old Testament. A popular preacher said in a printed sermon recently that he did not believe in 'that God who sat on the top of Mount Sinai issuing forth His wrath and His anger'. He believed in 'the God and Father of our Lord Jesus Christ'. The whole notion of wrath in God is regarded as utterly abhorrent.

How then do they interpret the Bible when it talks about wrath? They reply by saying that wrath is nothing but an inevitable consequence of sin. If I put my finger in a fire I get pain, I burn my finger. They say that wrath is something like that; the moment a man does something he should not do against God he suffers for it. They deny that there is any wrath in God. Wrath is the inevitable consequence of wrong-doing. If a man does wrong he is bound to suffer for it – it is inevitable, it is automatic. It has nothing to do with God. It is just in the nature of doing that which is evil. So they argue that for man to be reconciled to God did not necessitate that anything should be done on God's side. God is love, they say; God is always forgiving and always ready to forgive. Indeed God has already forgiven. The trouble is that man in sin does not know that; he is blind to it; sin blinds him. All that is necessary is that man's eyes should be opened to the fact of God's love. There is nothing necessary on the Godward side.

That is the commonly accepted position and teaching. Quite consistently, therefore, our critics say that all that is necessary is what is called 'expiation'. What is that? Expiation means that the guilt of the sin needs to be removed. Expiation is the process in which you cancel the guilt of sin and purify the sinner from it. So in their translations, and in their commentaries, they turn this word 'propitiation' into 'expiation' – 'Whom God hath set forth as an expiation'. They tell us that we must not use that other word that suggests that God is angry against sin, and against the sinner, and that there is some element of appeasement involved. That is an insult to God, it is almost blasphemous. What is needed is expiation. The sin must be blotted out from the sinner, and then all is well.

This is surely a matter which we have to face. What is our answer to this position? We can meet it on both counts, on both charges. First of all, from the standpoint of philology. There is scholarship on the side of propitiation which is quite as powerful as that on the other side. There is always this danger of following some expert on language. It has been the curse of the last hundred years. Men have fixed on particular words, they have tracked them through classical Greek literature and then they have tried to attach a new meaning to scriptural statements. They have ignored the context, they have ignored the whole tenor of the biblical teaching, and have decided and determined vital issues on an odd meaning or shade of meaning of a word. But I aver that purely in terms of linguistics this argument that propitiation should be turned into expiation can be completely answered.

The great exponent, or proponent, of the theory that you should do away with propitiation and call it expiation is the well-known biblical scholar, Dr C. H. Dodd, who is certainly a great expert on the Greek language. But there are others who are opposed to his teaching. The late Dr James Moffatt, who was not evangelical, was opposed to this and stood for propitiation. An up-to-date answer to the position of Dr C. H. Dodd is found in *The Apostolic Preaching of the Cross* by Dr Leon Morris. Let me explain that Morris's book is not a popular book; it is what is called a scholarly book. In it Dr C. H. Dodd's arguments are taken point by point and answered on their own level. As is to be expected in such a book, it has references to many other books and writers. Do not let anyone browbeat you therefore by saying, 'Ah, but Greek scholarship has now proved that it is not propitiation but expiation'. Just reply by saying that that is not the case. The Greek scholars, as is not infrequently the case with them, are almost exactly divided. It is very rarely indeed that the philologist settles any question!

The second matter, which is much more important, is the doctrine of the wrath of God. This was first introduced in the eighteenth verse of the first chapter. I have dealt with this thoroughly elsewhere, in *The Plight of Man and the Power of God*. Let me briefly summarize the teaching. Here is an idea, a teaching, that is to be found everywhere in the Bible. In the Old Testament alone more than twenty different words are used to describe the wrath of God, and these words in various forms are used 580 times in the Old Testament. These modern teachers do not believe in the wrath of God; they say it should be banished. But in the Old Testament this idea is put before us 580 times.

You have it also in the New Testament. Our Lord Himself talks about it, about the wrath of God. It is found repeatedly in the Gospel according to St John, known as the 'Gospel of love', as, for instance, 'the wrath of God abideth on him [*John* 3 :36]. Our Lord brings it out again in the parable of Dives and Lazarus. He speaks about the place in which 'their worm dieth not and the fire is not quenched'. He also spoke those three parables reported in the twenty-fifth chapter of Matthew's Gospel, emphasizing this doctrine. It is in the Book of the Acts of the Apostles: 'He hath appointed a day in which he will judge the whole world in righteousness', says the Apostle Paul in Athens [*Acts* 17]. Peter preached it on the Day of Pentecost in Jerusalem. It is everywhere. In this Epistle to the Romans this doctrine of the wrath of God is mentioned ten times. In the Book of Revelation you are confronted by it from the very beginning to the very end: 'The wrath of the Lamb' and how 'every eye shall see him'. In other words, if you go through the Bible without theories and preconceived notions, you will see at once that this notion that God is angry against sin, that God hates sin, that the wrath of God is upon sin is taught everywhere and is a basic proposition.

We must be very careful as we define this. The writer of the article from which I have just quoted ridicules and caricatures the evangelical position by saying that we are picturing God as some angry, wrathful Potentate. Of course we do nothing of the sort. The word 'wrath' tends to convey that impression to us, it tends to convey the idea of passion, uncontrolled passion. But you never get that in the Scriptures. The Scriptures do not use the word 'wrath' to depict God as Someone who is unreliable and capricious and who is always bursting forth into wrath. That element is not here at all, and it is not essential to the idea of wrath.

What does 'the wrath of God' mean? It means His settled opposition to all that is evil, arising out of His very nature. It is because 'God is light and in him is no darkness at all' that He is in settled opposition to everything that is evil. His nature is such that He abhors evil, He hates evil. His holiness of neces-

[75]

sity leads to that. Then, in addition, it seems to me that this other idea regards sin as if it were a sort of substance, and forgets that sin is something that is always attached to persons. The problem is this – the personal relationship between God and man. Sin is not a thing, it is not a substance. It is the condition of a human being, it is the condition of a soul. You cannot separate sin from persons, so when God deals with sin He has to deal with persons, and when He deals with persons He has to deal with sin. So the Bible teaches everywhere that God is opposed to sin and to the sinner. And this personal relationship must never be forgotten.

The Bible's view of sin is that sin is that which separates man from God; sin is that which comes between man and God. God, we are told, 'is not weary', 'His hand is not shortened nor his ear deaf that he cannot hear', but this sin has come between us and Him [*Isaiah* 59: 1–2]. Sin breaks this personal relationship, and we must always think of it in those terms.

But not only that; it can be shown quite easily that these authors are inconsistent with themselves. I have referred earlier to certain modern writers who say that wrath is just the inevitable consequence of sin. Well then, to be logical they ought to say that mercy is the inevitable consequence of goodness. They dislike saying that the wrath is in God; wrath is just the inevitable consequence of sin. We are then entitled to ask, What is mercy? Why not say that, if I am good, mercy comes automatically. But they will not have that and insist that mercy is something inherent in the character of God. On the one side they put it in the character of God, on the other side they take it out of the character of God. That is to be inconsistent. Surely both things are in the character of God.

But, indeed, they are guilty of another contradiction also. Take the whole idea of expiation. These critics say that this notion of expiation is an essential part of biblical teaching. Man's sin, they say, must be cancelled, and what Christ did was to cancel man's sin. But we must ask, Why does man's sin need to be cancelled? Why do you need expiation? What would be the position if no expiation were provided? If there were no expiation made, would it make any difference to God's attitude towards sin? Surely the very idea of expiation in and of itself leads to propitiation! If there must be expiation, why must there be expiation? There is only one answer – that there cannot be a true relationship between God and man until that sin has been expiated. But that is just another way of saying *propitiation*. There cannot be a happy relationship between God and man while sin is there. That is precisely what the biblical doctrine of the wrath of God says. So, in the last analysis, after all their protestations they seem to come back to precisely the same thing.

The Apostle John's way of putting it confirms this, 'If any man sin', he says, not only have we got a propitiation, which they call expiation, 'we have an advocate with the Father' [1 *John* 2:1–2] Why do I need an advocate? What is the business of an advocate? Is it not something in connection with this personal relationship between God and man? John does not merely say that we need to have our sins expiated, but adds that we have an Advocate also. That immediately suggests that there is something wrong in the personal relationship.

I trust it is now clear that we have not been wasting our time. That other idea is so common that people feel that it does not matter whether you say expiation or propitiation. But it does matter, and in this way, that if you really want to see what God's love is you must hold on to this notion of propitiation. It is a much bigger and more profound idea than expiation. In any case it is essential to the argument of the Apostle. From chapter 1, verse 18, right up to this point the Apostle has been dealing with one thing only, 'The wrath of God has been revealed from heaven against all ungodliness and unrighteousness of men', on Jew and on Gentile. 'All have sinned and come short of the glory of God.' All are under sin, all are under the wrath of God. That is the whole point. But here he says, Now I have some marvellous good news – 'But now'. Well, what is the good news? 'A propitiation has been provided.' Something has happened and has taken place as the result of which God's honour has been vindicated and His wrath appeased. How has that been done?

Here, once more, critics try to ridicule our position by saying that what we are teaching is a pagan notion. When pagans had done something wrong they said, 'The gods are against us, what can we do? We will take an offering, we will take a present to the god and try to bribe him. It will please him, and he will be so delighted with our offering that he will overlook our sin and will forgive us.' Surely, the critics contend, you are saying the same thing. You are saying that it is possible for a man somehow to influence God and to change God's mind. You are talking about doing something that is going to change God's attitude. But that is not our position. This has nothing to do with pagan mythology. This is in no sense borrowed from such a source, as I can easily prove. We are not even teaching that the Lord Jesus Christ has changed the mind of God. Let us be honest and admit that there have been certain zealous evangelical teachers who have said that. But they should never have said so. There are hymns that have taught that. They are equally wrong. Paul does not teach that the Lord Jesus Christ by dying has persuaded God to forgive us. Notice what Paul actually says: 'Whom God hath set forth'. It is God the Father Himself who is doing it. It is not even the case that the Lord Jesus Christ has changed the mind and the attitude of God towards sinners. It is God Himself providing the propitiation in His own Son and by His blood. It is God contriving a way whereby His own wrath upon sin has its full vent and yet that sinners might be saved. That is what the Apostle teaches here.

Are you clear as to the difference between expiation and propitiation? Propitiation carries this notion that there is Someone who has been offended, someone who has done the offending, that there is an offence, and that something is necessary on both sides. Something has got to be done from the side of the One who has been offended as well as from the side of the offender; and this great and glorious doctrine teaches us that the very God whom we have offended has Himself provided the way whereby the offence has been dealt with. His anger, His wrath against sin and the sinner, has been satisfied, appeased, and He therefore can now thus reconcile man unto Himself. So you see the importance of holding on to this great word 'propitiation'.

[78]

As we go on with our exposition we shall see this still more clearly. We shall see why we have to fight for this and to hold on to this. The word 'blood' will reinforce all the arguments.

I trust that certain things are plain and clear. It is not that sinful man, or even the Lord Jesus Christ, has to persuade God to do this. It is God Himself who has done it; and He has done it in the most amazing and marvellous manner. If you take out of the Bible this idea of the wrath of God against sin there is very little Bible left.

But why do people object to this teaching concerning the wrath of God? There is only one answer; it is that they substitute Greek philosophy for the biblical revelation. The Greek philosophers did not like the idea of wrath. They regarded the whole notion of wrath as something weak and discreditable. They said it was an unworthy emotion and therefore to attribute it to God was quite wrong. They said that even in a man wrath is a terrible thing, but in God . . .! The god of the Greek philosophers is impassive, he does not feel anything at all, he cannot be affected by anything that happens. He is incapable, therefore, of feeling wrath against sin or against the sinner. All the argument of the last hundred years is simply due to that influence. Scholars dominated by Greek thinking and philosophy say that the Hebrews had a wrong idea of God, and that we must get rid of it. God is love, and nothing but love, they say. So there is no wrath in God and there is no need of propitiation. Some of them go so far as to say that there is even no need for expiation, and that all that the death of our Lord upon the Cross does is to make me say when I look at it, 'If God forgives even that, then I must believe that He loves me'. As I once heard a man put it, 'God was not making a way of forgiveness on Calvary; what was happening is that God was proclaiming that He even forgives Calvary'.

You see, therefore, the importance of accepting the authority of the Scriptures. If you start with your philosophical idea of God instead of the biblical idea of God, you can throw out the idea of wrath, you can throw out sin, you can throw out propitiation, you can throw out atonement, you can throw out anything you like. But it is no longer the Bible, it is no longer the Christian faith. You no longer believe in 'the Lamb of God that taketh away the sin of the world,' and, as I hope to show, you will dislike the whole notion of blood and of sacrifice. We are all forced to this choice – I either submit to the Bible and accept its revelation of God in His Being and His character and activity; or else I say, 'Well now, I think . . .' That is philosophy; that has been the curse. The Church of God is as she is now because, since about 1840, men have been putting philosophy in the place of revelation, ideas before what God Himself has so graciously been pleased to reveal. It affects everything; it affects above everything else our view of the most glorious event in all history – the Death of the Son of God upon the Cross on Calvary's hill.

6 The Blood of Jesus Christ

*

Whom God hath set forth to be a propitiation through faith in his blood, to declare his righteousness for the remission of sins that are past, through the forbearance of God;   Romans 3:25

As we continue our study of this crucial statement I would remind you that the Apostle's fundamental pronouncement is that 'we are justified freely by his grace through the redemption that is in Christ Jesus'. How does the Lord Jesus Christ ransom us? Redemption means ransoming – how does He ransom us? The answer is that 'God hath set him forth as a propitiation' – as a propitiatory sacrifice – 'for our sins'. That brings us to this question: How has God done that? In what sense is the Lord Jesus Christ the propitiatory sacrifice? Or if you prefer to take it in that other way, how is He the propitiatory, the mercy-seat? There is a good deal, as we have seen, to be said for both those views which actually come to much the same thing.

So the question confronting us is this: In what sense is the Lord Jesus Christ this propitiatory sacrifice? The answer is given in the important term that is now before us. It is 'in his blood'. This is a thoroughly New Testament statement. 'The blood of Jesus Christ' in connection with our redemption and salvation is something that is frequently emphasized. Let me give you some examples. Take for instance Acts 20:28. In that most lyrical passage we read of the Apostle Paul saying farewell to the leaders of the Church at Ephesus. He has warnings to issue, he has advice to give. But above all he is anxious that they should 'feed the Church of God which he hath purchased with his own blood'. What a wonderful statement! The same thing

[81]

that we have here in Romans 3:25! Again, there is a very striking statement of it in the fifth chapter of this Epistle in the ninth verse: 'Much more then,' he says, 'being now justified by his blood . . .' In the Epistle to the Ephesians you find it in the first chapter and the seventh verse: 'In whom we have redemption through his blood, even the forgiveness of sins . . .'

The great Apostle clearly enjoyed writing these great phrases. It is the same thing almost everywhere. In the second chapter of Ephesians, verse 13, you have it again. He reminds these Ephesians that they were at one time 'strangers from the covenants of promise, and enemies and aliens from the commonwealth of Israel'; they were 'without hope and without God in the world'; they were once 'afar off'. 'But now', he says, 'you have been made nigh by the blood of Christ' – still the same thing. Whatever the particular line of approach, it is always 'by the blood of Christ'. Then in the Epistle to the Hebrews, chapter 9:12, 'Neither by the blood of goats and calves, but by his own blood he entered in once into the holy place, having obtained eternal redemption for us'. He is contrasting the Lord Jesus Christ and His work with all that was true of the Old Testament, the Levitical priesthood and all its ordinances. He is looking at this great High Priest, the Son of God, and he says, 'He has not gone in by the blood of goats and of calves, but by his own blood he entered in once and for ever into the holy place, having obtained eternal redemption for us' – precisely the same idea. And in the fourteenth verse of that same chapter he says, 'How much more shall the blood of Christ, who through the eternal Spirit offered himself without spot to God, purge your conscience from dead works to serve the living God'.

Yet another example is found in Hebrews 10:19, a most important one. 'Having therefore, brethren, boldness to enter into the Holiest by the blood of Jesus . . .' There is no more important text in the Bible, I sometimes think, than that. That is the whole secret of prayer; and we do not know what prayer is unless we really grasp the meaning of that great statement. Then you find it in the First Epistle of Peter, chapter 1, verse 19. He reminds them that they have been 'redeemed from their vain conversation inherited by tradition from their fathers; not with silver or gold'. Well, how then? 'By the precious blood of Christ, as of a Lamb without blemish and without spot.' Then go on to the First Epistle of John (and I am giving these quotations just to meet the objection which men are so ready to bring forward, that these are simply Paul's Judaistic ideas once more imposing themselves on to the Gospel). 1 John 1:7, 'But if we walk in the light as he is in the light, we have fellowship one with another, and the blood of Jesus Christ his Son cleanseth us from all sin.' Then, finally, in the Book of Revelation in the first chapter and the fifth verse: 'Unto him that loved us and hath washed us from our sins in his own blood.' I have selected these examples in order to show that this is the characteristic way in which the New Testament deals with and describes our redemption and our salvation. How is the Lord Jesus Christ the propitiatory sacrifice? The answer is 'by his blood'.

Now an interesting thing for us to observe is this. Why does the Apostle Paul, and why do the other writers talk about His *blood* and not simply say His *death*? Why say particularly His *blood*? This is the vital question, because it is obviously something that is done quite deliberately. And there is an obvious answer to the question. The term *blood* is used rather than *death* in order to bring this teaching concerning our Lord, and the way in which He redeems us, into line with the whole of the teaching of the Old Testament with regard to sacrifices.

You notice how important it is that we should pay attention to every single statement in the Scriptures. You remember how careful the Apostle was in the twenty-first verse to say, 'But now, the righteousness of God without the law is manifested' – then – 'being witnessed by the law and the prophets.' We emphasized that and drew certain deductions from it. One of them was that our interpretation of the New Testament must never contradict the Old Testament teaching. If it does, it is wrong, because the two fit in and belong together perfectly. All we have in the New was predicted in the Old. The New is the fulfilment of the Old. So, as the Apostle uses the term *blood* here, he reminds us that it is in line with the Old Testament teaching. It is the same

God, it is the same salvation. There it is in one form, here it is in another. The dispensations differ, the salvation is always one and the same. The New Testament doctrine about the death of the Lord Jesus Christ, you will find, is always couched and put in terms of the Old Testament sacrificial language.

That is a fundamental principle of interpretation, and it is because so many depart from that today, on account of their wrong views of the Old Testament, that they have to twist and turn and manipulate here, and turn this into something that fits in with their modern theories and ideas. But if you take it at its face value, and if you interpret it as it is meant to be interpreted, in terms of that other teaching, you will find that there is no difficulty, and that it all opens out before us in a perfectly simple manner.

The New Testament, then, always puts this doctrine in terms of the Old Testament sacrificial teaching. John the Baptist started this practice. He stood, you remember, with his disciples, and he pointed to our Lord and said: 'Behold the Lamb of God that taketh away the sin of the world.' That is the beginning of the New Testament, in a sense. 'Behold him', he says. 'Look at him.' What is He? He is the 'Lamb of God'. At once you are back in the Old Testament sacrificial teaching. And we must never lose sight of that. Indeed our Lord Himself said exactly the same thing. You will find that in the Sermon on the Mount in the fifth chapter of Matthew's Gospel, verses 17 and 18. He says, 'I have not come to destroy the law and the prophets; I came not to destroy but to fulfil. One jot or one tittle shall not pass from the law until all be fulfilled.' He has completely fulfilled all that is adumbrated and suggested and prophesied in the old Levitical teaching. He has brought all that to an end. He has fulfilled all. He is the great anti-type to which all the types were looking forward, and which they were foretelling. So you have it there. And, as we have already seen, it is in many of our Lord's own statements, for instance: 'The Son of man came not to be ministered unto but to minister, and to give his life a ransom for many' [*Matthew* 20:28]. What a vital verse! And again, you will find that in Luke 24:44 and 45 he goes through it all again. He took them through the Law and the Prophets and the Book of Psalms: '. . . all things must be fulfilled, which were written in the law of Moses, and in the prophets, and in the psalms, concerning me . . . Thus it is written, and thus it behoved Christ to suffer, and to rise from the dead the third day.' It is all there.

Here, in the Epistle to the Romans, it is looked at from the other angle. The Apostle is looking back at the thing which has happened, as the Old Testament was looking forward to that which was going to happen. There is a wonderful statement of it, made by this same Apostle, in his First Epistle to the Corinthians, chapter 5, verse 7: 'For even Christ our Passover is sacrificed for us.' And then John, in the last book of the Bible, the Book of Revelation, says, 'Unto him that loved us and has washed us in his own blood' [*Revelation* 1:5]. It is the typical, characteristic Old Testament sacrificial teaching; and if we are to understand the meaning of the death of our blessed Lord and Saviour we have got to approach it in this way. But, unfortunately, I have again to remind you that all this is made the subject of debate and dispute at this present time, and that there is much disputation and confusion concerning this word 'blood'.

One does this reluctantly but – as I have previously argued – owing to the fact that these loose notions are current, and that they are creeping into some of the new translations of the Scriptures, and are found in the books that are so often recommended, I regard it as my duty to issue a warning. I am but trying to follow the example of the Apostle Paul who, when he was bidding farewell to the elders at Ephesus, deemed it to be his duty to warn them against false teaching, and against certain wolves who would come in and try to destroy the flock. Such wolves are rampant at the present time; and it is a part of the duty of any man who claims to be a teacher of the Scriptures to warn men and women against these subtle heresies that subvert the Christian faith. That is why I call your attention to two attitudes towards this word *blood* that are so common today.

The first is one which just rejects it *in toto*, absolutely. It dislikes it altogether and it speaks of it in a blasphemous manner.

I have heard men talking about 'these Evangelicals who like to wallow in blood'. They speak with sarcasm and scorn and derision and blasphemy in that way. They say that this is nothing but Judaism; this is the Old Testament with its tribal God so closely related to paganism. They maintain that it has nothing to do with Christianity, and with the Lord Jesus Christ and His exposition of the love of God. They say it is about time we banished it, and all those hymns that mention it and glory in it. They ridicule the very idea; they hate and abominate it. The whole theology of blood is something that they detest and, indeed, despise. I have nothing to say about such people, except that I cannot see that they are Christian at all. I have nothing further to say about them.

But I must say a little more about the second group, because they are not guilty of dismissing the term altogether. They do something else, which, from the standpoint of this doctrine of the Atonement, it seems to me, is equally dangerous. It has been the custom and the practice now for some sixty to seventy years to say that the Church's conception of the blood of Christ – and, indeed, the whole conception of blood in connection with sacrifices even in the Old Testament – has always been completely wrong. In the past, they say, the Church always regarded the blood as representing the death, but, they maintain that the blood represents the life. Do not the Scriptures say that 'the life is in the blood?' Very well, they say, when those people under the Levitical Mosaic system went into the Temple or Tabernacle and presented the blood of the animals that had been sacrificed – what were they doing? They were not presenting a death they were presenting a life. 'The life is in the blood', so if you present the blood you are presenting a life. It was their way of saying that they wanted to give themselves to God again, so they gave themselves through the life of the animal which was in the blood of the animal. It was a means of self-dedication; they were renewing an act of dedication of themselves to God. And so they argue that when the Lord Jesus Christ died upon the Cross, and when the New Testament refers to His blood, what is really meant is that He was offering His life to God. It is not His death that

[86]

matters; it is His life that matters. He offered His life to God in a final act of dedication. He had dedicated Himself to God, He had obeyed God and His holy law in every respect. He obeyed this last commandment about going on even unto death. He gave His whole life to God. The blood, they say, stands for the life, and not for the death.

You may well ask the question, Why do they say all this? What is their object? There is only one answer to that – they do so in order to avoid the doctrine of the wrath of God, which we have already considered. They do not like that, indeed they abominate it. This is their way of getting rid of the idea of the wrath of God, of getting rid of the idea that God punishes sin, of getting rid of propitiation. It is because they dislike these fundamental ideas of God's wrath upon sin, the penal attitude, and therefore the necessity for propitiation, that they have to twist these words right round, and so 'the offence of the Cross' becomes something positive and beautiful and wonderful. The Lord was just presenting His life, and if we believe in Him we present our lives in Him and through Him.

I might add that they do this in terms of scholarship, and claim that this view is based upon a more thorough knowledge and understanding of language. Again there is only one answer as there was before. This contention cannot be established in terms of language and of scholarship. It is a subject that has been treated many times. There is a little booklet which does this very adequately, written by the Rev A. M. Stibbs. It is called *The Meaning of 'Blood' in Scripture*. He has taken up this argument point by point; and there are others who have done the same thing. Leon Morris in *The Apostolic Preaching of the Cross* does this also in an equally scholarly and linguistic manner.

In terms of language alone this theory simply cannot be established – indeed the reverse can be established. It can be shown clearly that the 'blood' in Scripture means 'life laid down in death'. Not 'life', but 'life laid down in death'. The blood is the final proof of the fact that death has been accomplished. It is not life preserved, it is life given up, it is life which has been laid down. It is very interesting and important to remember that the Hebrews, the Jews, never thought of life apart from the body; so that the idea that you can have life in the blood entirely separate from, and apart from, the body is something that was never known to the Hebrew. He always connected life intimately and of necessity with the body. So this idea that you can have life outside the body, in the blood, is something that is completely false to and contradictory to the basic Hebrew way of thinking. The blood always means the life poured out. So that in the animal sacrifices the blood means that the animal had been put to death, the life had been taken, and the blood was taken as proof positive of that – that the animal had suffered death. The punishment that should have come upon the Jews had come upon the animal as the substitute. The blood was presented in order to prove the fact of the death. 'Blood' means therefore 'a sacrificial death'.

What was the purpose of that? Why did God command these sacrificial killings? What was the purpose of the sacrificial death of the animals in the Old Testament? What is the Old Testament sacrificial teaching? It teaches four things which are of the greatest importance. First, their design was to propitiate God. The Old Testament animal sacrifices were not meant to affect man at all, they were directed towards God. There is not a scintilla of evidence in the whole of the Old Testament that those sacrifices were meant to do anything to the people. They made them in order, as it were, to affect God. That was the whole object, the whole purpose. That is their design, to propitiate God.

The second principle is that the propitiation was secured by the expiation or the cancelling of the guilt of the sinner. As we have already seen, expiation of necessity leads to propitiation; it is by means of expiation you procure propitiation. The sin is expunged, cancelled, and therefore you go to God who is now propitiated.

The third principle is that the propitiation was effected by the vicarious punishment of the victim substituted by the offender, and for him. The sinner, the offender, took a lamb or a bull or a goat, and he laid his hands upon it, thereby symbolically laying his sins upon the animal; and then the animal was slain. The animal is a vicarious sufferer, it bears the punishment vicariously. The sinner substitutes the animal for himself. That is a most important principle and you cannot begin to understand the Old Testament teaching in the books of Exodus and Leviticus unless you grasp that principle – the vicarious punishment of a victim which is substituted for the offender and by the offender.

Fourthly, the effect of sacrificial offerings was the pardon of the offender and his restoration into the favour and the fellowship of God.

Those are the four great principles which we must never lose sight of. Remember that the blood always had to be produced. It was not merely enough that the animal should be killed. No; it was bled; the blood had to be produced. This is the way in which the sacrificial system operated.

But still, someone may ask, and ask quite fairly and quite rightly, why was all this necessary? The answer is given in a great statement in Hebrews 9:22, 'Without the shedding of blood there is no remission of sins'. Why not? The answer is found in the last verse of the sixth chapter of the Epistle to the Romans. It is because 'the wages of sin is death'. That is the fundamental principle. God made it known to man – 'The day thou eatest thereof thou shalt die'. 'The wages of sin is death.' God's decreed punishment for sin is death. Sin can therefore never be dealt with apart from death. There is no remission of sins apart from the shedding of blood. You see how consistent this Scriptural teaching is from beginning to end. God lays it down even before the Fall, and when man fell it immediately came into practice. So you find it running right through the Old Testament. That is the meaning of all those sacrifices and offerings which you read of, and which continue right through the Old Testament dispensation, and which our Lord Himself, as we have seen, repeatedly tells us were prophecies of Himself and of what He had come to do.

We are now in a position therefore to say what this teaching is concerning the blood of Christ. What does the Apostle mean here when he says, 'Whom God hath set forth to be a propitiation through faith in his blood'? Surely it is obvious and inevitable that it means that Christ is our Substitute. The animals were the substitutes taken by the sinner; but what we are told here is that God Himself has made Christ our Substitute. It is God who has set Him forth as a propitiation for our sins. That is the marvel and the wonder of it all. There is nothing that we could provide; man cannot go beyond the animals. If he gives himself, that is the end of him; he is killed, he is dead, and he is lost to all eternity. Man could not produce a substitute; the whole glory and marvel of the Gospel is that God Himself has done so; and it is here we really begin to see the love of God. The very God whom we have offended has Himself provided the Substitute. He has set forth His own Son as the propitiation for our sins.

What does it mean as regards our Lord? It means that He has borne our sins and their guilt. 'God hath laid on him the iniquity of us all' [*Isaiah* 53]. His soul, His life has been made an offering for sin. Our sins have been laid upon Him; and the wrath of God upon those sins has come upon Him. That is what it means. Peter, quoting Isaiah 53 again at the end of the second chapter of his First Epistle, puts it like this: 'Who his own self bare our sins in his own body on the tree, that we, being dead to sins, should live unto righteousness; by whose stripes we are healed.' 'God', says Isaiah prophetically, looking forward to it, 'hath smitten him.' 'We beheld him, smitten of God.' That means that not only have the sins been laid upon Him, but that the wrath of God has been poured out upon Him. The punishment that should have come to you and to me on account of our sinfulness and our sins came to Him.

That is why you have these tremendous statements in the Gospel and elsewhere – John 3:16, 'God so loved the world that he GAVE . . .' That does not mean simply that He gave Him from heaven to come to earth. No! It includes everything. He gave Him up to the death of the Cross. 'He gave his only begotten Son, that whosoever believeth in him . . .' You remember the context is this, that 'as Moses lifted up the serpent in the wilderness, even so must the Son of man be lifted up, that whosoever believeth in him should not perish but have everlasting life'. 'He gave.' Or take the great phrase we shall find in this Epistle in the last verse in the fourth chapter: 'Who was delivered for our offences.' 'Given up to.' To what? Well, not merely to the death on the Cross, but to the wrath of God that led to the death, the punishment of sin. 'He that spared not his own Son', he says again in the eighth chapter, verse 32, 'but delivered him up for us all.' He did not spare Him. That does not just mean that He allowed Him to die. No! He did not spare Him all the punishment that sin deserved and that must be meted out. He did not spare Him the wrath of God. That was why the Son cried out there on the Cross, 'My God, my God, why hast thou forsaken me?' If you do not believe in the doctrine of the wrath of God, and this view of the blood of Christ, what possible meaning is there in that cry of dereliction? What likewise is the meaning of the agony in the Garden? Why did He sweat drops of blood? It was not merely the fear of death. Martyrs have not flinched from suffering and death, they have gone gladly and boldly. But the Son of God asked, 'If it be possible, let this cup pass by'. Why? Because He knew that He was going to feel the wrath of God against the sin He was to bear, and be separated from His Father. It is the only possible explanation.

Take the Scriptures as they are and it all fits in perfectly. But if you do not, and if you substitute your modern philosophical conceptions, there are statements which are simply meaningless and cannot be understood. This is what it means: He gave His life, as He says Himself, 'a ransom for many'. Then, as Hebrews 9, verses 12 and 14, go on to tell us, He was at one and the same time the Sacrifice and the High Priest, He offered His own blood. Not the blood of calves and of goats – that was not enough. That was sufficient for the covering of the defilement of the flesh for the time being; but it was not enough to purify the conscience from these dead works and sins. That is not what He takes. He takes 'his own blood', passes through the heavens and enters, not an earthly sanctuary, but the Holiest of all, the 'Heavenly Sanctuary' which He has purified by something better than the blood of bulls and of goats and of calves and the ashes of an heifer – even by His own blood. He entered in 'once and for all' and presented it, and it was accepted. His death was sufficient, the wrath of God against sin had been poured out; the holiness and the righteousness and the justice and the Law of God had been satisfied fully.

It is in that way, says the Apostle here, that we are 'justified freely by his grace'. It is thus, and thus alone, that we are forgiven. It is thus, as he puts it again in that glorious phrase in Ephesians 2:13, that we are 'made nigh' to God. It is thus that the Jews and Gentiles by one Spirit through Christ, have this access unto the Father – by the blood. 'Having therefore, brethren, boldness to enter into the Holiest by the blood of Jesus' [*Hebrews* 10:19]. It is thus we are reconciled to God. It is thus, and thus alone, we have fellowship and communion with God. We are 'walking with him in the light', says John in his First Epistle and the first chapter. As we do so, as we walk together, the 'blood of Jesus Christ his Son keeps on cleansing us from all sin' and unrighteousness.

Alas, we keep on falling, and we become defiled; but the blood of Christ keeps on cleansing. It is always 'the blood of Christ'. It is that which produces the fellowship and the communion; it is the only thing that guarantees its persistence and its continuance. 'If any man sin, we have an advocate with the Father, Jesus Christ the righteous, and he is the propitiation for our sins; and not for ours only, but also for the sins of the whole world.' It is always 'the blood of Christ' that secures everything.

Who am I? I am a creature who belongs to the new covenant. In Christ we are no longer under the old covenant; there is a new and better covenant. How do I know? What about its title deeds? Has it got a seal on it? How can I be certain of it? Oh yes, the seal is on! What is it? It is 'the blood of Christ'. That is the teaching of Hebrews chapter 9. He says that every testament, every covenant, was always sealed and ratified by blood. So was this, he says. The new covenant has been sealed and ratified by the blood of Christ. So when I come to the Communion Table to take the bread and the wine, what I am told is this: 'This cup is the new testament (the new covenant) in my blood.' What we do together at the Table is to remind ourselves of the new covenant, and that we are in it; that Christ has brought us into

it and under it. We are covered by the blood. Everything is
covered by the blood. And so we belong to the new covenant
and we can read the Will of Christ, the things He has bequeathed
to us and all the glory of our rich inheritance. And it is all, you
see, by His blood.

I am not surprised that the writers of the hymns have written
about it as they have done. Isaac Watts, William Cowper, John
Newton – oh how they delighted in it! and how every true child
of God must delight in it!

> *There is a fountain filled with blood,*
> *Drawn from Immanuel's veins;*
> *And sinners plunged beneath that flood,*
> *Lose all their guilty stains.*

'He died that we might be forgiven.'

No, He was not offering His life; His life was poured out in
death. He is the Lamb of God. He is our Substitute. He died for
us, and for our sins. 'By his stripes we are healed.'

Of whom is this true? It is true of all – and of them alone –
who have faith in Him, 'whom God hath set forth to be a propitiation through faith in his blood'. This does not cover everybody; this only applies to those who have faith in Him; those
who have seen the condemnation spoken of in the first part of
this third chapter of Romans and who have said, 'It is true; it
is true of me. "There is none righteous, no, not one." I am not
righteous, I am vile, I am sinful – the verdict is correct. I have
nothing, I am nobody, and I have no hope but that the Son of
God has "loved me and has given himself for me", given his
life unto death, has loved me even unto death, even the death of
the Cross.' He is 'a propitiation through faith in his blood'.
This grand atonement is ours and becomes ours only by faith.
This is the thing the Apostle has been emphasizing all along.
'But now', he has said in verse 21, 'the righteousness of God
without the law is manifested.' What is this? Well, this is it,
'being justified freely by his grace.' But how? 'Even the righteousness of God which is by faith of Jesus Christ, unto all and
upon all them that believe.'

What a salvation! Is it surprising that the enemy with all his ingenuity and malignity masses his attack upon this, and would rob these glorious terms of their real and profound meaning? 'Whom God hath set forth to be a propitiation through faith in his blood.'

7 The Vindication of God

*

Whom God hath set forth to be a propitiation through faith in his blood, to declare his righteousness for the remission of sins that are past, through the forbearance of God:
To declare, I say, at this time his righteousness: that he might be just and the justifier of him which believeth in Jesus.

Romans 3:25, 26

In directing your attention once more to the great words which are to be found in Paul's Epistle to the Romans in the third chapter, verses 25 and 26, I would remind you again that in many senses there are no more important verses in the whole range and realm of Scripture than these two verses. Here we have the classic statement of the great central doctrine of the Atonement. That is why we are considering it so carefully and so closely. I have said earlier that somebody has described this as the 'acropolis of the Christian faith'. We can be certain that there is nothing that the human mind can ever consider which is in any way as important as these two verses. The history of the Church shows very clearly that they have been the means that God the Holy Spirit has used to bring many a soul from darkness to light, and to give many a poor sinner his first knowledge of salvation and his first assurance of salvation.

Let me give one example and illustration out of history, a well-known and a notable one. I am referring to the poet William Cowper. He tells us that he was in his room in an agony of soul, under deep and terrible conviction. He could not find peace, and he was walking back and fore, almost at the very point of despair, feeling utterly hopeless, not knowing what to do with himself. Suddenly in sheer desperation he sat down on a chair by the window in the room. There was a Bible there, so he picked it up and opened it, and he happened to come to this passage. This is what he tells us: 'The passage which met my eye was the twenty-fifth verse of the third chapter of Romans. On reading it I received immediate power to believe. The rays of the Sun of Righteousness fell on me in all their fulness. I saw the complete sufficiency of the expiation which Christ had wrought for my pardon and entire justification. In an instant I believed and received the peace of the Gospel. If the arm of the Almighty God had not supported me I believe I should have been overwhelmed with gratitude and joy. My eyes filled with tears; transports choked my utterance. I could only look to heaven in silent fear, overflowing with love and wonder.' That is what the twenty-fifth verse of the third chapter of the Epistle to the Romans did for the famous poet, William Cowper. It has done the same thing for many another.

Let me remind you again of what it says. It is a continuation of what the Apostle has been saying in the twenty-fourth verse. It is his great good news that now it is possible for us to be 'justified freely by his grace through the redemption that is in Christ Jesus'. In other words there is a way of salvation now, apart from the Law, which does not depend upon our keeping of the Law. It is this free way which is in Christ. God has ransomed us in Christ and these verses 25 and 26 explain how that ransoming has taken place. But why did it have to happen like that? How does it happen like that?

We have already considered two of the great words which explain this. They are the two great words 'propitiation' and 'blood'. We know also that the redemption purchased in that way comes to us through the instrumentality of faith.

But the Apostle does not stop at that. He says something further. Look at the statement again: 'Whom God hath set forth to be a propitiation through faith in his blood, to declare his righteousness for the remission of sins that are past, through the forbearance of God. To declare, I say, his righteousness at this time, that he might be just and the justifier of him which believeth in Jesus.' Why did the Apostle go on to say all that?

Why did he not leave it at that first statement? What is the meaning of this additional statement?

The best thing we can do is to consider once more these terms. The first is the term 'set forth'. That means 'to manifest', 'to make plain'. Here is obviously something that is of vital interest to us; it tells us that at once. The death of the Lord Jesus Christ on the Cross on Calvary was not an accident; it was God's work. It was God who 'set him forth' there. How often is the whole glory of the Cross missed when men sentimentalize it away and say, 'Ah, He was too good for the world, He was too pure. His teaching was too wonderful; and cruel men crucified Him'! The result is that we begin to feel sorry for Him, forgetting that He Himself turned on those 'daughters of Jerusalem' that were beginning to feel sorry for Him, and said, 'Weep not for me but weep for yourselves'. If our view of the Cross is one that makes us feel sorry for the Lord Jesus Christ it just means that we have never seen it truly. It is God who 'set him forth'. It was not an accident, but something deliberate. Indeed the Apostle Peter, preaching on the Day of Pentecost, said that it all happened 'by the determinate counsel and foreknowledge of God' [*Acts* 2 : 23]. 'GOD hath set him forth.'

The term also emphasizes the public character of the action. It is a great public act of God. God has done something here in public on the stage of world history, in order that it might be seen, and looked at, and recorded once and for ever – the most public action that has ever taken place. God thus publicly 'set him forth as a propitiation through faith in his blood'.

That now brings us to this vital question: Why did God do that? Why did this ever happen? What was it (if I may ask with reverence) that led God ever to do that, that made Him ever purpose to do it? The best answer, still, is to be found by looking at the terms one by one. Then, we shall look at them as a whole and we shall see exactly why the Apostle felt that it was so vital and essential to add this to what he has already said.

The first term is this term 'To declare' – 'To declare his righteousness'. This means 'to show', 'to manifest', 'to give an evident token', 'to prove'. God has done this, says Paul, in order that

Christ might thus ransom us by giving the propitiatory offering. Yes, but in addition to that, God is 'declaring' something here, He is showing something, manifesting, giving an evident token of something. Of what then? 'Of his righteousness.' We must be careful with this expression, the term we have been looking at since verse 21. It is a little unfortunate that the same term is used to cover two slightly different ideas. So far, as we have looked at this term 'righteousness', we have seen that it means 'a way of righteousness'. Go back to verse 21: 'But now', he says, 'the righteousness of God without law is manifested.' In other words, 'God's way of making men righteous', 'God's way of giving men righteousness', is what that means. But here it does not mean that. Here he says that God has done something through which He declares His righteousness; not the righteousness which God gives to us, but rather one of God's own glorious attributes. It means God's equity; it means God's judicial righteousness; it means the essential moral, holy, just and righteous character of God. He says again in the next verse (verse 26): 'That he might be just and the justifier of him that hath faith (or believeth) in Jesus' – 'that he might be just'. At the Cross God is declaring His own righteousness, His own righteous character, His own inherent and essential righteousness and justice.

The next word is 'For'. 'To declare his righteousness FOR the remission of sins that are past.' 'For' means 'in respect of', or 'on account of'. He is declaring His righteousness on account of the remission of sins that are past.

The next word is the word 'remission'. Here is a most important word, and it is a pity that the Authorized translation is really most unfortunate at this point. It is one of those cases where the AV is really inferior to the Revised Versions, including the Revised Standard Version, which are right at this point. The AV is an unfortunate translation for this reason. Look up the word 'remission' in your Authorized translation and you will find that it is used a number of times; but if you take the trouble to look up the actual word used in the Greek you will make the very interesting discovery that the word which the Apostle used here,

and which is translated 'remission', is only used here in the whole
of the New Testament. The Apostle Paul did not use it anywhere
else, nobody else used it at all. There is another word which is
translated 'remission', and in its various forms you will find it
seventeen times in the New Testament; but this word which we
have here is only used once, and it really does not mean 'remission'. It means 'pretermission'.

This is an important word and we must look at it. What does
'pretermission' mean? What does 'to pretermit' sins mean as
distinct from 'to remit' sins? It is a word that was used in Roman
Law. When you find it in Roman Law it is generally used in this
sense – it refers to someone who has made a will and who has
left somebody out of his will. Imagine a man making a will and
leaving something to a number of his friends. But there is one
friend to whom he does not leave anything – that is 'pretermission'. He leaves him out of his will; he leaves him out of consideration. It means, if you like, 'to pass over'. The man gave something to all those friends and relatives but he passed over that
one – that is to pretermit. That is the very word that is used
here – 'to pass over', 'to overlook', 'to disregard', 'to allow to
pass without notice', 'to overlook intentionally'. Those are the
meanings which were given to this most important word which
the Apostle deliberately chose at this point.

Now when the Apostle does a thing like that he must have had
a very good reason for it. He does not do that sort of thing acci-
dentally. Why did he not use the word he had used elsewhere?
Why this word here, and here only? And why this particular
word that means 'passing over'? Clearly because he obviously
means to convey the idea of passing over. So instead of translating
'for the remission of sins that are past' we should read, 'for the
passing over of sins that are past', 'for the overlooking of sins
that are past'. We can put it like this. The difference between
'remission' and 'pretermission' is the difference between 'forgiving' and 'not punishing'. You may say that that is splitting hairs,
that it is a distinction without a difference. But that is not so.
Of course, in the end it comes to the same thing. If I do not
punish a man, in a sense I have forgiven him; and yet I have not

fully done so. If I forgive I certainly have not punished; but to forgive means more than not to punish. So this term 'pretermission', 'passing over', stops short of remission; and that is why it is such a pity that the Authorized Version has 'remission' here. It is 'the passing over', or 'the overlooking of sins that are past'.

The next phrase we come to is this phrase, 'that are past'. 'For the passing over of sins that are past.' Again the Authorized translation is not quite as good as it should be. Taking the AV you might well come to the conclusion that the Apostle is saying that it is the passing over of 'past' sins, anybody's past sins – my past sins, your past sins – 'sins that are past'. But that is not what the Apostle was saying; that is not what he meant. A better translation here would be 'sins that were formerly committed'. He is referring to a very definite time. It is the time which he contrasts in the next verse with, 'at this time'. There was *that* time, then *this* time. He says, 'God hath set forth Christ as a propitiation through faith in his blood, to declare his righteousness for the passing over of sins formerly committed, in the forbearance of God; to declare, I say, at this time . . .' At what is he looking back? He is looking back at the Old Dispensation. He says that God passed over sins under the Old Dispensation, under the old covenant, in the Old Testament times. His point is that God has done that, and has now set forth Christ to do something about what He did then.

That brings us to the last word we have to consider, which is the word 'forbearance'. What is forbearance? Forbearance means 'self-restraint', it means 'tolerance' or 'toleration'. What exactly is the Apostle saying here? 'Whom God hath set forth to be a propitiation through faith in his blood, to declare his righteousness for the passing over of sins formerly committed, through the self-restraint of God.' What does it mean? What Paul is telling us is that this public act which God enacted on Calvary has reference also to God's action under the Old Testament dispensation, when He passed over, when He overlooked, passed by, the sins of the people at that time in His self-restraint and His tolerance.

But what does all this mean? In a very interesting way we can answer that question by looking at the same kind of statement in two other places in the New Testament. Do you recall how the Apostle Paul addressed a congregation of Stoics and Epicureans and others at Athens? The account is given in the seventeenth chapter of the book of the Acts of the Apostles, beginning particularly at verse 30. The Apostle, working out his argument, says: 'The time of this ignorance God winked at, but now commandeth all men everywhere to repent.' Observe how he works out his great argument. He says, God has not left Himself without witness through all these generations and centuries. God has left His signs. The object was that people should seek the Lord 'if haply they might feel after him, and find him, though he be not far from every one of us. For in him we live and move and have our being, as certain also of your own poets have said, For we are also his offspring. Forasmuch then as we are the offspring of God, we ought not to think that the Godhead is like unto gold, or silver, or stone, graven by art and man's device. And the times of this ignorance God winked at, but now commandeth all men everywhere to repent: because he hath appointed a day, in the which he will judge the world in righteousness by that man whom he hath ordained; whereof he hath given assurance unto all men, in that he hath raised him from the dead.'

The other passage is verse 15 in the ninth chapter of the Epistle to the Hebrews: 'And for this cause he (Christ) is the mediator of the new testament, that by means of death, for the redemption of the transgressions that were under the first covenant, they which are called might receive the promise of eternal inheritance.' Now that is precisely the same thing. Hebrews 9 : 15 says exactly the same thing as the Apostle is saying here. The real commentary then on this verse is found in that statement in Hebrews. That Author was anxious that his readers should be clear about the old covenant and the sacrifices and offerings which the people took to God under the old covenant. They must be quite clear in their minds, and must see quite clearly, that they were never capable of producing a full forgiveness of sins; they did not expiate sin. They could do something, says this man, they were of value in 'the purifying of the flesh'. 'The blood of bulls and of goats, and the ashes of an heifer sprinkling the unclean, sanctifieth to the purifying of the flesh' [*Hebrews* 9: 13]. But they could not do any more. They could not deal with conscience. That is the difficulty. And yet the whole problem is with respect to the conscience. But if the blood of bulls and goats could purify the flesh, 'how much more shall the blood of Christ, who through the eternal Spirit offered himself without spot to God, purge your conscience from dead works to serve the living God?' All that 'was but a figure for the time then present, in which were offered both gifts and sacrifices, that could not make him that did the service perfect, as pertaining to the conscience; Which stood only in meats and drinks and divers washings, and carnal ordinances, imposed on them UNTIL the time of reformation. But (now) Christ being come an high priest of good things to come' – and so on.

Do you follow the argument? What he is saying is that under the old covenant, under the Old Dispensation, there was no provision for dealing with sins in a radical sense. It was simply a means, as it were, of passing them by, covering them over for the time being. Those old offerings and sacrifices gave a kind of purification of the flesh, they gave a ceremonial cleanness, they enabled the people to go on praying to God. But there was no sacrifice under the Old Testament that could really deal with sin. All they did was to point forward to this sacrifice that was coming and that could really do it, and could cleanse the conscience from dead works and truly reconcile man unto God.

Do you mean by that, asks someone, that the saints in the Old Testament were not forgiven? Of course I do not. They were obviously forgiven and they thanked God for the forgiveness. You cannot say for a moment that people like David and Abraham and Isaac and Jacob were not forgiven. Of course they were forgiven. But they were not forgiven because of those sacrifices that were then offered. They were forgiven because they looked to Christ. They did not see this clearly, but they believed the teaching, and they made these offerings by faith. They believed

God's Word that He was one day going to provide a sacrifice, and in faith they held to that. It was their faith in Christ that saved them, exactly as it is faith in Christ that saves now. That is the argument.

But that, in a sense, left a problem. The problem was this. God had always revealed Himself as a God who hated sin. He had announced that He would punish sin, and that the punishment of sin was death. He had announced that He would pour out His wrath upon sin and upon sins. And yet, here was God for centuries, apparently, and to all appearances, going back on His own statements and on His own Word. He does not seem to be punishing sin. He is passing it over. Has God ceased to be concerned about these things? Has God become indifferent to moral evil? How can God thus pass over sin? That is the problem. And it was a very real problem. It is clear that the blood of bulls and of goats, and the ashes of an heifer, cannot do this. And yet God has passed these sins by. How can He do that? What is it that justifies this 'forbearance of God'? Now, says the Apostle, God has really explained it all to us by what He did in public before the whole world, on the stage and in the theatre of the whole world, in Christ on Calvary. He held back His wrath throughout the centuries. He did not disclose it fully then; but He has disclosed it fully now. He has declared it now. Paul says, 'I will repeat that – "To declare, I say". . .' That was one of the things that was happening on the Cross. On the Cross on Calvary's hill God was giving a public explanation of what He had been doing throughout the centuries. By so doing, and at the same time, He vindicates His own eternal character of righteousness and of holiness.

How exactly did He do this? Let me answer that question; and as I do so you will see why I was at such great pains to defend that word 'propitiation' and to hold on to it at all costs because it was so vital. How has God done this on Calvary? How has He vindicated His character? How has He given an explanation of His 'passing over' of those sins in past times in His self-restraint and tolerance? There is only one way in which He could do it. God has stated that He hates sin, that He will punish sin, that He will pour out His wrath upon sin, and upon those guilty of sin. Therefore, unless God can prove that He has done that, He is no longer just. What the Apostle is saying is that on Calvary He has done that. He has shown that He still hates sin, that He is going to punish it, that He must punish it, that He will pour out His wrath upon it. How did He show that on Calvary? By doing that very thing. What God did on Calvary was to pour out upon His only begotten and beloved Son His wrath upon sin. The wrath of God that should have come upon you and me because of our sins fell upon Him. God always knew that He was going to do this. We read in the Scriptures of 'the Lamb slain before the foundation of the world'. It was a plan originating in eternity. It was because He knew that He was going to do this that God was able to pass over sins during all those centuries that had gone. Thus, you see, says the Apostle, God at one and the same time remains just and can justify the ungodly that believe in Christ. That was the tremendous problem – how can God remain holy and just, and deal with sin as He says He is going to, and yet forgive the sinner? The answer is to be found alone on Calvary. It is an essential part of what is declared upon the Cross.

That, according to the Apostle, was the first reason. God had to vindicate what He had been doing in the past under the old covenant. But He had something more to do, he tells us in verse 26: 'To declare, I say, at THIS TIME his righteousness.' He has now explained how He could pass over all those sins in the past. But how does He deal with sin now? How is He going to deal with sins in the future? The answer is still there in the Cross on Calvary's hill. The teaching in other words is this. The Cross on Calvary, the Death of the Lord Jesus Christ, as the Apostle John puts it in his First Epistle chapter 2, verse 2, 'is the propitiation for our sins; and not for ours only but also for the sins of the whole world' – the particular world that is meant there. Sins were dealt with once and for all on the Cross. It is on the Cross that all those sins under the Old Dispensation that God had passed by, and had as it were thus pretermitted – the sins that He had forgiven to Abraham and Isaac and Jacob, and all the believers in the Old Dispensation – it is there the means is provided for doing that. Their sins are included on Calvary. Yes, says Paul, and the sins that are being forgiven now are also dealt with there. And all sins that ever will be committed are also dealt with there.

That is the amazing thing about the Christ of Calvary – He died 'once and for all'. It is the great argument of the Epistle to the Hebrews, you remember. Those other sacrifices, it says, had to be offered day by day. There was a succession of priests, and they had to go on making their fresh sacrifices. 'But this man' has made a sacrifice for sins 'once and for ever'. He has dealt with all sins there. There is no need for anything further. There is no need for a fresh sacrifice. It has been done once and for ever. God laid them all on Him there – the sins you have not yet committed have already been dealt with. There, is the means of forgiveness: and there alone. Time past, sins committed formerly, sins committed now, all times – here is the justification of God for forgiving ANY sins whenever committed.

That is what the Apostle is saying here. All sin is forgiven on these grounds, and on these grounds alone. The Cross declares that God 'is just and the justifier of him which believeth in Jesus'. Let me put it in this way. The Cross of Calvary does not merely declare that God forgives us. It does that, thank God, but it does not stop at that. If it only declared that, the Apostle could have finished verse 25 at the word 'blood'. There was no need for more. But he does not stop there, he goes on; he goes on in verse 25 and adds verse 26. Why? Because the Cross is not merely the declaration that God is ready to forgive us.

Another way I can put it is this. The Cross is not merely meant to influence us. But that is what the popular teaching tells us. It says that the trouble with mankind is that it does not know that God is love, it does not know that God has already forgiven everybody. What is the meaning of the Cross? Well, they say, it is God telling us that He has forgiven us; and so, when we see Christ dying, it should break our hearts and bring us to see that. The Cross according to them is directed to us solely. It does speak to us; but it has a grander object than that; it does this other thing also.

Our forgiveness is only one thing; there is something infinitely more important. What is that? It is the character of God. So the Cross goes on to tell me that this is God's way of making forgiveness possible. Forgiveness is not an easy thing for God. I speak with reverence. Why is forgiveness not an easy thing for God? Because God is not only love, God is also just and righteous and holy. He is 'Light, and in him is no darkness at all'. He is as much righteousness and justice as He is love. I do not put these attributes against one another. I say God is all these things together, and you must not leave out the one or the other.

So the Cross does not merely tell us that God forgives, it tells us that that is God's way of making forgiveness possible. It is the way in which we understand how God forgives. I will go further: how can God forgive and still remain God? – that is the question. The Cross is the vindication of God. The Cross is the vindication of the character of God. The Cross not only shows the love of God more gloriously than anything else, it shows His righteousness, His justice, His holiness, and all the glory of His eternal attributes. They are all to be seen shining together there. If you do not see them all you have not seen the Cross. That is why we must totally reject the co-called 'moral influence theory' of the Atonement, the one I have just been describing – the theory which says that all the Cross has to do is to break our hearts and to bring us to see the love of God.

Above and beyond all that, Paul says, 'He is declaring his righteousness for the remission of sins that are past'. Why this, if it is merely a declaration of His love? No, says Paul, it is more than that. If it merely proclaimed His forgiveness we would be entitled to ask whether we can depend on God's word, and whether He is righteous and just. It would be a fair question because God has repeatedly stated in the Old Testament that He hates sin and that He will punish sin, and that the wages of sin is death. The character of God is involved. God is not as men. We think sometimes that it is wonderful for people to say one thing and then do another. The parent says to the child, 'If you do this thing you shall not have that sixpence to buy your sweets'. Then the boy does that thing, but the father says, 'Well, it is all right', and gives him the sixpence. That, we think, is love, and true forgiveness. But God does not behave in that manner. God, if I may so put it, is eternally consistent with Himself. There is never a contradiction. He is 'the Father of lights, with whom is no variableness, neither shadow of turning'. All these glorious attributes are to be seen shining like diamonds in His eternal character. And all of them must be manifest. In the Cross they are all manifested.

How can God be just and justify the ungodly? The answer is that He can, because He has punished the sins of ungodly sinners in His own Son. He has poured His wrath upon Him. 'He bore our chastisement.' 'By his stripes we are healed.' God has done what He said He would do; He has punished sin. He proclaimed this through the Old Testament everywhere; and He has done what He said He would do. He has shown that He is righteous. He has made a public declaration of it. He is just and can justify, because having punished Another in our stead, He can forgive us freely. And He does so. That is the message of verse 24: 'Being justified (being regarded, declared, pronounced righteous) freely by his grace through the redemption (the ransoming) that is in Christ Jesus; whom God hath set forth as a propitiation through faith in his blood.' Thus He declares His righteousness for having passed over those sins in His time of self-restraint. 'To declare, I say', His righteousness then, and now, and always, in forgiving sins. Thus He is, at one and the same time, just and the justifier of him that believeth in Jesus.

Such is this great and glorious and wonderful statement. Make sure that your view, your understanding of the Cross, includes the whole of it. Test your view of the Cross. Where does this statement about 'declaring' His righteousness and so on, come into your thinking? Is it something that you just skip over and say: 'Well, I don't know what that means. All I know is, that God is love and that He forgives.' But you should know the meaning of this. This is an essential part of the glorious Gospel. On Calvary God was making a way of salvation so that you and I might be forgiven. But He had to do so in a way that will leave His character inviolate, that will leave His eternal consistency still absolute and unbroken. Once you begin to look at it like that, you see that this is the most tremendous, the most glorious, the most staggering thing in the universe and in the whole of history. God is there declaring what He has done for us. He is declaring at the same time His own eternal greatness and glory, declaring that 'He is light and in him is no darkness at all'. 'When I survey the wondrous Cross . . .', says Isaac Watts, but you do not see the wonder of it until you really do survey it in the light of this great statement of the Apostle. God was declaring publicly once and for ever His eternal justice AND His eternal love. Never separate them, for they belong together in the character of God.

8 Boasting Excluded

*

Where is boasting then? It is excluded. By what law? of works? Nay: but by the law of faith.

Therefore we conclude that a man is justified by faith without the deeds of the law.

Is he the God of the Jews only? is he not also of the Gentiles? Yes, of the Gentiles also:

Seeing it is one God which shall justify the circumcision by faith, and uncircumcision through faith.

Do we then make void the law through faith? God forbid: yea, we establish the law. Romans 3: 27–31

In these verses we have a series of further consequences or characteristics of the great salvation of which the Apostle is writing in this section. God, he says, has done something new; there is a way of salvation, a righteousness of God by faith in Jesus Christ. He has explained to us how that has been brought to pass. He says, 'We are justified freely by his grace through the redemption that is in Christ Jesus'; and that redemption, that ransoming, he has told us, took place when God set Him forth as 'a propitiation through faith in his blood'. A further purpose served by that great act was 'to declare his righteousness for the remission of sins that are past, through the forbearance of God. To declare, I say, at this time, his righteousness, that he might be just and the justifier of him which believeth in Jesus.' This great way of salvation must be considered not only from our standpoint, but still more from the standpoint of God Himself; it 'declares him to be just and the justifier of him that believeth in Jesus'.

Here, we go on to look at further characteristics of this great salvation. To begin: we must never so describe this salvation as in any way to raise the question of the righteousness and the justice of God. Or to put it positively, our exposition of the way of salvation must always be one which asserts the justice of God as well as the love of God. That is the first characteristic. But now Paul goes on to consider three further characteristics. The first is, you notice, that it is a way of salvation that excludes all boasting. Secondly, it is a way of salvation that is open to Jews and Gentiles alike – such distinctions are abolished altogether. And thirdly, it is a way of salvation that asserts again and establishes the Law.

These, I say, are three further characteristics of this great salvation. We are equally entitled to say that these three points which are made in these three verses are also inevitable consequences of the doctrine of the Atonement, which the Apostle has just been expounding. These verses do the two things at one and the same time – they display characteristics of the salvation, and they are also corollaries of the particular way in which our salvation has been achieved. As we look at this we must surely feel like asking why the Apostle goes on to say these things? Why did he not end with that magnificent statement of the doctrine of the Atonement and leave it at that? What verses they were, and what a climax he had reached! We have been looking at them in detail: 'Being justified freely by his grace through the redemption that is in Christ Jesus. Whom God hath set forth to be a propitiation through faith in his blood; to declare his righteousness for the remission of sins that are past through the forbearance of God. To declare, I say, at this time his righteousness, that he might be just and the justifier of him that believeth in Jesus.' What a sublime statement, what a glorious climax! Why did he go on to add these three things? Why did he not leave it at that positive statement of the doctrine of the Atonement which we have in verses 25 and 26?

I suggest that the question must be raised, and that a further reason for raising it is the fact that the Apostle has already said these three things several times during the first three chapters. Yet he brings them in again, he says them once more. Why do you think he does so? I am raising the question because this is to me an extremely important matter. This great Apostle does not do a thing like this merely for the sake of doing it; he obviously has a very good reason for the repetition. For the moment I am just dealing with the question of how to read the Scriptures. This is in a sense purely mechanical, but it is a very important question in the mechanics of the study of the Scriptures. We must always watch what the Apostle does. When he goes on to do a thing like this we must stop and ask ourselves why he has done so. Why did he not leave it at that great climax? Why come back again to these three things which he has been saying so frequently? He has already dealt with the tendency of the Jews to boast, in the seventeenth verse of the second chapter: 'Behold, thou art called a Jew and restest in the law and makest thy boast of God', and of circumcision and of the Law, and also elsewhere. Yet here he is coming back to it again. Why?

I suggest that there are definite answers to that question. The first is: He does it because of the greatness of the subject. This subject is so great, so important, so vital that there must be no misunderstanding whatsoever with respect to it. The Apostle was much more concerned about that than about mere literary form or literary style. From the literary standpoint it is always a bad thing to go on after you have reached your climax. Paul was not a literary man, he was a preacher of the Gospel, an evangelist and a teacher, an ambassador for Christ. He is not interested in the literary form of his letters. What he is anxious to know is whether these people have really seen this truth, and grasped it. Are they quite clear about it? He is taking no risks at all with them. Having said the thing many times, and at the risk of producing a kind of anti-climax, he comes back to it again in order to make absolutely certain. The thing is so central and crucial that there must be no mistake about it. That is the first reason.

The second reason is this. Because of our sinful state it is essential that truth should be stated negatively as well as positively. If man had not sinned it would have been enough to give him the truth positively, but because he has sinned that is never enough. So you will find in the Scriptures everywhere, in the teaching portions, that there are negatives as well as positives. It is not enough to tell people what the truth is positively; you have also to point out that it is not this or that. That is because we are sinful. The negative helps to focus attention on the teaching; it helps to underline it; it helps to define it. I must not labour this point, but I am emphasizing it because I have the impression that this modern generation of Christians does not like negatives. They say, 'All we want is the positive truth; you need not bother about those negatives'. But the very fact that they say that means that they need the negatives very badly. They are displaying their ignorance, they are in the position described by this Apostle in his Epistle to the Ephesians. They are 'like children tossed to and fro and carried about by every wind of doctrine' [*Ephesians* 4:14]. The Scriptures safeguard our position by emphasizing negatives as well as positives. We have here a perfect illustration of that.

A further reason for his doing this is that Paul was dealing with actual difficulties in the minds of many at that very time. For instance, the Jews were in real difficulties about the Gospel. It seemed to them, on the surface, to be doing away with the whole of the Old Testament. The Apostle had already referred to that at the beginning of chapter 3, but he comes back to it again. He knew that they held on to these things tenaciously. What prejudiced creatures we are! We hold on to our prejudices, or perhaps I should say, the prejudices hold on to us. Now the Apostle wanted to explain this thing clearly to the Jews. And not only to the Jews who were outside, but also to many Jewish Christians who were still in trouble about these same points.

There is a classic illustration of this – the case of the Apostle Peter. Do you remember what Paul tells us about Peter in the second chapter of the Epistle to the Galatians? Peter had come to see this truth about the Gentiles being admitted. God had taught him this truth in connection with Cornelius when he had given him the vision [*Acts* 10]. And Peter had preached the Gospel to the Gentiles, and had even defended himself for doing so [*Acts* 11]. But then, later on, even Peter suddenly began to wander away from the truth. Certain dissemblers and Judaisers came down to Antioch who were so plausible that even Peter was led astray. The old Jewish prejudices rose up, and Paul had to 'withstand him to the face'. So the Apostle was anxious that the Jewish Christians who were members of the church at Rome should be quite clear about this matter. There was still a lingering tendency in these Jews, though they had become Christians, to feel that somehow they were different after all from the others and that they were in a superior position, and that they had some special privileges, even as Christians, because they were Jews. They could not see that the middle wall of partition had been really demolished once and for ever. Now the Apostle knew that, so he comes back to the matter again.

My final remark about this matter is to point out that the great Apostle never confines himself to mere positive statements but often indulges, because he feels that he must do so, in arguments, in polemics. I make this point because I think there is a great deal of very loose and very false and flabby thinking on the whole question of polemics and of argumentation at the present time. The attitude of many seems to be, 'We do not want these arguments. Give us the simple message, the simple Gospel. Give it to us positively, and do not bother about other views.' It is important that we should realize that if we speak like that we are denying the Scriptures. The Scriptures are full of arguments, full of polemics. And the Apostle sees the necessity for it here. Having just reasoned up to that tremendous climax on the doctrine of the Atonement, he suddenly asks, 'Where is boasting then?' 'Is he the God of the Jews only, or is he the God of the Gentiles also?' 'Do we then make void the law?' In doing so he is arguing, he is disputing; this is sheer polemics.

Disapproval of polemics in the Christian Church is a very serious matter. But that is the attitude of the age in which we live. The prevailing idea today in many circles in the Church is not to bother about these things. As long as we are all Christians, anyhow, somehow, all is well. Do not let us argue about doctrine, let us all be Christians together and talk about the love of God. That is really the whole basis of ecumenicity. Unfortunately that same attitude is creeping into evangelical circles also and many say that we must not be too precise about these things. But if you begin to object to clear statements about the doctrine of the Atonement you are beginning to argue. It is important that we should be clear about the doctrine of the Atonement. 'Ah but, you are beginning to argue now,' they say. 'You must not argue, that is upsetting, that is going to divide people.'

What I am trying to show is that if you hold that view you are criticizing the Apostle Paul, you are saying that he was wrong, and at the same time you are criticizing the Scriptures. The Scriptures argue and debate and dispute; they are full of polemics. You cannot read this Epistle to the Romans, or the Epistle to the Galatians, or indeed any one of these epistles, without seeing that very clearly. Let us be clear about what we mean. This is not argument for the sake of argument; this is not a manifestation of an argumentative spirit; this is not just indulging one's own prejudices. The Scriptures do not approve of that, and furthermore the Scriptures are very concerned about the spirit in which one engages in discussion. No man should like argument for the sake of argument. We should always regret the necessity; but though we regret it and bemoan it, when we feel that a vital matter is at stake we must engage in argument. We must 'earnestly contend for the truth', and we are all called upon to do that by the New Testament. The Apostle Paul thanks the members of the church at Philippi, and thanks God for them, because they have stood with him from the very beginning in the 'declaration and the defence of the truth'. And there is nothing that is so utterly contrary to the New Testament method as to say, 'Let us be positive, let us forget the negatives, let us never argue about these things'. While men and women are not clear in their minds as to the truth, while they are liable to be carried away by that which is false, we must contend for the truth, we must engage in the type of argumentation that we have illustrated in these verses we are considering. We must know why Paul has done this. And there, it seems to me, are the reasons.

Now let us look at the things he says. The first is: That God's way of salvation through Christ's blood leaves no room for boasting. That is the statement of verses 27 and 28: 'Where is boasting then? It is excluded. By what law? of works? Nay, but by the law of faith. For we reckon (or if you like, we therefore conclude) that a man is justified by faith without the deeds of the law.' What does he mean by asking, 'Where is boasting?' This word translated 'boasting' is one of the Apostle's favourite words. You will find it constantly in all his writings. It is one of his great words, of course, because boasting was one of his greatest troubles before his conversion. Indeed I think we may venture to say that it troubled him somewhat after his conversion. That is why he mentions it so frequently. You do not always find it translated in the Authorized Version as boasting; quite frequently, perhaps more frequently, the same word is translated 'glorying'. Take for example that great statement at the end of the first chapter of the First Epistle to the Corinthians: 'He that glorieth, let him glory in the Lord.' What that really amounts to is, 'he that boasteth, let him make his boast in the Lord'. Why has God made the way of salvation in this particular fashion? That is what Paul is arguing there with the Corinthians. 'Well,' he says, 'in order that no man may glory in his presence.'

The Apostle brings in this word because he knew it was the essential trouble with the Jews as it had been his own trouble. He introduces it in chapter 2, verse 17: 'Behold, thou art called a Jew, and restest in the law, and makest thy boast of God.' The Jew said, 'I am one of God's people. God is my God.' He boasted in that respect. He boasted of the law, he boasted of circumcision. He was always boasting and setting himself up and despising the Gentiles – the dogs without the pale. Boasting! And if ever a man had done this it was Saul of Tarsus before his conversion. Read Philippians chapter 3 again, and you will see it clearly – 'Circumcised the eighth day, of the stock of Israel, an Hebrew of the Hebrews'. It comes out in almost every word! He knew the list so well, he had thought it out so frequently, he had repeated it so often. There he was, a Pharisee trained at the feet of Gamaliel, better than most others, understanding more, 'excelling all my contemporaries' as he says to the Galatians. Boasting! Boasting of his nationality, his birth, his train-

ing, his knowledge, his understanding, his religiosity, his morality – always parading it and proud of it, and despising
others.

Our Lord has painted the perfect picture for us, as usual, in
the eighteenth chapter of Luke's Gospel in His parable of the
Pharisee and the publican who went up together to the temple
to pray. The Pharisee went right forward as far as he could go
and said: 'I thank Thee, O God, that I am not as other men are',
and then he brings out all his virtues and his good deeds. Boasting! It was the central trouble with the Jews; and it is still the
central trouble with unregenerate men.

That is why the Apostle has to take it up. He makes this bald
statement and says in effect: Now I have just been describing
God's way of salvation, I have been holding you face to face
with the Cross and the death of the Son of God. Have you understood it or are you still boasting? Are you still holding on to
something? Is there any vestige of self-righteousness left? Is
there anything you are clinging on to? Can you cling on to it
in the light of the glorious message of the Gospel? He had
already in his exposition of the Law shown quite clearly that the
Law condemns us and removes any possibility of boasting.
'There is no difference, all have sinned and have come short of
the glory of God. There is none righteous, no, not one. The whole
world lieth guilty before God.'

But the exposition of the way of salvation removes the boasting in a yet more glorious way. 'Where is boasting then? It is
excluded.' It is turned out of court once and for ever. It must
never put in an appearance again; there is no room for it in this
way of salvation. But he does not leave it at that. He goes on to
ask, 'By what law is this true? By what law is boasting turned out
entirely, swept out of the house and the door slammed behind
it? How has it happened?' He is not content with just saying
that boasting is excluded, he knows the people with whom he
is dealing, he knows human nature in sin, he knows this Jewish
prejudice, this religious, moral prejudice that follows us even
into the Christian life and keeps on trying to come back. If you
drive it out of the front door it tries to come in again by the back

door. It is always there, and you always have to be sweeping it out. So he takes it up again – 'By what law?'

The fact that he uses the term 'law' here has often confused people. 'Is it the law of works?' 'No', he says, 'but by the law of faith.' What does he mean by 'law' here? Well, obviously he does not mean the Mosaic Law, the Law that God gave to the Jews through Moses, because he uses the same expression with regard to faith. No, what he means by the law here is 'principle' – on what principle has it gone out? Is it on the principle of works that a man does? 'No', he says, 'it is on the principle of faith'. Law, here, stands for principle or system. You will find that he uses the term 'law' in that way many times in this great Epistle. What we have here, then, is, 'On what principle do you say that boasting is excluded? Is it on the principle of works that a man does? No, it is on the principle of faith.'

What does this mean? Here, again, we see the importance of taking up these matters and arguing them out. Alas, there are certain popular forms of evangelical teaching today that claim that what the Apostle says here is quite simple. They say it means that God first of all gave to mankind the Law of works, and particularly to the Jews. He gave them that Law and said, 'If you do those things you shall be saved'. But, they go on, they did not do them, nobody could do them, everybody failed to keep that Law. So what did God do? He brought in a new law. He put aside that first Law which man could not keep, and now He comes to mankind and He says: 'In my love I am going to offer you something that is easier. I am no longer going to ask you to keep the law which was given through Moses; you could not keep it, nobody could. Very well, in order to show my great love to you, I am now going to ask you to do something that is within your competence. All I am asking you to do now is to believe on my Son and if you do so you shall be saved.'

I am not imagining this. It is something that is actually being taught – that the way of salvation in Christ is simply that God is now asking us to do something we can do; it is 'just believing'. He is no longer asking us for works which we could not do; He is now asking us simply to believe on His Son. They say he

[117]

calls it 'the law of faith'. The Law of works no longer applies;
it is now a question of keeping 'the law of faith', and this is
something we can do.

But that is an impossible exposition; let me show you why it
is so and why it is thoroughly wrong. The last verse in this
chapter is enough alone and in and of itself to show how terribly
wrong that is. He asks the question, 'Do we make void the law
through faith?' He is there referring to the Law given through
Moses, and he answers, 'God forbid' – 'far be it from you',
'out upon the suggestion'. Far from cancelling or nullifying the
Law, this way of salvation 'establishes' the Law. That other
teaching says that it does not establish the Law, that it has done
away with it, and puts another law in its place. In other words,
that interpretation is the exact opposite of what the Apostle is
saying here.

Moreover, if that way of putting this is right, then boasting is
not excluded. If you say that the difference between the Old and
the New is that, before, I was asked to do certain works, and
now I am simply asked to believe, and if I believe I am saved,
you have then turned faith into a work. You are saying that it
was works in practice before: 'Do not commit adultery; do not
steal; do not kill'; and so on. Now it is simply belief. Yes, but
thereby you are turning faith and belief into works, and therefore, because you believe, you have something whereof you can
boast. I have believed, the other man has not believed. My belief
saves me. Very well, my work of faith has saved me.

For those two reasons that interpretation of the phrase 'the
law of faith' is false; it does not exclude boasting and it does not
establish the Law. Twice over in this bit of argumentation the
Apostle goes out of his way to say that it is wrong; yet many are
teaching it. They say this is a marvellous Gospel because God has
reduced the standard and has put before us now something that
is within our competence. By believing we can save ourselves.
Thus all the boasting comes back, and the Law of God has been
made void and swept aside, and has been replaced by another
law. Do you now see the importance of argumentation? Thank
God that the Apostle went on after his great climax in verse 26.

Thank God that he came down to the level of our stupidity, and laid out this matter before us so clearly, and showed us how easily we can go wrong. We must not boast of our faith. If your view is one that makes you boast about it, it is wrong. Boasting is excluded in every shape and form. If in any way you are proud of the fact that you believe, then you do not believe; you are in the position of the religious man the Apostle is denouncing. 'Boasting is excluded.'

Then in verse 28 he reinforces all this by putting it in another way more positively. 'Therefore', he says, 'we conclude that a man is justified by faith without the deeds of the law.' What does this mean? This is one of those telling phrases that has played such a great part in the history of the Church. The great Martin Luther translates that like this: 'Therefore we conclude that a man is justified by faith only, without the deeds of the law.' A great argument began between him and the Roman Catholic Church over the word 'only'. What is the position? It is this, that the word 'only' is not in the Greek text, it is not in the original text. Why then, you ask, did Luther say 'justified by faith only?' He was quite right in doing so. He was doing what Paul was doing – he was preaching at that point. What the message teaches is that it is by faith only, and that was the thing that Luther was anxious to emphasize. Though it is not strictly accurate as a translation, it is justified from the standpoint of teaching.

What is the Apostle saying? He is saying, 'We conclude, therefore, that a man is justified by faith only, without the deeds of the law'. He means this, that our works – your works and mine – in response to the demands of the Law do not come in at all. We could not keep the Law, and we did not keep the Law. God's way of salvation is one which announces that the Law has been kept and fulfilled for us by the Lord Jesus Christ. It still makes the demand, but God has provided a way whereby we can be saved, though we do not keep the works of the Law, and though we cannot do so. That is what he means by 'apart from works of the law'. As far as you and I are concerned, the works of the Law do not come into our salvation, because, as Paul shows at great length in chapters 2 and 3, the works of the Law simply condemn us. But God's way in Christ has delivered us from that.

We must be careful, however, about our definition of faith, and what faith does, and where faith comes in. Faith is nothing but the instrument of our salvation. Nowhere in Scripture will you find that we are justified because of our faith; nowhere in Scripture will you find that we are justified on account of our faith. That is where that teaching I have just been denouncing goes wrong; it says that we are justified on account of our faith. The Scripture never says that. The Scripture says that we are justified BY faith or through faith. Faith is nothing but the instrument or the channel by which this righteousness of God in Christ becomes ours. It is not faith that saves us. What saves us is the Lord Jesus Christ and His perfect work. It is the death of Christ upon Calvary's Cross that saves us. It is His perfect life that saves us. It is His appearing on our behalf in the presence of God that saves us. It is God putting Christ's righteousness to our account that saves us. This is the righteousness that saves; faith is but the channel and the instrument by which His righteousness becomes mine. The righteousness is entirely Christ's. My faith is not my righteousness and I must never define or think of faith as righteousness. Faith is nothing but that which links us to the Lord Jesus Christ and His righteousness.

Or, to put it in other language, we must never think of faith as something in and of itself. Faith is never something isolated or alone. You must never divorce faith from its object. Faith is always linked to an object. The object is the Lord Jesus Christ and His perfect work and His perfect righteousness; and as long as you always remember that, you can never go wrong. So we must not boast of our faith; it is not faith as such that saves us. Faith is merely that channel, that instrument, that link that connects us with the righteousness of Christ which saves us. His is the righteousness that saves, and faith simply brings it to us. It is His righteousness that saves us by faith, through faith.

At this point, of course, we have of necessity to consider the Apostle James and his teaching. 'This is all very well,' says someone, 'but as evangelical Christians we believe in the inspiration of the whole of the Scriptures, and we believe in the inerrancy of the Scriptures. You have been impressing this truth upon us, "we conclude that a man is justified by faith only apart from the deeds of the law"; and yet here is James saying in the second chapter of his Epistle, verse 24: "Ye see then how that by works a man is justified, and not by faith only." Put them over against one another: Romans 3:28. "We conclude that a man is justified by faith only apart from the deeds of the law"; James 2:24. "Ye see then how that by works a man is justified, and not by faith only." What about the Bible now? Must we not all become "higher critics" and say that the Scriptures contradict themselves, and that James and Paul are blankly contradicting one another?'

This is a very important question. Even Martin Luther fell into this trap and called the Epistle of James 'an epistle of straw'. He should not have fallen into it. Is there a contradiction between James and Paul? Let us see again how to approach our study of the Scriptures. The danger, of course, is to pull out verses, as I have done deliberately in order to show you what not to do; you pull out Romans 3:28 and you pull out James 2:24. There you are, the case is proved. But to do that would be unfair to both Paul and James. Every statement in the Scriptures should always be taken in its context and in its setting. Furthermore, you must always read the whole and discover what the author is setting out to do. That is the key to this problem. James and Paul, while believing the same truth, were setting out to do two different things; they had a different immediate objective. Paul is concerned to show that our works under the Law do not count at all in salvation; James is concerned to do something very different. The problem James had to confront was that there were people in the early Church who were talking about faith in an utterly wrong way. He puts that clearly in verse 14 in the second chapter. 'What doth it profit, my brethren, though a man say he hath faith and have not works?' James was dealing with the kind of people who said, 'I have faith, I am a believer' and then went on to say that, because they had faith and were believers, it did not matter what they did, that what saves a man is that he

[121]

says he is a believer. In other words, they had the problem of 'believism' in the early Church. James is dealing only with men who claim to have faith – men who use the word 'faith' but who mean nothing by it but intellectual assent.

Look at the way in which James deals with that and you will see clearly what he is saying. Look at his illustrations, verses 15 and 16. 'If a brother or sister be naked and destitute of daily food, and one of you say unto them, Depart in peace, be ye warmed and filled; notwithstanding ye give them not those things which are needful to the body; what doth it profit?' You do not help that poor person who is naked or destitute or starving by just saying, 'Well, God bless you, carry on'. That does not help them. Mere talk is of no value. If you really want to help, in addition to saying something you must do something. That is the context, that is his argument. Then he applies that in verse 17: 'Even so' – in that same way exactly – 'faith, if it hath not works, is dead, being alone.' Then he goes on with his argument in verse 19: 'Thou believest that there is one God; thou doest well' – that is very good. You say, 'I believe there is one God'. Excellent! 'The devils also believe and tremble.' The devils say in the same way that they believe there is one God. That is valueless. Merely to say that you believe there is one God is of no value if you do not submit to that one God, if you do not obey that one God, if you do not love and worship that one God. The devils do not do so, so that their saying that they believe is useless.

That is the sort of person James has in his mind, and he gives proof of that in verse 20: 'But wilt thou know, O vain man, that faith without works is dead.' He is talking about this vain person, this man who says, 'I believe; therefore, because I believe, all is well'. 'Simply believing, that is all.' Vain man, you do not realize what you are saying. Then he goes on in verse 24: 'Ye see then how that by works a man is justified, and not by faith only.' Why does he say that? Because that is his conclusion as the result of what he has just been saying about Abraham. 'Was not Abraham our father justified by works, when he had offered Isaac his son upon the altar? Seest thou how faith wrought with his works, and by works was faith made perfect? And the Scripture was fulfilled which saith, Abraham believed God and it was imputed unto him for righteousness: and he was called the friend of God.' Abraham believed God. How do you know? Was it merely a statement? Not at all! He took his son Isaac and put him on the altar and was on the point of offering him as a sacrifice. It was not mere talk, he did it. That is James' argument. Abraham is one of his proofs that faith is not merely a matter of saying, as a vain man does, that you believe something. Abraham in practice proves that he has true faith; not this thing that is without works which is dead, but the living thing and the real thing. In other words, faith does not mean the kind of belief that the devils have. Faith indeed does not just mean believing certain things. In faith there is always the element of trust, the element of committal, the element of obedience, the element of abandoning oneself to what you believe. James was concerned to emphasize that.

He puts it in the clearest statement of all in the last verse, verse 26: 'As the body without the spirit is dead, so faith without works is dead also.' So that when James is arguing about faith – and again you notice it is an argument – he has in mind a belief which is distinct from faith. He is concerned about people who separate these elements in faith. Faith is not just intellectual assent. A man can give intellectual assent to the teaching of the whole Bible and go straight to hell. Faith means, first of all, that you are aware of the truth. It means, secondly, that you believe it and accept it. And, thirdly, it means that you commit yourself to it and abandon yourself to it. What James is saying is that if you separate these things, what you call faith is worthless. It is exactly like taking the spirit out of the body; the body is then dead and lifeless, and it is useless. There must never be a wedge between belief and committal, belief and trust.

This is of very great importance. There is no contradiction at all between Paul and James. Paul is asserting that this great thing called faith has nothing to do with 'works under the law'. James is asserting that faith is a very great thing and does not mean mere intellectual assent, merely saying 'I believe'. They are both saying the same thing, but they are looking at it from different angles. You see how this becomes urgently important for those of us who are unhappy about rushing people into decisions in evangelistic meetings. You can rush a man into saying: 'All right, I do believe it.' You take him through the Scripture, then you say to him, 'Do you believe that?' 'I believe it', he says; and then the tendency is to say, 'Very well, you are saved, you are converted.' I remember a man telling me years ago about his own conversion. He said he was in an evangelistic meeting. He was not quite clear about things and he went to the Inquiry Room at the end and there he was dealt with. He said a man spoke to him and his friend, and just put these facts before them. The enquirer was waiting for something more, but the man said, 'No, you do not need anything further, here are the plain statements. Do you believe?' He said, 'Yes, I believe it.' 'Ah,' this man said, 'You're in.' 'Where am I in?' asked the enquirer. 'You're in the Kingdom of God. If you say you believe those things you are in the Kingdom of God,' said the counsellor. He should not have said that. A man can say that he believes that Jesus of Nazareth is the Son of God, and yet be outside the Kingdom. There are many people in the world today who are not Christians but say they believe that Jesus Christ is the Son of God. It does not influence their lives at all; they go on living as they did before. He is not 'the Lord' of their lives. They know nothing about the Atonement, they may ridicule this doctrine of blood, but they give assent to His Person. The devils can do that sort of thing. The devil recognized Him as the Son of God, you remember. So, merely to believe a number of propositions is not faith; it does not mean of necessity that we are in the Kingdom. I would not venture to say that any man is in the Kingdom of God until he gives some manifestation of the fruits of the Spirit, until he shows certain signs that he has a living faith, that he is really in Christ. He may be in it without knowing it. All I say is that I would not dare to say that he is. I cannot say that I am, or that anybody else is, a Christian merely because we say 'Yes' to a number of intellectual propositions. That alone is not faith. James makes that clear once and for ever; and Paul asserts the same thing in his own way. The whole of chapter 6 of this Epistle is really designed just to say that, as we shall see. That is Paul's way of saying what James says in chapter 2 of his Epistle.

So the Apostle makes this first great point – 'Boasting is excluded' in every shape and form. You must not boast even of your faith; boast of nothing. Faith is the instrument and the channel by means of which, and through which, the righteousness of Jesus Christ becomes ours, and we can conclude with Paul and James that 'a man is justified by faith only, apart from the deeds of the law', but 'faith without works is dead', and not faith at all.

9 Distinctions Abolished

*

Is he the God of the Jews only? is he not also of the Gentiles?
Yes, of the Gentiles also;
Seeing it is one God, which shall justify the circumcision by faith,
and uncircumcision through faith.
Do we then make void the law through faith? God forbid; yea, we
establish the law. Romans 3:29–31

Here, we come to the second and the third of the series of three deductions which the Apostle draws from the doctrine of Redemption through the blood of Jesus Christ, who is set forth as a propitiation for us. At the same time we are reminded of certain characteristics of this way of salvation in which the Apostle glories. We have considered the first, namely, that all boasting has been removed, there is nothing for anyone to boast of. 'He that glorieth, let him glory in the Lord.' This man who used to boast so much about his own merit, and his birth, and all his achievements and understanding, this man who has boasted of all those things has come to see them now as 'dung' and 'loss'. All he can say is: 'God forbid that I should glory, save in the Cross of the Lord Jesus Christ.'

The second deduction is this: that God's way of salvation abolishes all distinctions between people. This is the message of verses 29 and 30. 'Is he God of the Jews only? is he not also of the Gentiles? Yes, of the Gentiles also, seeing it is one God, who shall justify the circumcision by faith, and the uncircumcision through faith.' The distinction between Jews and Gentiles as regards salvation has been abolished; they are in exactly the same position. There is a mechanical point here which is of some importance. You notice that in the Authorized Version the reading is,

[126]

'Is he the God of the Jews only?' But there should be no 'the' there. It should read: 'Is he God of Jews only, is he not also of Gentiles?' – not 'the' Jews, or 'the' Gentiles. 'Yes, of Gentiles also, seeing it is one God, who shall justify circumcision' – not 'the' circumcision – 'by faith, and uncircumcision through faith.'

The correction is important in this way only, that some might argue from AV translation that God is going to save all Jews and all Gentiles, that everybody is going to be saved. They might argue that the whole world is going to be saved. But the Apostle is not saying that. He has made it abundantly clear that the only people who are saved are those who have faith in Jesus Christ. The salvation is to 'everyone that believeth in Jesus', whether he is Jew or Gentile, in circumcision or uncircumcision; it does not matter. So it is not 'all' the Jews and 'all' the Gentiles, but it is Jew and Gentile, whosoever is a believer in Jesus.

Having cleared that matter we must consider exactly what the Apostle is saying. In a sense he has prepared us for this by a word or expression he employed in the twenty-eighth verse, where we read: 'Therefore we conclude that a man' – that is it, 'a man' – 'is justified by faith without the deeds of the law'. 'A man' – the man who is justified. He has put it there in a manner which now enables him to go on to say: 'The man I am talking about, the man who is justified by faith, may be a Jew, he may be a Gentile, he may be circumcision, he may be uncircumcision'. He is not talking of all Jews and all Gentiles, but just this man, the man who is justified by faith. 'We conclude that a man is justified by faith.'

It is interesting once more to notice how the Apostle comes back to and repeats this point which he has been making so frequently. All the way from verse 18 in the first chapter to the twentieth verse of the third chapter the Apostle has been at great pains to show that the Law had proved that finally there was no difference between Jew and Gentile. 'There is no difference,' he says, 'for all have sinned and come short of the glory of God.' Yet he comes back to it and says it again. What he is saying in effect is that the Law negatively, as it were, demonstrated that there is no difference between the Jew and the Gentile in this matter of salvation, because neither could keep the Law. It was immaterial whether it was the Law given externally through Moses, or that law, that moral sense that was in the heart, all have failed. But now, he says, that is shown much more clearly by the Cross of the Lord Jesus Christ. It is here you see every division and distinction entirely abolished, and for ever banished, because that is the only way of salvation. And because it is the only way of salvation, all these other distinctions have gone. They are irrelevant, and it is no use talking about them any longer. That is the argument here. Here is God's only way of salvation, and there is therefore no purpose or point in your talking about being different, or about the Law; it is an utter irrelevance.

In the second chapter of his Epistle to the Ephesians Paul says this still more plainly and at greater length. 'The middle wall of partition', he says, 'has been broken down.' By what? 'By the blood of Christ, by his death upon the Cross.' The Jew and the Gentile now both come together in Christ, and by the one Spirit, unto the Father. They both have to be saved in the same way; and they have been saved in the same way. So the Law of ordinances has been put aside because Christ has completed it, and has fulfilled it, and there is this equal opportunity for the Gentiles. That is his precise argument here, that the Cross of Christ has broken down and demolished for ever the middle wall of partition between Jew and Gentile. 'And of twain he has made one new man, so making peace.' The Gentiles are now 'fellow-citizens with the saints and of the household of God', and they are being built together in this great Temple of the Lord in which He dwells by the Spirit.

That is the first part of the argument; but there is more. You notice how he puts it in verse 30: 'Seeing', he says, 'it is one God who shall justify the circumcision by faith and the uncircumcision through faith.' What does this mean? Sometimes it is taken in two different ways. Some say that instead of reading, 'Seeing it is one God who shall justify', it should read, 'Seeing that God is one, and this one God shall justify the circumcision by faith and uncircumcision through faith . . .'. I am prepared to accept that and the AV translation because I believe that both are true.

So the Apostle's argument can be put like this. The fact that there is only one God must mean that this distinction and division between the Jew and the Gentile must no longer be perpetuated. The Jews were tending to do this but there is only one God; they were wrong. There is not one God for the Jews and another God for Gentiles. That is entirely wrong, that is quite false, that in reality is the error of Paganism with its multiplicity of gods. There is only one God, and if there is only one God, everybody in the world must be under that one God, Gentiles as well as Jews. There is one God, and the human race is one in its relationship to Him. The Apostle therefore argues that this one God has provided His one way of salvation; and therefore it must be for Gentile as well as for Jew. If you do not admit that, he argues, then you are saying that He is not the God of the Gentiles. But if He is not the one and only God, there must be some other God for the Gentiles. But that is wrong, and indeed blasphemous. He is the one and only God who is over all; and everybody is under Him.

Or you can take it the other way. This fact that God is one was the great argument of the Old Testament. Then, because God is one, the argument inevitably follows that He has not a number of different ways of saving people. He has only one way of saving people, and it is the one way we have been considering. It is the way for Jews and for Gentiles because it is the only way. God is always consistent with Himself, and He does the same thing in this respect for all who believe. So the second argument is, that not to see that Jews and Gentiles are in the same position is really to impugn the character and the being of God. God is one – one God. He has this one way of salvation, and it is for all. In that sense we speak of the Lord Jesus Christ as 'The Saviour of the world'.

That leaves us with this one question which has often perplexed people. They ask, 'What is this distinction in verse 30, where Paul says, "Seeing it is one God who shall justify circumcision by faith and uncircumcision through faith?"' What is the difference between 'by' and 'through?' Is there some subtle point here when he says the Jews are going to be justified by faith and the Gentiles through faith? The answer, it seems to me, is that there is no doubt at all that ultimately there is no material difference between the two. The Apostle is merely varying his expression, as he is very fond of doing, and as, I suppose, every speaker or writer frequently tends to do.

But let me produce some evidence to substantiate what I am saying. You will find, for instance, in the Epistle to the Galatians in the second chapter and the sixteenth verse, that the Apostle there uses terms interchangeably, 'Knowing that a man is not justified by the works of the law but by the faith of Jesus Christ, even we have believed in Jesus Christ, that we might be justified by the faith of Christ and not by the works of the law.' Now there in the Authorized Version you notice that both times it was 'by' faith in Christ. But actually in the first instance the Apostle said 'through' faith – 'Knowing that a man is not justified by the works of the law but through the faith of Jesus Christ'. Then he goes on, 'even we have believed in Jesus Christ, that we might be justified by the faith of Christ'. He is talking about the same people, he is talking about himself and others; once he says 'through', then he says 'by' of the same people. Obviously there is no difference between the two.

In Galatians 3:8 there is a still more interesting example. There we read: 'And the Scripture, foreseeing that God would justify the heathen through faith, preached before the Gospel unto Abraham, saying, In thee shall all nations be blessed.' That reading is from the Authorized Version. Unfortunately its translation is not accurate; it has 'through' faith where it should have put 'by' faith. The word the Apostle used there was exactly the word that he uses in Romans 3:30 where we have, 'shall justify circumcision by faith'. Now here in Galatians 3:8 he says, 'The Scripture foreseeing that God would justify the heathen by faith'. So we must not make too much of this difference. We must not argue, that as Paul says that the Jews are justified by faith, but the heathen are justified through faith, it is clear that the heathen are not justified by faith. For, in Galatians 3:8 he says that the heathen are justified *by* faith. Obviously, therefore, it is not a material point at all.

Yet I find myself in some sympathy with those who argue that he must surely have had some reason in his mind for making the difference and the slight change. They say that what he was really bringing out was this. The first term, which is translated 'by', points to the source. The Apostle is talking about the Jews, and he wants to nail this point, that the source is never 'works'. In order to get rid of that error he deliberately uses this word as a hint and as a suggestion of a source. So it is *by*. Whereas in the case of the Gentiles there was not the same danger. They were not in the same danger of saying that they could justify themselves *by* their works, so he says that the 'means', the 'method', the 'intermediate agency' is faith. You can accept that or not, as you like. Ultimately it really does not make any difference at all, because the fundamental proposition is, 'Therefore we conclude that a man is justified by faith without the deeds of the law'. However, as many have felt that there was some subtle and important and vital distinction, I felt that I should call your attention to it.

Summing up, then, the great point, the principle the Apostle is emphasizing again is that there is only one way of salvation, and that that one way of salvation is for all who are saved. There is no other, there is no alternative. We can surely see how essential it was for the Apostle to establish this point in those early days of the preaching of the Gospel. The Jews found this to be a real stumbling-block; this idea that the same message should be preached to the Gentiles. It was an offence to them, and so the Apostle has to go on repeating it. Also, as we have seen, it was still a kind of lingering difficulty in the minds of many Jews who had actually become Christians. When they listened to Judaizing teachers who emphasized the Law and circumcision they tended to go back. You remember that even Peter did so at Antioch, and he had to be put right and to be withstood to the face by the Apostle Paul. So it was essential that Paul should make it perfectly plain and clear that this one way is for the Gentile as well as the Jew, and that the Jew needs it in exactly the same way as the Gentile.

This constant repetition and re-emphasis was essential in those early days of Christianity. But it is equally essential today; and that is why I am emphasizing it. There are those who still seem to think that the Gospel and its message, and Christianity, is not for all. There are many false distinctions still being drawn. I have known good people, religious people for instance, who have been brought up in a church, who seem to think that the Gospel of salvation is really not needed by them, and by people like them. They believe that you are a Christian because your parents were Christians, and therefore they do not need this Gospel in that way. They are ready to think that this Gospel of salvation, and the need of conversion, may be necessary in slum work or something like that; but not among respectable people, not among those brought up in Christian homes. That is a denial of the very thing the Apostle is arguing. He says we are all in exactly the same position, all of us, every one of us. We all need the same Gospel in precisely the same way. The Gospel is not only for good people; neither is it only for bad people. It is for all people. All need it. 'All have sinned and have come short of the glory of God.' This is the only way whereby anybody can be saved. It is this message, it is the Person and the work of the Lord Jesus Christ received by faith; and until there is that faith there cannot be salvation. It is still essential for all. 'We conclude that a man is justified by faith apart from the deeds of the law.'

It has another urgent application which we can put like this. You will sometimes read in the Press, and indeed, alas, in the religious papers, of what they call a World Congress of Religions. This kind of thing is very popular today. And there is also a Society or Association – 'The Society (or the Association) of Christians and Jews'. It has an annual meeting in which Christians and Jews come together for common worship and fellowship. But as I say, it goes beyond that, and extends to Buddhism, Confucianism, Hinduism, Christianity – a World Congress of Faiths. This is now a fact in the modern world; it is a fact in which the modern man tends to glory. He says, 'At last we really begin to understand the love of God. People used to be so rigid and so narrow in the past. They criticized one another and they refused to have fellowship with one another. But we have come to see that there is only one God, and we all worship the same God – the Christian, the Hindu, the Mohammedan, the Buddhist, the Confucianist, we all worship the one God. It is like climbing a great mountain where God dwells on the summit. Christians make their approach to the summit from this side, the Mohammedans come up the other side, and others by different paths. Because of these different approaches people used to think we could have no fellowship at all, and therefore had none. But we are all going to the same summit, we believe in the same God, and therefore we should have fellowship together. So let us have a "Congress of World Faiths". Let us stop criticizing, is the modern cry, let us stop saying that we are right and others wrong, that because I am a Christian I alone am right and all these others are wrong. Let us thank God rather for the insights of these other religions, and let us come together and pool our insights. Let us rejoice that we all in our different ways worship the only God.'

You are familiar with that argument. All we have to say about it is that it is an argument that is based on nothing but ignorance of what the Apostle teaches here. It is a complete denial of the very thing the Apostle is saying. The Apostle says, 'There is only one God.' But the Congress of World Faiths says that also. Where, then, is the difference? It is that the Congress of World Faiths starts there, and then stops. But Paul goes on, and says, 'Because there is only one God there is only one way of dealing with people in the matter of salvation'. That is the whole point of his argument. There are not 'many' ways of arriving at God; there is only 'one' way. Jew and Gentile – all must come by the one way, the only way. It is because He is 'one God' that the Congress of World Faiths is wrong when it says that the one God deals with different people in different ways. Whereas Paul's whole argument is that, because He is one, He has only one way, and He has already declared what that one way is. He has 'set forth' Christ in public as the 'propitiation'; that is His only way of salvation.

So we must not hesitate to make these assertions. There is only one way to God, there is only one way to know God; it is in

'Jesus Christ and him crucified'. Did He not say so Himself? 'I am the way, the truth, and the life: no man cometh (can come) unto the Father but by me [John 14: 6]. The Mohammedan cannot come to God by his way nor can any one of the others by their different ways. They cannot truly worship the same God because they are not reconciled to the same God. And until they are, the Christian cannot have spiritual fellowship with them. They must come to Christ before they can ever come to God. They must come to Christ as the Saviour of the world, and be reconciled to God by His blood, before they can be 'fellow-citizens with the saints and of the household of God'.

This Congress of World Faiths, this Association of Jews and Christians is a denial of the Gospel; it is a denial of what God has so plainly 'set forth'. Far from being an indication of a deeper understanding of the love of God, it betrays an utter ignorance of the love of God: it is a denial of the most glorious manifestation of the love of God. It is a trampling under foot of 'the blood of Christ', because it says that man can go to God, and know Him, and worship Him, without going 'by the blood of Christ', which is the only way whereby man can ever enter into the Holiest of all [*Hebrews* 10: 19].

Are we still surprised that the Apostle took the trouble to deduce these principles? Should we not thank God that He led this man by the Holy Spirit, not simply to state the way of salvation, but to go on and to be careful to underline it and to show that it was crucial, that without it there was nothing? It is the only way, there is none other. No man knows God, or is reconciled to Him, or is forgiven by Him, except through the one and only way that God Himself has appointed. 'There is one God, and one mediator between God and men, the man Christ Jesus' [1 *Timothy* 2: 5]. The Apostle in later chapters of this Epistle argues this matter out at great length. The Jews, he says, still think they are worshipping God; but they are blinded, they are in unbelief; they are outside and not inside. All who are in, are in only by 'the blood of Jesus Christ'. A Jew is not reconciled to God except by Jesus Christ. A Gentile is not, either. They both come in the same way – 'Through him we both have access by one Spirit unto the Father'. And there is no other way. To pretend that you are manifesting the spirit of love by saying that you have fellowship with the other man because he believes in the same God, though he denies Christ, is simply to deny the Lord Christ yourself. May God open our eyes to this, and keep us from this subtle delusion, this most subtle heresy, that, in the name of love, is denying the greatest manifestation of the love of God.

Thirdly, I want to emphasize one other thing which we should bear in mind. There is another error which perhaps comes a little nearer to us who are evangelicals in outlook, than the one which I have just mentioned. It is an error that, alas, seems to me to be guilty of a similar denial of what the Apostle is teaching here. It is what may be described as the dispensational error. I mean the teaching that emphasizes that there is still a real distinction and difference between the Jews and the Gentiles. It is a teaching which says, that though, in a sense, now in the time of the Gospel, they are both one, nevertheless the old fundamental distinction is still there; and it will come back again, for it is still a real one. Indeed, some go so far as to say that it will persist throughout eternity, that the Church will be in Heaven and the Jews, the nation, will be on earth – this distinction between Jew and Gentile will be perpetuated to all eternity.

But not only that; it teaches that there are several Gospels, that there is a 'Gospel of the Kingdom' which is not the same as the 'Gospel of the grace of God'. This teaching has achieved great popularity. It maintains that, when our Lord first came, He, like John the Baptist, preached the Gospel of the Kingdom. But that when the Jews rejected that, then God brought in the Gospel of the grace of God, the present Gospel which we preach, which says that both Jew and Gentile can be saved by faith in the Lord Jesus Christ. That is the Gospel of the grace of God, which is not the same thing as the Gospel of the Kingdom; and this Gospel of grace, they say, will go on being preached until the end of the great tribulation, then it comes to an end. There is disagreement as to details; some say it will end earlier, and that then the Gospel of the Kingdom will come back again, and that there will be people who will be saved through believing the Gospel of the Kingdom which the Jews rejected of old.

You see the implication of all that. It means that there will be some people saved in eternity, not through believing the Gospel of the grace of God but through the Gospel of the Kingdom. In other words, it is possible for people to be saved apart from the grace of God in and through our Lord Jesus Christ and Him crucified.

You cannot reconcile that with this clear and plain teaching. There is only one Gospel, it is the Gospel of the grace of God. That is the only Gospel that admits anyone into the Kingdom; it is the only way into the Kingdom of God. There is only one way to be reconciled to God, and it is through this 'propitiation' which He hath set forth in the blood of Christ. There is no other, there never has been another, there never will be another. It is the only way. So to insist upon this perpetuation of the difference between Jew and Gentile, and to talk of different types of Gospel, is to deny the very teaching that the Apostle has gone out of his way to stress and to emphasize. There is no more, no longer, 'Jew or Gentile, Barbarian, Scythian, bond or free'. The 'middle wall of partition' has gone; and it has gone for ever.

What is the position? The position is, that the Gentiles are made 'fellow-heirs with the saints', with the Jews who had believed before, and who were saved through trusting to what God was going to do in Christ. God's great method of salvation has always been by faith. The distinction between Jew and Gentile has gone, and it has gone for ever, and will never come back. It is the only way of salvation, and we must never hint at, or even suggest in the slightest manner, any other way. There is only one Gospel for Jews and for Gentiles alike. 'Is he God of the Jews only? is he not also of the Gentiles? Yes, of the Gentiles also. Seeing it is one God who shall justify circumcision by faith and uncircumcision through faith.'

Let me commend to you once more a careful consideration of these two verses. Above all, let me press upon you the importance of working out the implications of biblical statements. Every error and every heresy that has ever troubled the Church, is always the result of men being governed by something other than the Scripture. How subtle these errors are! They come at this present time to the modern Christian in this form. There is this atmosphere, this climate of opinion, which would have us believe that our fathers were too legalistic and too rigid, that they were too harsh, but that we have made this wonderful discovery about the love of God. Starting with that, they begin to sit loose to the Word of God.

Then the second form which the error takes makes a great point of always being positive. You must not be negative, you must not criticize wrong or false teaching. That shows a bad spirit. After all, the erring ones may not see things clearly, but surely that does not matter; the great thing is that they want to be Christians. And so the argument goes on. You must not be too particular, otherwise you are setting yourself up as the authority; and you are saying that everybody else is wrong. That is to be critical and to be lacking in love, and so on. It enters in that subtle way, and before you know where you are you have denied the Gospel, you have 'sold the pass'. God forbid that any one of us should desire to be controversial, or delight in it as such. There is such a possibility, and may God have mercy upon us if we are guilty of it. But when a message like this deliberately and specifically calls our attention to these things, we have no right to ignore them, whatever the consequences. If we do, we shall not further the interests of the Kingdom of God, because the Holy Spirit will never honour anything except the truth.

The argument that is being used says: 'The position is desperate; the people, the masses are outside the Christian Church. Let us get them in somehow. Do not be too particular. Let us bring them to Christ and then perhaps we can set about teaching them. But the vital question is: Are we absolutely clear that He is the only way, and that salvation in Christ is only through His blood, and that justification by faith only is vital and essential doctrine? And that there can be no compromise on these matters? These are foundations, fundamentals. There are other matters about which we cannot and must never be dogmatic. But here surely there can be no argument at all. This one passage alone is enough once and for ever: 'We conclude that a man is justified by faith only, apart from the deeds of the law.' The blood of Christ is essential; He is the propitiation. And that applies to everybody. All must come this way. There is no fellowship possible between those who rely on Him and on Him alone and on His blood, and those who claim that they know God without Him.

It is not for us to judge, but it is for us to pronounce the truth; and for myself I cannot even pray with a man who tells me that he can go to God without the blood of Christ. For I cannot, and I believe that nobody else can. I therefore am driven to say that, though he may be in the posture of prayer by my side, we are not doing the same thing. How can we be? No! boasting has gone; divisions and distinctions are abolished; 'the whole world lieth guilty', in exactly the same way, 'before God'. No man will ever know God, and His forgiveness, and His Fatherhood, except it be in and through Jesus Christ and the merit of His blood. May God awaken us to the realization of the importance and the urgency of these things. The Protestant Reformers did not die in vain, our fathers did not suffer for these things for nothing. Let us be careful lest in our ignorance, and with a desire to be affable and friendly, and to have so-called 'fellowship', we not only deny the Faith but deny these men of God who held to these things even to the point of laying down their lives for them. May God have mercy upon us and open our eyes to see the truth clearly, to rest upon it, to live by it, to contend for it earnestly, and to enjoy it and all its wondrous blessings!

10 The Law Established

Do we then make void the law through faith? God forbid: yea, we establish the law.   Romans 3 : 31

This brings us to the third and last illustration of what I have been describing as characteristics of the Gospel way of salvation. We can also describe them as three deductions which the Apostle draws from his description of the way of salvation. In other words he says that because this is the way of salvation we must always deduce from it that there is no boasting, and that there is no difference between different kinds of people. But that is not all. The third deduction is that the Gospel, this way of salvation in Jesus Christ and Him crucified, this way of salvation which has been brought to pass because God hath 'set him forth as a propitiation through faith in his blood', establishes the Law.

The Apostle puts that in an interesting way. He asks another rhetorical question, 'Do we then make void the law through faith?' But actually the order in which the Apostle put it is this: 'The law, do we make it of no effect through this faith?' (or 'through the faith?') Now that is a better way of putting it: 'The law, do we make it void or of no effect through the faith?' It is not 'faith', but 'the faith', 'through the faith'. By 'the faith', of course, he means this message, this particular message concerning the way of righteousness that has now come in. He is not talking about our faith, he is talking about the message – 'Do we make void the law through this preaching of salvation by faith in Jesus Christ?' The message, the faith, the faith principle, if you like, in contradistinction to any kind of works.

Having put his rhetorical question, the Apostle answers it at

[139]

once by the words here translated, 'God forbid', which really mean, 'May it not be', 'It is unthinkable'. The Apostle is speaking very frankly and bluntly. He has already used the same expression at the beginning of this chapter where he says, 'For what if some did not believe? Shall their unbelief make the faith of God without effect? God forbid.' He uses these expressions because there were people who were very ready indeed to draw these false deductions. And there are still people who are ready to draw them. But the thing is so abhorrent that he says, 'May it not be, do not even think of it, do not even come near to suggesting it. The thing is unthinkable.' We must discover, therefore, the reason for this sense of abhorrence which the Apostle feels at the mere suggestion of such an error. Indeed he himself gives us the reason at once. He says, 'Yea, rather, we establish the law'. Far from making the Law of none effect we are helping it to stand, we are establishing it, we are really showing its essential importance.

Our task, therefore, is to show that there is really nothing which so establishes the Law as this doctrine that we are saved by the redemption that is in Christ Jesus, 'Whom God hath set forth to be a propitiation through faith in his blood'. In other words, we have to show, and to establish the fact, that it is only as we interpret this teaching in the way we have been doing that this verse really follows. Negatively, we must show that other interpretations of this teaching concerning the Atonement do not establish the Law. That is our final way of proving that they are wrong. Any way of salvation that we believe in, any doctrine of the Atonement that we may hold, must always 'establish' the Law.

How, therefore, have we to interpret this statement? It has been interpreted in two ways. There are some who say that what the Apostle means by 'the law' here is the Old Testament Scriptures, and that therefore what he is saying at this point is, that in giving this teaching concerning the Lord Jesus Christ and His ransoming work upon the Cross, and the value of His shed blood, he was not making the Old Testament of no value, with all its history and all it has to say about the Jews. And they would argue that that is the right interpretation because, they say, the Apostle goes on immediately, in what we know as chapter 4 in our Bibles, to say: 'What shall we then say that Abraham our father, as pertaining to the flesh, hath found?' In other words, they argue, he goes back to the Old Testament history, and talks about Abraham and about David. Surely, therefore, they deduce, he is using this term 'the law' as a term to mean the whole of the Old Testament.

Now it is true that the Jews did sometimes refer to the whole of the Old Testament as 'the law'. Believing as they did that the Law of Moses was the most important thing in the Old Testament, they tended to regard the whole Book as the Book of Law. But there are some very good reasons for not accepting that interpretation. Here are some of them. In the whole context from verse 21 onwards, the Apostle has really been speaking about the Mosaic Law, the Law given through Moses, the Moral and the Ceremonial Law, and especially the Moral Law. That is the thing about which he has been speaking, and therefore it would be a strange thing if, suddenly and without giving any notice or warning or any indication that he was doing so, he should suddenly change the meaning of the word and begin to use it to describe the whole of the Old Testament. That is a good principle which we should always bear in mind when we are interpreting the Scriptures. If a term has been used in a given sense in a number of verses, it is not likely that its sense will suddenly be changed without any indication to that effect. And there is certainly no indication whatsoever at this point.

Then, taking up this other matter that what we are told in the fourth chapter certainly does go back into history, notice that it does not start with the word 'For'. Surely if the Apostle were speaking here in verse 31 of the Old Testament history, which he certainly goes on to do in chapter 4, the connecting word would have been the word 'For' – but it is not. In chapter 4 he is obviously taking up a new subject, as I hope to show. If it were but a direct continuation of this matter dealt with in chapter 3 from verse 21 to the end, then the natural connecting link would have been 'For'.

On those two grounds we must reject that interpretation and suggest that the Apostle is referring here to the Mosaic Law, the

[141]

Law which God gave to the Children of Israel through Moses, saying unto them as He gave it, 'If you can keep it, it will save you'.

The Apostle's assertion is that God's way of salvation establishes the Law; it holds it up, it shows what a wonderful thing it was. Indeed, nothing else so establishes it. We see therefore once more that the teaching which is current today, which tells us that under the new dispensation the Law of the Old Testament has been entirely abolished and put aside – and that we are now confronted by a new law which is the law of faith, and that henceforward we have nothing to do but just to believe on the Lord Jesus Christ – we see that that is entirely wrong. Because if we teach that the old Law has really been thrown overboard and has been replaced by a new law, we are obviously not establishing that old Law. We are dismissing it, we are jettisoning it. But the Apostle is concerned to say the exact opposite. So we must never teach that that Law has been abrogated, and that all the sinner now has to face, and all he will ever have to face at the bar of judgement, is this new law of faith, of believing in Christ. We see that that is entirely wrong; indeed the Apostle has already made that plain and clear in verse 27. That cannot be the explanation.

What, then, does Paul mean? How does this teaching 'establish' the Law? Here again there is a popular teaching at the present time to which, unfortunately, I am compelled to call attention. It is very common and is not only taught by those who are regarded as liberals in their theology, but has crept in now and again also into the writings of those who are considered to be evangelical. It is this. What the Apostle means, they say, is that by means of our faith in the Lord Jesus Christ we are now enabled to live the Law, we are enabled to keep the Law. Christ gives us strength and power which enable us to keep and honour and fulfil the Law, by living the good life, the Christian life. That means we are establishing the Law.

What a spurious argument and exposition that is! It is often put in terms of the Easter message, that we are really saved by the Risen Christ; not saved by the death of Christ, but by His resurrection life and power. The Cross is by-passed, and salva-

[142]

tion is described in this way. The great fact is the Risen Christ, who is still alive. If we look to Him and ask Him for help to live the Christian life we shall be saved. And as we live the Christian life we are incidentally honouring the Law, keeping the Law, and thereby 'establishing' the Law.

We must examine this teaching because, as I want to show, it is entirely false, and completely negatives the very thing the Apostle is saying. The first answer to that teaching is this. The Apostle in this third chapter is not considering sanctification at all; he is only considering justification. But the moment you begin to talk about living a life, and living the Christian life, and living a good life, you are talking about sanctification. What that teaching really comes to in the end is that you are justified because you are sanctified. That always was, and still is, the Roman Catholic teaching on justification. They say that a man is justified before God because he is enabled to live the good life by the grace and new life he received in baptism, and as he is enabled by grace to live this good life he justifies himself. This teaching we are evaluating really amounts to the same thing.

But, here, the Apostle is not dealing with sanctification at all. It is not mentioned. He is dealing with justification by faith. Surely we should be clear about that. In verse 20 he has said, 'Therefore by the deeds of the law there shall no flesh be justified in his sight'. That is not the way of justification. Well, what is that way? We find the answer in verse 24, 'Being justified freely by his grace through the redemption that is in Christ Jesus'. That is the way, and this is his theme right through to the end of the chapter, and as it will be right through chapter 4. So we reject that teaching because it introduces the element of sanctification into a paragraph which is dealing with nothing but justification.

But not only that, it is also a complete denial of the Apostle's teaching of the doctrine of justification by faith only. As we have just seen, it takes us back to the doctrine of justification by works. The fact that the Lord Jesus Christ enables us to live a life that honours the Law does not make any difference at this point. This wrong interpretation states that it is our works, however produced, that really are the means of our justification. So we must reject it, because the Apostle's whole point, as we have seen, is that justification is something essentially forensic and declaratory. Justification is that declaration of God that we are regarded in His sight as just, because of the righteousness of the Lord Jesus Christ. It is a forensic, a legal declaration, by God that though we are still as it were in our sins, He regards us as just; He gives us the righteousness of Christ through faith, and pronounces us to be just and accepted and righteous in His most holy sight.

What the Apostle maintains here is that God's way of declaring those who believe in Christ to be righteous honours and establishes the Law. How does it do so? Here are the answers to the question. The Apostle is in a sense just repeating what our Lord Himself said in the Sermon on the Mount. You remember the statement in Matthew chapter 5, verses 17 and 18: 'Think not that I am come to destroy the law, or the prophets; I am not come to destroy, but to fulfil. For verily I say unto you, Till heaven and earth pass, one jot or one tittle shall in no wise pass from the law, till all be fulfilled.' And, of course, our Lord Himself 'established' the Law by fulfilling it in every respect. That is what the Apostle is saying here. He, as it were, asks, 'Does somebody suggest that by stating that the only way of salvation is in and through Jesus Christ and Him crucified – by His blood, which is the purchase price to ransom us out of the clutches of the Law and of the devil and of death – does anyone argue that by preaching this I am somehow or other putting the Law entirely aside and saying that it does not matter at all? On the contrary, I am asserting that this way of salvation and redemption, above everything else, honours the Law in all ways'.

How is this true? First of all, the Lord Jesus Christ honoured the Law in His active obedience. We are told of Him by the Apostle in the Epistle to the Galatians, 'He was made of a woman, made under the law' [*Galatians* 4: 6]. He deliberately placed Himself, and God placed Him, 'under the law' as a Man. Though He was entirely free from sin, He came, and was made under the Law. He set out to obey and honour God's Law in every jot and tittle, and He did so perfectly and completely. You remember

His words to John the Baptist, who was reluctant to baptize Him, and who remonstrated with Christ, saying, 'I have need to be baptized of thee, and comest thou to me?' 'Suffer it to be so now', says our Lord, 'for thus it becometh us to fulfil all righteousness.' He put Himself under the Law, and He gave a perfect obedience to it. He never sinned. He could say, 'Which of you convinceth me of sin?' He said, 'the prince of this world cometh and hath nothing in me'. If Satan could have found anything he would have brought if forward; if the authorities could have found anything they would have done the same thing. They had nothing to bring forward, so they tried to invent a case; they concocted a lie which they could not prove. No one could point a finger at Him. He never sinned, He never disobeyed God. He honoured the Law of God perfectly and entirely in His holy life of obedience.

But then, and still more strikingly, as the Apostle emphasizes here, Christ honoured the Law in His passive obedience upon the Cross on Calvary's hill. The Law not only demands obedience, it also pronounces judgment upon failure to keep it. And mankind had sinned: 'All have sinned and come short . . . There is none righteous, no, not one.' The Law demands and claims its penalty. It must be fulfilled in every respect. If this way of salvation does not answer that demand of the Law for the punishment of sin and transgression it does not establish the Law. But it does. The Apostle has already put that in his great phrase, 'that he might be just and the justifier of him which believeth in Jesus'. Here, he is saying that in a slightly different form, but it is essentially the same thing. By taking upon Himself the punishment of our sins demanded by the Law, the Lord Jesus Christ was establishing the Law. So, by making His soul an offering for sin, by going, and being led, as 'a lamb to the slaughter', in this passive obedience in submitting to God to lay upon Him the iniquity of us all, without murmuring or complaining, or running away from it, He establishes the Law.

But there are other ways also in which He does this. There are a number of other things which we must always bear in mind as we consider this most important verse. The Lord Jesus Christ, by His work, and indeed God Himself by what He has done in and through Christ, confirm and reveal more clearly than ever before what the Law says about the holiness and the righteousness of God. We must never lose sight of that fact. One of the primary functions of the Law was to reveal the holiness and the righteousness of God. Read again the Ten Commandments as they are given in the twentieth chapter of the book of Exodus, and there you will find that that is the Law's great emphasis. It is all summed up elsewhere in Scripture in the phrase, 'Be ye holy; for I am holy, saith the Lord'. That is what God demands of us. 'I am holy, and you are to be holy because I am holy.' The first function of the Law is to make clear to us the utter, absolute, indescribable holiness and righteousness of God. Now there is nothing that shows that so plainly and clearly as what happened on the Cross; and if we do not see first and foremost in the Cross a manifestation of the holiness and the righteousness of God, we are not seeing it truly. It establishes the Law in that way; it brings that out.

The Cross does it, secondly, in this way; it confirms everything that God had said in His law about His holy wrath against sin. God in that Law had said that He hates sin, that sin arouses His holy wrath, and that He will most certainly and surely punish sin. It is not I who am saying that; the Law of God says that. God goes on repeating it – 'I hate these things', He says, and He threatens punishment upon all who are disobedient. If His people obey, they will be blessed; if they disobey they will be cursed – Mounts Gerizim and Ebal – blessing and cursing. God laid it down clearly in that Law that He would certainly punish sin and all who are guilty of it. All that we have in this third chapter brings that out in a most amazing manner. There is nothing in the whole of history, there is no point in the whole course of mankind's story, there is no place in the universe which has so manifested the wrath of God against sin, His detestation of it, and His determination to punish it, as the death of our Lord upon the Cross. We have seen that in detail already as we considered the word 'propitiation'. That word brings out the wrath of God; and you do not establish the Law unless you show the wrath of God and its being poured out upon sin. The thing God said He would do He has done, and thereby this way of salvation establishes the Law. But a way of salvation which does away with propitiation does not establish the Law and therefore it cannot be the true way.

Again, this way of salvation confirms everything that the Law has said about sin and about our sinfulness. The business of the Law, Paul has already told us, is this: 'By the deeds of the law there shall no flesh be justified in his sight; for by the law is the knowledge of sin.' 'We know that what things soever the law saith, it saith to them that are under the law; that every mouth may be stopped and the whole world become guilty before God.' Does the Cross say that? If it does not it does not establish the Law. But it does! What the Cross says is that nothing but it can save any soul; that all are lost and are helpless and hopeless. It proclaims that. If our view of the Cross does not proclaim that, I say once more that it must be false. And there already my fourth point has been mentioned, namely, that it confirms also our utter inability and our complete helplessness and hopelessness.

That brings us to the fifth point, which is this. In the Law given through Moses we have a great deal of instruction concerning burnt offerings and sacrifices, and we read that the High Priest once every year was to go into the Holiest of all in the Tabernacle or Temple and take and present blood – the blood of bulls and of goats. He was to offer sacrifices on behalf of the people. What is the meaning of all this? This way of salvation, says Paul, shows us their meaning, and therefore establishes them, and therefore the Law that commanded them. It shows that they were but types given by God and used by God to teach the one and only way of salvation that was to come – the great Anti-type. Christ by dying upon the Cross has fulfilled that Levitical Ceremonial Law perfectly, and all that it foreshadowed. He established that aspect of the Law by offering His soul as a sacrifice for sin. He is 'the Lamb of God that taketh away the sin of the world'.

The sixth way in which this salvation through Christ as a propitiation through faith in His blood also confirms and establishes what the Law said is that it confirms that 'without shed-

ding of blood there is no remission' of sins [*Hebrews* 9: 22]. As we
have seen, there are many popular modern views of the Atonement that do not like 'the blood' at all. But God Himself had
shown plainly in the Law that 'without shedding of blood there
is no remission of sins'. Therefore, unless this way of salvation
confirms that, and establishes that, there is a contradiction. But
it does confirm it. What I see as I look at the Cross, and 'the water
and the blood from His riven side which flowed' is that – 'without
shedding of blood there is no remission of sins'. In every respect
the Law is established by this view of the Atonement that the
Apostle teaches here – but by no other.

So I come to the last point, the seventh. It is only as we look
at the Atonement as taught here that we have a truly spiritual
conception of God's Law. Apart from this we are liable to think
of the Law in terms of particular actions and deeds and things
that we do or omit to do. But the Law is much bigger than that.
It is essentially spiritual, and its whole intent is to bring us to the
place in which we shall 'love the Lord our God with all our heart
and soul and mind and strength'. It is spiritual and personal, and
it is in that summary of it given by our Lord that we see that.
It is my relationship to God that matters, not simply my morality,
not simply my behaviour. No, it is my total relationship to Him.
And as I see it in that way it creates within me a desire to keep
the Law myself and to honour it. Christ died, as Peter reminds
us in his First Epistle, 'in order to bring us to God' [3: 18]. Not
merely forgiveness but the restoration of a broken personal
relationship.

These are some of the ways, the chief ways, in which this way
of salvation establishes, holds up, the Law and honours it. I say
again, that any view of the Cross that does not bring out these
particular elements is wrong, is false, and it is to be rejected.
We really must discriminate in these matters. We must not allow
ourselves to become sentimental and believe men who say, 'Ah,
the message of the Cross is this. There is the Son of God being
crucified by men, and yet He says to them from the Cross, and
in His terrible agony, "I still love you so much that I am ready to
forgive you for even doing this".' If you accept that as the real

meaning of the Cross you are denying the teaching of the Apostle. There is no 'blood' there, there is no 'establishing' of the Law, there is no explanation of all these great things that are found in the Old Testament concerning the Law, and, indeed, in the New Testament also. We must insist always upon all these points being made plain and clear in our understanding of the Atonement. This alone shows the truth, the sanctity, the inviolability of God's holy Law, which is an expression of God's character.

There, then, is the exposition. That brings us to the end of this third chapter, and especially to the end of this classic passage on the doctrine of the Atonement. It is a foolish thing to say, perhaps, but I was going to say that if I were asked which in my opinion is the most important and crucial passage in the whole of Scripture, I would have to include Romans 3: 21–31. Here is the very heart and centre of the Gospel; and the history of the Church throughout the centuries shows this clearly. It is when men and women have gone wrong here that they have gone into heresy, have gone astray, and the Church has lost her power. This is the message: 'Jesus Christ and him crucified.' It is the heart of the Gospel. So we really cannot afford to be uncertain as to its teaching.

Let us therefore, in a footnote, look at some of the reasons which men give today for not interpreting this in the way that we have tried to do. There are three things that are commonly said. There are those who do not hesitate to say, without any apology at all, 'This is admittedly a correct exposition of Paul's teaching but the Apostle Paul after all was the child of his age. He was a Jew, he had been trained as a Pharisee, and he was steeped in that Jewish teaching with all its doctrine of Law and blood and of sacrifice.' Some even say that the teaching did not actually come from the Old Testament but that the Jews had been slowly incorporating into their teaching Egyptian ideas with regard to sacrifices and offerings. So they say, 'Your exposition is quite right, but Paul was wrong; he had a wrong view of God, he had a wrong view of salvation. We now know better. We know that God is a God of love, and that wrath is incompatible with love, and that the idea that God ever instituted blood sacrifices is just monstrous and ridiculous.' That is their explanation, that our exposition of Paul's teaching is right, but that Paul himself was wrong, and therefore the whole teaching is wrong. We need waste no time in contradicting such ideas; they are unworthy of contradiction.

If anyone ever says that to you, what you need to discuss with them is not this particular teaching; you must discuss with them the meaning of the term 'Apostle'. What is an apostle? Make them start with that. Paul starts off by describing himself as a 'called Apostle'. The question is, what is an apostle? If an apostle is a man who has been called by the risen Lord to receive a revelation and a commission directly and immediately from Him to go out and to preach in an authoritative manner, well then we need say no more – everything the Apostle Paul writes is correct. But these men set up themselves and their own ideas; they do not believe the Scripture to be the inspired, infallible Word of God. And the moment you reject the authority of the Scripture and its writers, you can say whatever you like. In other words, they are forming a gospel of their own, and there is no point in their using the Old Testament or the New. They are rather dishonest in using either; for what they beleive is merely what they themselves, and others like them, think.

That is one school; but there is another, and this is a little more dangerous. The second school is represented by Dr C. H. Dodd in his Commentary on this Epistle. What he says in effect is that though this is the teaching of the Apostle Paul, yet this teaching of Paul's has been misunderstood since about the second century. About the second century certain Greek ideas came in, and these Greek ideas monopolized the minds of the Fathers of the Church. Then, still worse, certain ideas of Roman law came in, with their ideas of equity and of righteousness, and so on. As Christianity spread in the Roman Empire so the ideas of the Roman Empire began to spread into Christianity. The tragedy is that these Greek and Roman ideas have been controlling the teaching of the Church right down the centuries. He refers to the Middle Ages and to the Protestant Reformation, when a

supposedly Pauline theology was re-framed. A 'supposed'
revival, you observe, of Pauline theology under Luther and
Calvin! Ancient ideas of sacrifice were no longer alive, and the
language which derived from them was not understood, he says,
and so this passage was unintelligible to them, and current or
traditional theological ideas were read into it. And so it has gone
on until . . . Until when? Ah, he says, 'In our own day the fresh
study of ancient thought and language, both Hebrew and Greek,
gives us a better prospect of coming in to touch with the Apostle
Paul's mind.' Somewhat patronizingly he goes on to say that,
while he rejects some of the historic statements of Pauline
theology, he must admit that they were not untrue to his intention, in so far as they enabled men to believe reasonably, in terms
of the thought of their time, that God in Christ has done whatever
needed to be done in order that men might be freed from the
guilt of their sin, and start upon a new life in the strength of
divine grace. He adds that many theological doctrines which
we must think alien in their detail from Paul's thought have
nevertheless safeguarded for their time the Gospel which he
preached. Remember that the 'detail' to which Dr Dodd refers
includes ideas such as 'the wrath of God' and all penal notions
and also the substitutionary suffering of our Lord, and the great
and controlling teaching concerning propitiation, which, as we
have seen, is crucial in the Apostle's argument. are Those the
doctrines taught, not only by the Reformers, but also by the great
Puritans, and likewise preached by all the great evangelists, that
are thus patronizingly dismissed. Any teaching which says that
the Church has been mistaken throughout the centuries and that
we alone know the truth and are right as the result of modern re-
search and knowledge should be immediately suspect. When
modern scholars find the founders of the various cults saying
that kind of thing they rightly charge them with arrogance. But
they do not seem to realize that they are guilty of precisely the
same thing. Why is this? Because they dislike the notion of propitiation, because it does not fit in to their philosophical ideas of
God and His love. They do not like us to talk about the 'blood'
of Christ. It is 'the offence of the Cross' that ultimately explains it.

It was an offence and foolishness to the Greek mind in the first century; and it is the same today.

The third and last view which is put forward today is not as arrogant as the last one, but it is still arrogant. It is the teaching which seems to argue that we must never teach anything which is objectionable to the modern mind. We are told that to talk about 'blood' and about sacrifices and about wrath is objectionable to the modern mind, and therefore we are not to do so. Here again is very popular teaching which is being followed by large numbers. The modern mind becomes the standard of all truth. They do not stop to consider that what is modern today may be out of date in twenty years. They are already having to confess that things about which they were quite certain, and which were described as the 'assured results' of scholarship fifty years ago, were mistakes. Yet we are still told that the modern mind must determine these things. This modern mind which is so delicate that it cannot abide talk about blood and propitiation, but which can make and use atomic and hydrogen bombs, is to be our standard. These matters are not determined by the scrupulosity of the modern mind, thank God. We must go back to a true authority, and that authority is to be found in this Apostle, a 'called apostle', a man who was apprehended on the road to Damascus, and who says that the Gospel he preached was not given to him by men, neither was he taught it by men, but by the revelation of God; the one who does not hesitate to say, 'If we or an angel from heaven preach any other Gospel unto you than that which we have preached unto you, let him be accursed' [*Galatians* 1: 8–9]. Let the moderns believe what they will. There is no Gospel apart from 'Jesus Christ and him crucified' – Jesus Christ, the Son of God, 'set forth to be a propitiation through faith in his blood', God visiting upon Him the punishment of our sins, God 'making him to be sin for us who knew no sin, that we might be made the righteousness of God in him' [2 *Corinthians* 5: 21]. That other teaching is not only entirely wrong, the Holy Spirit will not honour it. He does not honour it, He cannot honour it. No one is ever converted by such preaching; and you will never get revival as the result of such preaching. Dismiss it, and have nothing to do with it. Hold fast and firmly to this Gospel of Redemption, of ransoming by the blood of Christ, which has been preached throughout the centuries and has ever been honoured by God the Holy Ghost, not only in the conversion of individuals, but also in the great revivals in the history of the Church. At all costs, whatever it may mean to us, we must hold on to this word 'propitiation through faith in his blood'. Let us be ridiculed, let us be ostracized, let us be dismissed as fools by men and their supposed learning and academic knowledge, and their 'recent discoveries'. Let them say what they will. There is only one 'Gospel of the glorious God' – it is this. This alone saves, this alone justifies. Thank God for it.

11 *Abraham Justified by Faith*

*

What shall we say then that Abraham our father, as pertaining to the flesh, hath found?
For if Abraham were justified by works, he hath whereof to glory; but not before God.
For what saith the scripture? Abraham believed God and it was counted unto him for righteousness.   Romans 4: 1–3

Here we come not only to a new chapter, but also to a new thought. Yet we must be careful to notice that we are not starting an entirely new section in this great Epistle. The Apostle still continues the same subject that he has already been dealing with – justification by faith. But he is now going to deal with an objection which he imagines certain people, particularly the Jews, might raise against his teaching.

Why does he do this? I believe he does so for the reason that he has already stated twice, that this great salvation about which he is writing, and which now has been made manifest in the coming of the Son of God into this world – and by all that He did and all that happened to Him – is something which had previously been 'witnessed to by the law and the prophets'. You remember that he says this very thing in the second verse of the first chapter of the Epistle. He says, 'Paul, a servant of Jesus Christ, called to be an Apostle, separated unto the Gospel of God,' – then in brackets '(Which he had promised afore by his prophets in the Holy Scriptures)'. He was careful to say that right at the beginning, and he had an object in doing so. Then we noticed that when he announces the way of salvation in Christ in the twenty-first verse of the third chapter he says it again: 'But now the righteousness of God without the law is

[154]

manifested, being witnessed by the law and the prophets; even the righteousness of God which is by faith of Jesus Christ.' So twice over he has told us in passing that we must never fail to observe and to grasp clearly the fact that this salvation, this way of salvation, which is now so plain and clear in Christ, had been witnessed to before by the Law and by the Prophets. Indeed, we have seen already that he has been at pains to prove this. That is what he was doing at the end of the third chapter. There he says: This is not making void the Law; I am establishing the law by preaching what I am preaching. I have told you that it was witnessed to by the Law, and I have shown that it fulfills the Law. There is no contradiction.

But even that is not enough! He feels he must go on because he imagines someone putting a question like this: 'Now this way of justification, this way of righteousness you are teaching, is it something entirely new? Are you saying that, whereas the Law and the Prophets did predict it and foretell it, nevertheless it is something quite new in itself, and was quite unknown under the Old Testament dispensation?' That, it seems to me, is the point which he now takes up in this fourth chapter. In other words I suggest that the purpose of this fourth chapter is to show that under the Old Testament dispensation this way of salvation was not merely predicted, it was also God's way of dealing with men, and saving them, at that time also.

This is a very important point; and I want to show how the Apostle establishes it. The Old Testament does not merely prophesy and predict this way of making men righteous by imputing the righteousness of Christ to them, and justifying them by faith – that was God's way of forgiving men and dealing with them even in the time of the Old Testament dispensation itself. The Apostle feels constrained to establish this point. Why must he establish it?

There are at least three main reasons for that necessity. He must do this, of course, for the sake of the Jews. After all, the Gospel was first preached to the Jews, and a number of Jews had believed, and had been converted, and were members of the Christian Church. The Apostle is anxious to help them. We know from experience that when we are born again and become new creatures, there is an old nature that still remains within us. Now these Jews who had been truly converted and born again had been so long in the habit of thinking in a Jewish way that they found it rather difficult to break with that and to become quite free. We have seen, for instance, in Galatians 2 that even Peter fell into trouble along that line on one occasion and had to be corrected by Paul; how much more so then the common people who were not Apostles. The Apostle is anxious to help such people. At the same time he is anxious to preach the Gospel to the Jews who were right outside. They were outside because they had completely misunderstood the message of the Old Testament. That was why they were rejecting the Gospel of Christ. Paul puts this in a very striking manner in the Second Epistle to the Corinthians in the third chapter. He says, The veil is upon their hearts when Moses is read, Sabbath by Sabbath. They read the Scriptures but do not perceive their meaning. They are spiritually blind. There is this veil before their eyes. It was because of their misunderstanding of the Old Testament that they felt that the Gospel was contradicting the Old Testament. So the Apostle is very much concerned to clear up this Jewish misunderstanding.

Further, Paul wished to show that, because God is one, His way of dealing with men in the matter of salvation is always the same. We have already seen something of that in the third chapter, in the twenty-ninth verse: 'Is he the God of the Jews only? Is he not also of the Gentiles? Yes, of the Gentiles also; seeing it is one God', or 'that God is one'. And we made the point that God, because of that, has only one way of salvation for everybody. But here the Apostle adds another thing – not only one way of salvation for everybody, but one way of salvation at all times also. This is, obviously, a most important and material point.

The third reason is, I believe, that he is still holding in his mind the idea that this way of salvation does away with all forms of boasting. He is going to use the term. He says, 'For if Abraham were justified by works he hath whereof to glory (to boast of), but not before God'. And he is concerned that this idea that any-body can boast of anything in the presence of God must be dis-missed and got rid of once and for ever. Let me put it like this. The theme of this chapter, to put it in a more doctrinal manner, is that there is only one covenant of grace, and that men in all dispensations are saved in exactly the same way. It is the same covenant of grace under the Old Testament as it is under the New. There is a difference in administration, but it is the same covenant of grace. There is only one way of salvation always, whether in the past, present, or future. People often get confused about this. There are some, indeed, who seem to make an abso-lute division between the Old Testament and the New; there are even Christians who seem to think that there is no value in the Old Testament. It is because of this that I have never been happy about the practice of printing the two Testaments apart; it leads some people to read only the New Testament. We should be interested in the whole Bible, because the two Testaments are one. That is where we see the wisdom and guidance of the Holy Spirit in leading the Early Church, which by that time was mainly Gentile, to incorporate the Old Testament literature with their new literature. There is only one great covenant of grace. The Old Testament saints were saved in exactly the same way as we are.

The Apostle is particularly fond of making this point. In many ways the classic statement of it is to be found in the Epistle to the Ephesians. 'Ye', he says, 'who sometimes were afar off, who were aliens from the commonwealth of Israel, who were strangers from the covenants of promise, who were without hope and without God in the world, are made nigh by the blood of Christ'. 'Ye are no more strangers and foreigners, but fellow-citizens with the saints (the Old Testament saints) and of the household of God', [*Ephesians* 2:11-22]. What is the message? In the third chapter of that Epistle he says that it was revealed to him by revelation, that the Gentiles should be fellow-heirs with the Jews. Let us never forget this. We Gentiles are simply brought into that which was already in existence. It is not something entirely new. The Jews were in it before; we are brought into it with them. We are fellow-heirs with them, fellow-possessors, fellow-citizens.

Furthermore, in this very Epistle to the Romans, in chapter 11 he puts it still more clearly in his analogy of the olive tree. The olive tree is a picture of the true Church. There were first natural branches in it – that is, the Jews. But some of these have been plucked out because of their unbelief; and now un-natural branches, the Gentiles, are grafted in. But it is the same tree, it is the same trunk. He also uses another picture there; he talks about all belonging to the same 'lump'. That is the theme he begins to deal with in this fourth chapter – that because God is one there is only one way of salvation, whether under the Old Testament or the New. And, more, there never will be another. There is only one Gospel. There is only one way of salvation. There is only one way of being reconciled to God. It is the same covenant of grace then, now, and in the future. There will never be a time when man can enter the Kingdom of God by any way or by any means save this one and only way.

Let us now follow the Apostle as he works this out. He proves it in a most striking manner. What he does is to choose two of the most illustrious – if not the two most illustrious – persons who have ever appeared in the long history of the Jews. He takes Abraham and David. In doing this he does precisely what Matthew does in the first verse of his Gospel. Here it is: 'The book of the generation of Jesus Christ, the Son of David, the Son of Abraham.' These are the two that Matthew also picks out – Abraham and David. Why? Abraham was the father of the nation, the man out of whom the whole nation came; the original progenitor. Why David? Because it was to David the special promise was given that out of his loins the Messiah should come. God made a covenant with Abraham; He repeated it to David. That was why Paul, in writing to Timothy later on, says, 'Remember (always bear in mind) that Jesus Christ of the seed of David was raised from the dead according to my gospel'. David the king, David, who is in himself such a wonderful type of the Messiah that was to come.

So the Apostle, in taking up Abraham and David, is obviously taking the two crucial cases in the entire long history of the Jewish people. The Jews were very proud of these two men. They looked back at their memories and were for ever praising them and lauding them. 'Our father Abraham' – 'David the king,' 'the sweet singer of Israel', 'the man who was raised up and blessed of God.' The question to be considered is this: how did these two men come to be so favoured by God? How did these two men ever attain that position, that situation, in which God so signally manifested His good pleasure in them? The Apostle's answer is that it was precisely in the same way and by the same method as He was now redeeming and rescuing and justifying men. He shows it first in the actual history of Abraham, and in what the Scripture says about Abraham. Then he puts it in terms of what David himself says in Psalm 32, verse 2.

That is his argument in this chapter and we can analyse the contents of the chapter in this way. In verses 1 to 5 he takes the case of Abraham, giving the facts and the statements of the Scriptures on the facts. In verses 6, 7 and 8 we have what David said explicitly in Psalm 32. Then from verse 9 to verse 12 he points out that all this had happened to Abraham before he was circumcised; so circumcision cannot be the vital thing. Then in verses 13 to 17 he proves that this also was before the Law had been given. Indeed God had ordered things in this way in order that He might show once and for ever that salvation is by grace, through faith, not by circumcision or by the Law, because grace is the only way whereby it can be made certain and sure. From verse 18 to the end of the chapter he gives an exposition of how this faith was manifested in the case of Abraham and how it all redounds to the glory of God. At the end he brings it back to the point at which he originally started, by saying, As God did it then He is still doing it now: 'Now it was not written for his sake alone, that it was imputed to him; but for us also, to whom it shall be imputed, if we believe on him that raised up Jesus our Lord from the dead; who was delivered for our offences and raised again for our justification.' Are you not moved to admiration at the wonderful way in which this Apostle is able to deploy a great argument? His epistles always remind me of a great advocate. He starts by giving a general outline of his case, and the arguments he is going to employ. Then he works each one out in detail; and having done so, he sums it all up and repeats the original contention.

There, in general, is the scheme and analysis of this masterly chapter which we are now to consider. But someone may have a question in his mind, perhaps even a possible objection, and may ask, 'That is all very interesting, but life is very busy at the present time, and I have a great deal to do; so what I really want is a positive message. All I want to know is the way to be saved and how to live. I really am not concerned to follow into all this argumentation and all this Old Testament business.' Such people feel that they are wasting their time when they try to follow a great argument like this, and would like to miss out chapter 4 and get on to chapter 5, which they feel is more practical and comes nearer to us. Need we, they say, really go over all this? My reply is that this chapter, as I shall demonstrate, explains justification by faith yet more clearly. The Apostle has put it quite clearly in chapter 3 but he puts it still more clearly here. He is taking no risks at all. Paul knew sin, and he knew human nature, and he knew very well that people tend to say, 'Oh yes, I am all right; I have got hold of that justification by faith doctrine. Let us go on now to sanctification.' But Paul is not so sure of us, and he wants to make certain that we have really understood.

The second reason is this: I feel that this chapter is invaluable as a key to the understanding of the Old Testament. People sometimes get confused as they read the Old Testament, and then give up, saying, 'I really cannot be bothered with all this, I will go on to the New'. But you must read the Old Testament; and this chapter throws great light on it, as I hope to show you.

Again it is essential that we should grasp the argument of this chapter if we really want to help other people. The Apostle, as I told you, wrote this because he wanted to help those Jews who may have been in trouble about salvation. You will find that there are still people who are in trouble about it; and if you really want to help them and to be able to explain things to them, you have got to learn how to follow these arguments and then in turn use them yourself.

Finally, I know of nothing more strengthening to faith than to take a chapter like this and to watch the Apostle standing back, as it were, and taking a bird's-eye view of salvation. He looks at it in the Old Testament, he traces it along and shows that it is the same thing everywhere. Here, I am brought to realize that my salvation is not something contingent or uncertain or almost accidental; I see that God had planned it before the very beginning of time, and that He was already putting it into practice in the dawn of history. And he has gone on with the same method. And He will go on. It is God's way, and it is therefore a perfect way. These panoramic views, I always feel, are particularly strengthening to faith.

His first argument is the argument about Abraham. Verses 1–5 put it in general. Verses 6–8 give us David's confirmation of it from Psalm 32. In verse 1 he just puts the question: 'What shall we say then that Abraham our father, as pertaining to the flesh, hath found?' The Authorized Version puts a comma after father, and I think rightly. It is not, 'What shall we say then that Abraham our father as pertaining to the flesh hath found?' That is not what he is saying. Let me suggest another translation. 'What then shall we say that Abraham our father has found according to the flesh?' That is what he means. Not 'our father according to the flesh', but 'What did our father Abraham find with respect to, or according to, the flesh?' Or if you wish, you can even translate it thus: 'What then shall we say that Abraham our father has attained by the flesh?'

What is the meaning of 'flesh? That is the important question. He means by 'the flesh' that which is external and opposed to that which is internal and spiritual. The Apostle himself gives a very wonderful exposition of what he means by the flesh in the Epistle to the Philippians, chapter 3, beginning at verse 3: 'For we are the circumcision which worship God in the spirit, and rejoice in Christ Jesus, and have no confidence in the flesh.' Then he goes on, 'Though I might also have confidence in the flesh.

If any other man thinketh he hath whereof he might trust in the flesh, I more.' What had he attained by the flesh? Here is the answer: 'Circumcised the eighth day, of the stock of Israel, of the tribe of Benjamin, an Hebrew of the Hebrews; as touching the law a Pharisee; concerning zeal, persecuting the Church; touching the righteousness which is of the law, blameless.' That is what the flesh means. The flesh means anything that a man is prone to rely on in the matter of salvation. Some rely upon their nationality – 'because I am a Jew I am one of God's people; I need no more'. Some have even said, 'Because I am brought up in a Christian country I am all right'. Others rely upon circumcision, or the fact that they were christened when they were children. That is the flesh. Flesh means works of any kind, or anything that may be true of us, or that may belong to us, on which we tend to rest for our salvation, and of which we tend to boast.

That is the meaning of 'flesh' in the first verse. He goes on with that in the second verse, which in the AV reads, 'For if Abraham were justified by works, he hath whereof to glory'. We may put that like this. Was Abraham then justified before God and accepted by God on the grounds of what he was and did? Was Abraham, the friend of God, so signally blessed by God, because of his character and good deeds? If so, says Paul, he has grounds for glorying before God. He can say: God has thus dealt with me because I am what I am, and because I have done what I have done. He can boast of it and he can say to God, 'Because I am thus I have a right to be blessed'. He would have grounds for glorying in the presence of God. But, says Paul, that is impossible – 'not before God'. It seems to me that the Apostle was so moved at this point, and so stirred in his spirit by the very suggestion, that he almost forgot words, and just says, 'but not before God'. He seems to say: I have already shown you abundantly that no flesh can glory in His presence; all have sinned and have come short of the glory of God. No man can glory in the presence of God; the thing is unthinkable. But, he goes on, I need not leave it at that, I need not leave it as a general argument (verse 3), I have a specific statement of Scripture to prove this – 'for what saith the Scripture?' Incidentally, notice that he does not say, 'What saith the Scriptures?' It is in the singular – 'What saith one particular Scripture?'

I am tempted to digress for a moment, but I must avoid the temptation. Nevertheless, in a day like this, when people criticize the Scriptures and especially the Old Testament, and Genesis in particular, it is interesting to notice how the Apostle is ready to base everything on one statement out of Genesis 15. 'What saith the Scripture?'

What it says is, 'Abraham believed God, and it was counted to him for righteousness'. There is the clinching proof. There is no need to speculate, there is no need to argue in general. The Scripture itself has settled it once and for ever [*Genesis* 15:6].

This statement in Genesis 15 is a most important declaration. This is the first time in the Bible that the doctrine of justification by faith only is stated clearly. Had you always thought that the doctrine of justification by faith only was only to be found in the New Testament? Had you realized that it is found in Genesis 15:6? That is the first place in which it is stated explicitly and clearly, though it is there implicitly before that.

It is such a crucial statement that we must be quite clear in our minds as to its meaning. 'Abraham believed God.' What does that mean? Our first reply is that it is not just a matter of giving an intellectual assent to teaching about God and various other propositions. It includes that, but it goes well beyond that. The word used by the Apostle conveys the whole idea of trust and committal. Abraham, if you like, trusted God and it was counted to him for righteousness. But here again we have to be most careful because of the way in which people have misinterpreted this very statement.

Let us look at some of the misinterpretations, and let us examine ourselves as we do so. Some say that it means this, 'Abraham believed and it was counted to him for righteousness': Abraham was a godly man, Abraham was a God-fearing man, Abraham was a pious man. Abraham delighted in obeying God and in doing what God told him, and it was because he was such a man that God dealt with him as He did. Is that justification by faith?

Is that what Genesis 15 says? They argue that it is, and that it is still the way of salvation. If a man really takes a serious view of life, and is out to please God, and to live a good and godly life, he will be forgiven and he has nothing to fear. It is this intention of his that God is concerned with; and if He sees that intention He will forgive such a man and will bless him. It is almost incredible that anyone should be able to interpret it like that, but many do so. What they are doing, of course, is to say that we are justified by works, that we are saved because we are good men, because we are pious, because we say our prayers, because we are religious. That is just sheer 'justification by works'. If that were true such a man would have a right to boast. He could say that whereas the majority of people are not interested in God at all, and never say their prayers, and never go to a place of worship, he does all these things. He is like the Pharisee in the parable of the Pharisee and the Publican who went up into the temple to pray. He goes right to the front and says, 'I thank thee, O God, that I am not as other men are . . . or even as this publican. I fast twice in the week, I give tithes of all that I possess.' In effect, I am a godly man and a good man; I thank You for it [*Luke* 18:9–12]. He is boasting. He is justifying himself by works. Obviously, that is just a sheer contradiction of everything the Apostle is setting out to say in this great Epistle.

Yet there are people who read this very Epistle and interpret it like that. A very popular Commentary, to which I have already referred, expounds it like that. It teaches that all that the Lord Jesus Christ did when He came into this world was to encourage men to be godly, and to give us an example of living a godly life. He obeyed, and we are to look at Him, and to follow His example, and so we shall be saved. It is a complete negation of the Apostle's whole argument. How subtle these things are!

Then another interpretation – and this is the more common one among evangelicals – is, as I have had to say several times already, that it was once the position that men had to keep the Law. It is no longer that. God has done away with the Law. Now, all you need to do is believe, and you are saved. Your believing saves you. But this turns believing into works. If it is our belief that saves us, we have got something to boast of and to glory in. We have believed while the majority of people have not believed, therefore we are proud of it and can glory in our belief. It brings back the whole element of boasting. This phrase cannot mean that, for it would mean that the Apostle is just contradicting himself.

What then does it mean? The Apostle shows us quite plainly here. When the Scripture says that 'Abraham believed God and it was counted to him for righteousness', it means that Abraham was justified in exactly the same way as we are justified now. What does Abraham's believing mean? It means that God appeared to Abraham and He said, 'Abraham, I want to make a covenant with you'. God made a great covenant with Abraham. He gave him great promises with regard to His way of redemption. He said, 'Through thee . . . and thy seed shall all the nations of the earth be blessed: I am going to make of your seed a great multitude and I am going to bless the whole world through you and your seed.' In other words God spoke to Abraham about the Lord Jesus Christ. God revealed to Abraham the way of salvation in Jesus Christ, who, He told him, was going to come out of his loins. Read Genesis, chapters 15, 16 and 17, and you will find it is all there. But Paul puts it here in this fourth chapter. Notice verse 13 where he says, 'For the promise that he should be heir of the world was not make to Abraham or to his seed through the law, but through the righteousness of faith'. Then notice verses 17 and 18: 'As it is written, I have made thee a father of many nations, before whom he believed, even God, who quickeneth the dead, and calleth those things which be not as though they were.' To what is the Apostle referring? 'Who against hope believed in hope, that he might become the father of many nations; according to that which was spoken, So shall thy seed be.' God came to Abraham when he was aged ninety-nine and said, From you and Sarah – an old woman, well beyond the child-bearing age – the Messiah is ultimately going to be born. He announced to him the plan of redemption in the Lord Jesus Christ. And Abraham believed it.

Not only that! In the incident of the sacrifice of Isaac, God revealed it again to Abraham. He gave him a foreshadowing of the death upon the Cross, and showed him how He was going to redeem man. Of course Abraham did not understand it fully. But you remember what the Lord Himself said, 'Your father Abraham rejoiced to see my day; and he saw it and was glad [*John* 8:56]. That is what the Lord Jesus Christ Himself says. When therefore, you read this phrase 'Abraham believed God', do not assume that it just means that Abraham believed in God, and Abraham did what God told him. It goes well beyond that. Abraham believed in God's way of redemption as you and I do. He did not see it clearly, but he saw it 'afar off'. It has happened now; it has been manifested in all its fullness. But Abraham saw it afar off about two thousand years before it happened, as did David afterwards in exactly the same manner. This means a belief of God's way of salvation. It is there away back in Genesis.

This term 'belief' must be made to include that, otherwise there is no meaning in that statement of our Lord – 'Your father Abraham rejoiced to see my day; and he saw it and was glad.' In other words, Abraham was saved by faith in exactly the same way as we are – without works, without any merit. He saw that his salvation lay entirely in the merits of the Son of God, who was going to come, and who after the flesh was going to be born of his seed, and also of the seed of David. You see now that this is something that illumines the whole of the Old Testament. It shows the one-ness of this covenant of grace and redemption. Abraham saw it. He trusted himself to it. That was the means of his salvation. He saw that it was this righteousness that God was going to give him – so boasting is entirely excluded.

We must also glance at this other word, the word 'counted'. 'Abraham believed God and it was counted to him for righteousness.' It is a pity that the Authorized Version employs this word 'counted' here. In the next verse it uses the word 'reckon', and then in verse 6 it uses the word 'imputed'. Actually the Apostle Paul used exactly the same word in the three instances. So it is good to translate it each time as 'reckon'.

What does this mean? It is something that we have already considered in the third chapter. This word to 'reckon' or to 'impute' means to put something to somebody's account. You make up a deficiency in someone's account. For instance, you remember what Paul says in writing to Philemon about Onesimus. He says, 'If he has defrauded you and if he owes you anything, put that down to my account, I will repay it.' The Apostle did not owe Philemon anything; but he tells Philemon to put it down to his account as if he did owe something. That is 'imputing'. We employ the term when we may be having an argument with somebody. We say, 'Ah, but now you are imputing a statement to me which I did not make.' Or we may say, 'You are imputing motives to me and you are not fair.' What we mean is that that man is putting something into our mouths, or into our position, which is not there at all; he is imputing it. The thing is not there but it is put there by somebody else.

That is exactly the meaning of the term here, and it is the whole essence of this matter of justification by faith only. It puts that to our account. When we have nothing at all; God puts in the righteousness of Jesus Christ. He imputes it to us, He reckons it to us. He just takes it and puts it there, as it were in our account, and thereby clears our guilt and debt. He does not *make* us righteous in so doing, as we have seen. We are left, in this matter of justification, exactly where we were; but God puts this to our account and thereby clears our debt. He pronounces that all His claims against us are satisfied. Let us never forget that justification is forensic, is legal. It does not make us righteous; it declares us to be righteous. And we are declared righteous because the righteousness of Jesus Christ is put to our account.

The vital point so far is that we should have understood and grasped that when we are told that 'Abraham believed God' it means that Abraham was given to understand that God's way of justification is not by works, not by law, not by circumcision, not by any of these things; but that it is God imputing the righteousness of His Son to us, and enabling us to see that by faith. It comes to us by the instrument of faith, but the righteousness is that of Jesus Christ.

What an amazing doctrine, and how wonderful that Abraham saw it, saw the day of Christ, believed it, rejoiced in it! So did

David, and so did others under the Law! Here they were under the Old Dispensation looking forward – to what? To the day when all this would really be enacted and done. They saw it clearly enough to be saved by it. It is that that saved them, because it is God's plan from all eternity and nothing can upset it. That is our position still – not our righteousness, nothing in us. The saved are still those who look only unto Jesus Christ and rejoice in Him. 'We are the circumcision, which worship God in the spirit and rejoice in Christ Jesus, and have no confidence in the flesh' [*Philippians* 3:3]

12 *Justifying the Ungodly*

*

Now to him that worketh is the reward not reckoned of grace, but of debt.

But to him that worketh not, but believeth on him that justifieth the ungodly, his faith is counted for righteousness.

Even as David also describeth the blessedness of the man, unto whom God imputeth righteousness without works,

Saying, Blessed are they whose iniquities are forgiven, and whose sins are covered.

Blessed is the man to whom the Lord will not impute sin.

Romans 4: 4–8

We continue our consideration of the argument of the Apostle Paul in this fourth chapter.

We have seen that what the Apostle is saying is that God revealed the way of salvation in Jesus Christ to Abraham. Abraham did not understand it fully nor clearly, but he saw it. 'Abraham rejoiced to see my day: and he saw it and was glad.' What Abraham did was to believe this way of salvation, this justification by faith, this giving to man of a righteousness by God Himself – and it is the righteousness of Jesus Christ. Now that is the content of this word 'believed'. Abraham's belief did not just mean that when God said to him, 'Come out of your country Ur of the Chaldees and go to Canaan', he believed Him and did it. Of course it includes that, but there is much more. What God revealed to Abraham can be read in the book of Genesis chapters 12–18 and you will see there that Abraham was given a preview of the Gospel. God made a covenant with him in terms of Jesus Christ. Abraham believed, and it was that that justified him and was counted to him for righteousness.

But the Apostle, having said that, is not content to leave it

[169]

there. That is the basic statement. He then goes on in verses 4 and 5 to substantiate this, or to put it, if you like, in a still clearer manner. He expounds it, he elaborates it a little in order that it might be clear beyond any doubt. How does he do that? Well, in the fourth verse he makes a general proposition which will appeal to everybody's reason and understanding. Here it is: 'Now to him that worketh is the reward not reckoned of grace, but of debt.' In other words he uses a simple illustration taken from ordinary life. If I do a piece of work for a man and he pays me for doing it, that man in paying me is not being gracious toward me, but is just paying what he owes me. I have done the work and I present my account, and he pays my account. You must not say that his paying that account is a gracious act on his part. It would be very wrong if he did not pay me; he is in my debt. I have rendered the service, I have done the work, and therefore when he pays me it is not a matter of grace, it is a matter of debt. It is a legal matter. He is not, out of the kindness and the munificence and generosity of his spirit, doing something to me and for me which he need not do. It is a matter of debt and I can put him into court if he does not pay. There is no grace in that. That, says the Apostle in effect, is a general proposition about which everybody is prepared to agree.

Then in the fifth verse he puts it positively. Verse 4 was the negative. But now, positively, 'But to him that worketh not (who does not work, who does not produce works) but believeth on him that justifieth the ungodly, his faith is counted for righteousness.' This is, I do not hesitate to assert, one of the most important verses in the whole of the Bible. I mean from a practical standpoint, from the standpoint of evangelism if you like, or from the standpoint of becoming a Christian. Therefore it is important that we should be clear about it. It is in many ways the strongest statement concerning justification which this Apostle ever made. He who makes the clearest statements about justification by faith, here goes beyond anything that he says anywhere else. Take, as a comparison, the way in which he put it in the twenty-sixth verse of the previous chapter: there he says, 'To declare, I say, at this time his righteousness; that he might be just, and the justifier of him that believeth in Jesus.' It says there that the man who is justified is the man who believes in Jesus. But here it is much stronger. It is the difference between saying 'the justifier of him that believeth in Jesus', and that 'he justifies the ungodly'.

To see the importance of the distinction, let us look at the terms. Who is the man that is justified? The Apostle tells us two things about this man. The first thing he tells us about him is that he is a man who 'worketh not' – he does not do any work, he does not produce any works. The man of whom he speaks in his illustration is a man who did work. 'To him that worketh the reward is not reckoned of grace.' But now in contrast to 'him that worketh' is 'him that worketh not'. Here is a man who has no good works to show, he has nothing to recommend himself. He certainly cannot present an account and a bill because he has done nothing. He is a failure, he has not worked and therefore he has no works to show. That is the first thing. The Apostle is very concerned to emphasize that and to bring out the contrast with the other.

But then he goes beyond that. The man who is justified is not only a man who has no good works to show, he is actually ungodly – 'justifieth the ungodly'. To whom is he referring? He is referring to Abraham. But, you say, Abraham was a very good man. I know that in one sense Abraham was a very good man, but nevertheless it is right to describe Abraham, as he was by nature, as ungodly. Indeed we are all by nature ungodly. The Apostle has put that plainly in the previous chapter where he said, 'Therefore by the deeds of the law there shall no flesh be justified in his sight'. He says, 'the whole world has become guilty before God'. 'All have sinned and come short of the glory of God' – even Abraham. And to come short of the glory of God, to be under the dominion of the Law and of sin is to be ungodly. This is, of course, what he says everywhere about the entire human race. 'We are all by nature the children of wrath, even as others' [*Ephesians* 2: 3]. 'There is none righteous, no, not one.' Those are the statements of Scripture; and when we become Christians, looking back, we see clearly that we never were godly.

These Jews thought that they were godly and that they were pleasing God.

A perfect instance of this is to be found in the account of a discussion between our Lord and such Jews in the eighth chapter of the Gospel of John. They were arguing with the Lord Jesus Christ. They said, God is our Father. 'We have one Father, even God.' Our Lord replies, in effect 'No, God is not your Father. He cannot be, because if He were your Father you would not reject my words. I come from Him, and if you were God's children you would not be persecuting Me. You are of your father the devil' [*John* 8: 33–47]. They thought they were godly; they thought they were pleasing God. But our Lord says that they were ungodly. We all tend to manufacture a god for ourselves. There are many people who think they are worshipping God but who are really simply worshipping themselves, worshipping their own goodness. They have made a god of their own, and when they are truly confronted by God as He has manifested Himself in the Bible they hate Him, they dislike Him. When God tells them that they are so sinful and so hopeless that they cannot save themselves, they resent it. When God tells them that nothing but the death of His Son can redeem them they feel it is a personal insult. To them the Cross is an offence. Now that is to be ungodly.

Abraham, then, by nature, like the rest of mankind since the Fall of Adam, was ungodly. That does not mean that before conversion we are all as bad as we can possibly be. It does not say that. But what it does say is that we have 'all sinned and come short of the glory of God'. The Apostle's statement is that God justifies such people. What does this tell us about the doctrine of justification by faith only? It establishes the fact that this is the clearest statement ever made concerning justification. It proves once and for ever that justification is entirely God's action – 'who believeth' says the Apostle, 'in him that justifieth the ungodly'. It is He that justifies. It is entirely God's act and is in no sense based on our activities.

The second thing that it shows clearly is something we have already noted several times. I must repeat it because people will persist in falling into this error. It shows that justification does not make us righteous – 'God justifies the ungodly'. He does not first make us godly and then justify us. What Paul says is that He justifies the ungodly, not the ungodly made godly, not the unrighteous made righteous or become righteous. They are justified as they are, without works and while still ungodly. This vital point must be emphasized. It is just here that the Roman Catholic teaching is not only dangerous but a complete denial of the biblical teaching. It teaches that by our baptism we are made righteous and godly; righteousness is infused into us, injected into us, put into us: and because we have been made righteous by our baptism we are justified. But that is to say that we are justified because we are sanctified, which is the exact opposite of what the Apostle is saying. No, we are justified while we are still ungodly. There is the prisoner at the bar; he is guilty before the law. He has no plea whatsoever to offer, nothing to say for himself. It is he as he is, standing in the dock, who is acquitted and who is pronounced free and righteous. 'He justifies the ungodly.' If this verse does not make us see the true meaning of justification by faith, nothing will. There is nothing beyond this in Scripture.

The third point is that this statement establishes that it is entirely a forensic, a legal matter. Justification is a declaration by God that He is now acquitting that person, and that He is going to put on him the righteousness of Christ and regard him as righteous. That is the meaning of this act. It is legal. It does not do anything to the man; it does not change him; it does not make him any better. It puts on him this righteousness of Christ, and God pronounces him to be just and righteous.

In other words – the fourth point – to use the term that the Apostle uses so much, it is entirely a matter of 'reckoning' or 'imputing' or 'putting to one's account'. Let me put it like this. The doctrine of justification by faith does not say that God now regards us as if we were righteous. That is not true, that would be a lie. God cannot regard a man who is unrighteous as righteous. That is not what the doctrine says. What it says is that God imputes this righteousness of Jesus Christ to us, puts that to our account, and because He has done that He regards us as righteous. We have the righteousness of Christ. He sees us in

Christ. Let me use the kind of illustration that was obviously in the mind of Count Zinzendorf when he composed his great hymn on this theme. In John Wesley's translation as printed in the Congregational Church Hymnary it reads:

> *Jesus, Thy robe of righteousness*
> *My beauty is, my glorious dress.*

This is the picture. There is a man standing in his rags, in his filth. There is the condemned, guilty sinner before God, the prisoner in the dock. What happens? Well, God puts on him this robe of righteousness; He puts on him the white robe of Christ's perfection, and now sees that and nothing else. That is the doctrine of justification. He puts that to our account. We shall draw certain practical lessons from it later.

What comes next? In verses 6, 7 and 8 he says that we have a marvellous confirmation of this. Paul is not the only one who says this; David has said it. 'Even as David also describeth the blessedness of the man unto whom God imputeth righteousness without works, saying . . .' Then he quotes from Psalm 32: 'Blessed are they whose iniquities are forgiven, and whose sins are covered. Blessed is the man to whom the Lord will not impute sin.' The Apostle Paul was a mighty debater and has no equal in handling a matter of controversy. Watch his method. He has already referred to Abraham, and now he produces David because he knew what David meant to the Jews. He knew that they looked back to David, the great king, as the greatest of all their kings. And he knew the great promise concerning the Messiah that had been made to David, and that all the Jews knew that also. Indeed he knew, and the Jews knew, that 'David was a man after God's own heart'. David stood with Abraham in the estimation of the Jews in the first position. Paul quotes him therefore. And he is able to prove that David says this precise thing that he is teaching.

It is interesting to notice the way in which the Apostle uses this quotation from the thirty-second Psalm. David actually put it negatively. He said, 'O the happiness, O the blessedness of the man whose iniquities are covered; the happiness of the man to whom the Lord will not impute sin.' Here is the happy man, here is the man who is blessed, who is right with God, whose iniquities are forgiven. He is a man whose sins are covered; something is put over them. But you notice this other interesting statement; he is a man to whom the Lord will not impute sin, He will not reckon sin to him. What does that mean? The man has committed sin, how then can he be a blessed man? The answer is that though he has sinned and is guilty of many sins, God will not put down sins to this man's account in His Heavenly ledgers. He might do so, He has a perfect right to do so. But, says David, 'Blessed is the man to whom God does not reckon the sins.' He does not put them down in the account. He leaves them out; He has sent them away; He has covered them up; He has forgiven them.

It provides invaluable support for the Apostle's doctrine that David had said this very thing long ago in the thirty-second Psalm. David certainly puts it in a purely negative manner. He says, 'Blessed is the man whose iniquities are forgiven and whose sins are covered, to whom the Lord will not impute sin.' That is forgiveness, and it is negative, and actually in the thirty-second Psalm David does not go any further. But notice how Paul interprets it. He says, 'Even as David also describeth the blessedness of the man unto whom God imputeth righteousness without works.' Now this is a most important point. That is Paul's interpretation of David's Psalm. And of course it is right. God never leaves us in a negative position. God does not merely forgive us our sins. It is possible for somebody to forgive you, and yet to feel rather distant toward you. Someone whom you have offended, or against whom you have done some wrong may say, 'Well, I will not put you in court, I will not punish you, I will let you off, I will forgive you.' But that does not mean of necessity that you are reconciled fully, that you are in a position of harmony with one another, that you are fully received back. Forgiveness is only the negative aspect, and God never stops at that. God always goes on. God is never satisfied with anything less than reconciliation. So Paul's interpretation of David's Psalm is right for this reason, that forgiveness is the first step in the process that leads to full reconciliation. David only mentions the first step, eaning by that that the first step will certainly lead to the rest. The Apostle Paul, in an interesting phrase, does exactly the same thing himself elsewhere. In the Epistle to the Ephesians in the seventh verse of the first chapter he writes, 'In whom', referring to the Lord Jesus Christ, 'we have redemption through his blood, the forgiveness of sins', as if the whole of redemption were nothing but the forgiveness of sins. It is Paul himself who says constantly that redemption means justification, sanctification, and final deliverance – glorification! Redemption includes everything; and yet he seems to describe it here as if it were just the forgiveness of sins. That is merely a manner of speech; he knows that the first step implies all the others. If God takes the first step He will always take all the others. So, in a sense, you need only mention the first step for it suggests and adumbrates the entire redemption. Here Paul reminds us that David in Psalm 32 was doing exactly that very thing. He puts it in terms of iniquities forgiven, sins covered, and God not imputing our sins to us.

Let me put it like this. The man who is truly blessed is the man whose sin is forgiven as debt, whose sin is covered up so that God will never look at it again. He is one to whom it is never going to be imputed as a crime. There is the negative aspect. But it goes beyond that; he is also one to whom God reckons this righteousness of Jesus Christ. That is the doctrine of justification by faith. Here are we – all of us – sinners in the sight of God. What does the doctrine tell me? It tells me that as I stand there on trial, my debt is cancelled, my sin is covered. God has cast my sin 'behind his back'. He will never look at it again, He will never see it again. It is blotted out – out of His sight for all eternity. And I shall never be charged with it as a crime. I am completely delivered from it. But over and above that, God puts to my account, and reckons to me, this righteousness of Jesus Christ His Son.

What the Apostle has clearly demonstrated is that that has always been God's way and method of dealing with man in sin. It was what He did to Abraham. David says that He does it. So from the lives of the two greatest Jewish leaders we find proof of the doctrine of 'justification by faith only'. Moreover we have seen again that it is always a question of reckoning, it is always a matter of imputation.

So let me once more state this great and most blessed doctrine. God does not reckon our sins to us. But you may say, How can He do that and still be God? We have committed these sins, how is it possible for God not to reckon them to us though we have committed them and are guilty of them? The answer is that He has reckoned them to His only begotten, beloved Son. A great statement of that is to be found in 2 Corinthians, chapter 5, where the great Apostle puts it plainly and clearly, 'God was in Christ reconciling the world unto himself, not imputing (not reckoning) their trespasses unto them'. Well, what does He do then? He reckons their trespasses unto Him. 'God', he says in the last verse, 'hath made him (Christ) to be sin for us, who knew no sin . . .' [2 *Corinthians* 5: 19–21]. God took our sins, and instead of imputing them to us and to our account, He put them to His Son's account. He put them on Him and He punished them in Him. Christ came into the world to bear that. He volunteered to do it. He came into the world deliberately in order to do it. This is how we are saved and reconciled to God – instead of reckoning my sins to me God reckoned them to Christ, and punished them in Him. As Peter puts it, 'Who his own self bore our sins in his own body on the tree, that we, being dead unto sins, should live unto righteousness; by whose stripes ye were healed' [1 *Peter* 2: 24]. Go back to Isaiah 53 – 'We esteemed him smitten of God . . .' 'God hath laid on him the iniquity of us all.' Instead of reckoning them to us He reckoned them to Christ, and He bore them and the punishment due to them. That is the first part of justification.

That brings us to the second part, which is the reversal of the previous process. The first step is that our sin is reckoned to Him. The second step is that His righteousness is reckoned to us. What an amazing piece of book-keeping! What a tremendous manipulation of the accounts, if I may so put it! We had no righteousness at all. He has a perfect righteousness. God reckons His righteousness to us – 'God was in Christ reconciling the

[177]

world unto Himself, not imputing (not reckoning) their trespasses unto them.' And then, 'He hath made him to be sin for
us, who knew no sin.' Why? In order that 'we might be made
the righteousness of God in him' [2 *Corinthians* 5 : 21]. That is
what is meant by justification. It is all God's action. We do nothing
at all, we cannot do anything at all. We have no works, our
righteousness is 'as filthy rags', it is 'dung', refuse. We have
nothing at all. We are ungodly, we are helpless, we are hopeless.
God does it all. It is entirely God's action. It is what He does with
these sins of ours which He puts on Christ and punishes them in
Him. It is what He does with Christ's righteousness which He
puts on us. It is all done to us, and we receive it passively from
God.

A Christian, a person who is saved, is one who believes and
realizes that. That is how we become Christians. The Christian
is one who, having realized this truth, does not attempt to do
anything to save himself. If you try to do anything it means that
you do not understand this. Of course, realizing this great truth,
you will afterwards strive with all your might and main to please
Him and to do all you can. But that does not save you, and you
do not rely upon that in your salvation. The man who believes
this repents, but it is not his repentance that saves him. You are
not saved because you repent, you are not saved because you
believe the Gospel, though both are involved in salvation. You
are saved because God justifies you by the righteousness of Jesus
Christ. We produce no works at all to earn our salvation. Faith is
not a form of works. We have nothing whereof to boast, nothing
whatsoever. It is entirely the action of God. A Christian is one who
sees that and who rests upon it.

Let us be clear about this. Let me put it in the form of a
question. Are you a Christian? This is how you discover the
answer. Have you ceased altogether to look at yourself, or to
yourself, in every possible way? And are you looking only and
entirely and utterly to the Lord Jesus Christ the Son of God,
and what He has done on your behalf? Would you know for
certain whether you are a Christian? Here is the answer. Do you
realize that you can do nothing – nothing at all – about making

yourself a Christian? I will go further. Have you ceased to attempt to do anything? Salvation is entirely the free gift of God. It is a gift which comes to the ungodly. If you start saying, 'Oh but . . . I feel I ought to do . . .' you betray your position. The moment you say, 'Oh but . . .' you show that you are not a Christian.

That brings me to the most searching test of all. Do you believe now, at this moment, just as you are, that you become a Christian entirely through what God has done in Jesus Christ on your behalf? This 'time' element is very important. If you say, 'Ah now, but wait a minute; you do not really expect me to be able to settle that here and now; ought I not to go back and decide that I must pray more, that I must read my Bible more, that I must stop doing certain things and start doing others?' The moment you begin to talk like that you show that you have not grasped this doctrine. If you feel that you have still something to do about this, that you ought to weep, or that you ought to feel sinful, or that you ought to have a greater sense of conviction, or anything else – I do not care what it is – if you are going to bring in anything that you should be doing you have not seen it. For the doctrine of justification tells us that God justifies the ungodly as they are – does not wait to make them godly first, does not expect them to do anything. He says they can do nothing, they have got no works. That is the whole doctrine. Abraham just believed, he did not do anything. David says, 'Oh the blessedness of this man whose sins are thus dealt with', which really means ultimately, says Paul, that he accepts this doctrine that God imputes righteousness to him. If you cannot see that you can become a Christian immediately, at this moment, you have not grasped the doctrine. The moment one sees this doctrine one says, 'Yes, I see that it is as possible for me to become a Christian now as it will be in a thousand years. If I withdrew from the world and became a monk or a hermit and spent my whole days in fasting and sweating and praying, I would be no nearer than I am now.' God justifies the ungodly!

Nothing in my hand I bring,
Simply to Thy Cross I cling.

[179]

Justifying the Ungodly

Just as I am, without one plea,
But that Thy blood was shed for me,
And that Thou bidd'st me come to Thee,
O Lamb of God, I come!

Just as I am, and waiting not
To rid my soul of one dark blot,
To Thee, whose blood can cleanse each spot,
O Lamb of God, I come!

That is the Christian's confession. You realize that you are ungodly, that you are guilty before God, that you deserve nothing but punishment and hell, that you have nothing to recommend you, that you can never produce anything to recommend you; but that God in His infinite love and kindness sent His Son into the world in order to deliver you by His perfect life of obedience, His atoning, sacrificial, substitutionary death upon the Cross, when He took your sins upon Him and received their punishment, by His glorious resurrection, and the power of His endless life. You realize that you do not have to do anything, that you do not say, 'Give me a moment, give me time'. You realize that if you had a thousand years it would avail you nothing. You can see it now. It is God who does it all, and He does it in spite of our being what we are. We become Christians immediately because it is this giving to us, this reckoning to us, of the righteousness of Jesus Christ. Our iniquities are pardoned, our sins covered, all this sin will never again be imputed to us; and, positively and gloriously, we are clothed with a righteousness Divine. We are therefore ready to say with Count Zinzendorf and with John Wesley, that clothed with this we are ready to face anybody or anything:

Jesus, Thy robe of righteousness
My beauty is, my glorious dress;
'Midst flaming worlds, in this arrayed,
With joy shall I lift up my head.

Bold shall I stand in Thy great day;
For who aught to my charge shall lay?

Romans 4: 4–8

Fully through Thee absolved I am
From sin and fear, from guilt and shame.

When from the dust of death I rise
To claim my mansion in the skies,
This only then shall be my plea,
Jesus has lived and died for me.

13 Faith Only

*

> Cometh this blessedness then upon the circumcision only, or upon the
> uncircumcision also? for we say that faith was reckoned to Abraham
> for righteousness.
>
> How was it then reckoned? when he was in circumcision, or in
> uncircumcision? Not in circumcision, but in uncircumcision.
>
> And he received the sign of circumcision, a seal of the righteousness
> of the faith which he had yet being uncircumcised: that he might be
> the father of all them that believe, though they be not circumcised;
> that righteousness might be imputed unto them also:
>
> And the father of circumcision to them who are not of the circum-
> cision only, but who also walk in the steps of that faith of our father
> Abraham, which he had being yet uncircumcised.
>
> For the promise, that he should be the heir of the world, was not to
> Abraham, or to his seed, through the law, but through the right-
> eousness of faith.
>
> For if they which are of the law be heirs, faith is made void, and the
> promise made of none effect:
>
> Because the law worketh wrath: for where no law is, there is no
> transgression.
>
> Therefore it is of faith, that it might be by grace; to the end the
> promise might be sure to all the seed; not to that only which is of the
> law, but to that also which is of the faith of Abraham; who is the
> father of us all.   Romans 4: 9–16

As we come to look at two series of verses in this chapter,
verses 9 to 12 and also, briefly on this occasion, verses 13 to 16, let
me remind you of what exactly the Apostle is doing in this chapter.

Having stated his great doctrine of justification by faith alone
at the end of chapter 3, in this chapter he deals with various
objections that the Jews were likely to put forward against this
teaching. We have seen that they were likely to bring up the
objection that, surely, works must play a part in our salvation.
The Apostle has already dealt with this in verses 1 to 5 in parti-

cular, where he shows quite clearly that Abraham was justified by his faith and not by works. He has then gone on to show how the teaching of Psalm 32 also supports this doctrine.

In the section now before us he deals with two further objections. The first is dealt with in verses 9 to 12, where he refutes the argument that, even if works are not thus essential, surely circumcision is essential. The third objection he deals with in verses 13 to 16, in which he shows that in the same way to be 'under the law', as the Jews alone were, is not the vital matter in connection with justification, and that the promise to Abraham was given not only before he was circumcised but also long before the giving of the Law by God through Moses. The argument of the Jews with regard to circumcision was that surely it must be essential to salvation; otherwise why should God have ever given it as a sign. The Apostle takes up this argument and refutes it in his customary thorough manner.

However, before we look at his argument, I must turn aside for a moment to comment on the powerful, tenacious and subtle character of unbelief. Notice how when one argument is demolished another argument is immediately brought up. It is the whole tragedy of mankind that it keeps on arguing against its own salvation. Man in sin is always anxious to claim a little credit for himself. He resents the doctrine that salvation is solely and entirely the free gift of God. We must notice also the patience of the Apostle. He realizes, as one who had held those Jewish views himself, how deeply rooted all these misconceptions were, and therefore he deals with each in turn in a patient and exhaustive manner. In all his arguments one can always see the pastor's heart and his great concern for his fellow-countrymen after the flesh.

Turning now to our particular text, in verse 9 we find the Apostle states the question in these words: 'Cometh this blessedness then upon the circumcision only, or upon the uncircumcision also? for we say that faith was reckoned to Abraham for righteousness.' Now this he shows at once is purely a question of history, the history that we can read in the Old Testament. Once more we are reminded of the place of the Old Testament and its teaching in the thinking and the life of the Christian.

[183]

Nothing is more foolish than to imagine that the Christian no longer has any need of the Old Testament. It is quite impossible to follow the argumentation of the New Testament, and especially of the Epistles of Paul, without a knowledge of the Old Testament; for these matters are deeply rooted in the history that is to be found there.

Paul's answer to this question raised in verse 9 is given in a plain and categorical manner in verse 10, and it is to the effect that Abraham was justified not 'when he was in circumcision, but in uncircumcision'. Abraham had in fact been justified and had received the gift of justification long before he was circumcised. His righteousness was imputed to him 'by faith', fourteen years before his circumcision. There is a sense, therefore, in which there is no need to say anything further; but actually the Apostle goes on and, in verses 11 and 12, gives us additional reasons which help us to understand why circumcision was ever given.

Now the assertion made in these two verses is most important and is truly wonderful. I always feel that it is one of those statements which it is well to read out aloud, for by doing so we are more likely to give it the proper emphasis, and shall therefore be able to understand it in a better manner. It is legal language and Paul repeats himself to ensure that there is no misunderstanding. How well he knows the human heart! Therefore he takes no risks.

What, then, are the reasons why circumcision was ever given? First, circumcision was an outward sign given to Abraham as a seal of the righteousness which he had received fourteen years before. Now to 'seal' means to authenticate. This is illustrated elsewhere in the Scriptures. You remember that we are told in John 6, verse 27 – 'for him hath God the Father sealed'. All commentators are agreed that that statement refers to our Lord's baptism, and it means that at His baptism He was publicly sealed with the sign of the descent of the Holy Spirit in the form of a dove upon Him. The word 'seal' is used in exactly the same way in referring to the Holy Spirit in Ephesians 1: 13, 14, 'In whom also after that ye believed (or having believed), ye were sealed with that Holy Spirit of promise, which is the earnest of our inheritance until the redemption of the purchased possession, unto the praise of his glory.' The Holy Spirit seals to us God's promise of our ultimate redemption and of our receiving our great inheritance in glory. Having the Holy Spirit I know that all that God promises to me is already mine in a very real sense. It is sealed to me. What the Apostle is saying here is that in the same way circumcision was given to Abraham as a sign to authenticate the imputation of righteousness to him fourteeen years before.

In other words the teaching is, that circumcision of itself did not do anything to Abraham. The real reason for it was that Abraham should have the promise made sure to him; it was to seal it to him. And so we are right in saying that circumcision played no part in Abraham's justification. Indeed it is exactly the other way round. Justification is the basis upon which circumcision is given. There is no other conceivable way of interpreting the Apostle's statement here.

The second object of circumcision the Apostle explains in verse 11, namely '. . . that he might be the father of all them that believe, though they be not circumcised; that righteousness might be imputed unto them also: and the father of circumcision to them who are not of the circumcision only, but who also walk in the steps of that faith of our father Abraham, which he had yet being uncircumcised'. Now what does this mean? The central declaration is that Abraham is the father of all who believe. He is the father, the pattern, the leading example, the archetype, the first in a great succession.

To put it in another way, it is in the case of Abraham that God defines righteousness and establishes and declares explicitly the principle on which anyone is made righteous. We must not think that Abraham was the first man to be justified; that would be patently wrong. People like Abel and Enoch and Noah and others were equally justified in the sight of God, but it is in the case of Abraham that God makes plain and clear and explicit the way in which He justifies men. While it had always been God's way before, it had not been thus declared in a legal manner.

But Paul does not leave it even at that. He knows how prone we are to misunderstand such profound teaching. So he further explains it by defining who exactly are the children of Abraham. Here we have to look at two statements; the first is found in the second half of verse 11 where we read, 'that he might be the father of all them that believe, though they be not circumcised; that righteousness might be imputed unto them also'. Here, obviously, the Apostle is referring specifically to the uncircumcised, the Gentiles. It was necessary that he should emphasize this because of the view held by the Jews, that people who were uncircumcised could not possibly be justified. He therefore teaches clearly that Abraham is the father of all that believe, even though they are uncircumcised; and the proof he gives is in the statement that Abraham himself was justified by faith while he was yet uncircumcised, as we have seen, even fourteen years before he was circumcised.

The second statement is found in verse 12, where we read, 'And the father of circumcision to them who are not of the circumcision only, but who also walk in the steps of that faith of our father Abraham, which he had yet being uncircumcised.' We have to be very careful as we face this verse because it is one that can be, and often has been, misunderstood and misinterpreted. It is taken by some to mean 'both those who are circumcised together with those who believe'. It cannot possibly mean that, for if so, it would be tautology and simply a partial repetition of what had already been said. No! What the Apostle is saying here is, that Abraham is also the father in the faith of those who belong to the circumcision if they have also believed. Notice the way in which he puts it. He does not say simply that Abraham is the father of the circumcision and leave it at that, for the good reason that a person can be circumcised and yet be lost. He therefore adds the qualification that the circumcised person to whom he is referring is one who has also believed, one who walks in the same faith as Abraham.

In other words, Abraham is not only the father of all the uncircumcised who believe, but also the father of all the circumcised who walk in the same faith as Abraham. It is very important to remember the negative that Paul has put into this verse in this way.

Let us then sum up the teaching. Circumcision in and of itself is nothing. To be circumcised avails nothing by itself. The Apostle states this very clearly in Galatians 5, verse 6: 'For in Jesus Christ neither circumcision availeth anything, nor uncircumcision; but faith which worketh by love.' That is the right way to view circumcision. The children of Abraham are those, and those alone, who have the faith of Abraham. The failure to understand this teaching largely explains the tragic element not only in the history of the Jews but also of the Christian Church. The Jews in general completely failed to understand that circumcision is but a seal of the righteousness which is by faith. They took it to mean the exact opposite. They turned it into something which was meritorious in itself and regarded it as something by which they were justified. They assumed that they were right with God because they were circumcised. However, the whole emphasis of the Apostle's teaching in this great Epistle is that what matters is not circumcision but the principle of faith. Indeed the Apostle had already said this earlier in chapter 2, verses 28 and 29. 'For he is not a Jew, which is one outwardly; neither is that circumcision, which is outward in the flesh. But he is a Jew which is one inwardly; and circumcision is that of the heart, in the spirit, and not in the letter; whose praise is not of men, but of God.'

This particular line of argument that the Apostle employs here is of great and vital importance to us all. It emphasizes that this principle of faith is the vital matter. We in our day and generation must remember that our natural birth, or the fact that we may have been born into a Christian family or a Christian home, does not save us. We must realize equally that baptism does not save us. In the same way, being religious does not save us. We are saved and justified by faith alone; by the same faith that Abraham had; this channel, by which the redemption purchased through the work of our blessed Lord and Saviour is conveyed to us. Baptism is nothing but a seal. The teaching of baptismal regeneration is a plain denial of the doctrine of justification by faith only, and is to be utterly rejected. To build anything on baptism save God's sealing to us our justification by faith alone is to deny this vital teaching.

In verses 13 to 16 the Apostle turns to the third objection which he knew was in the mind of the Jews. They were clutching at every straw, and they fought the doctrine of justification by faith only, with every conceivable argument. Here he deals with the relationship of the Law to this matter, and the question he raises is, whether the Law justifies, or, what is the relationship of justification by faith to the Law?

Once more the Apostle argues in very much the same way; in verse 13 he makes a categorical statement and assertion: 'For the promise, that he should be heir of the world, was not made to Abraham, or to his seed, through the law, but through the righteousness of faith' – that is once more a sheer statement of history, again in the story of Abraham. But then the Apostle goes on to elaborate this and to work it out for us.

What does Paul mean by the term, 'the promise'? The direct words which he uses here were not actually uttered verbatim to Abraham, but the sense was certainly conveyed by what we read first in Genesis 15: 7: 'And he said unto him, I am the Lord that brought thee out of Ur of the Chaldees, to give thee this land to inherit it.' But still more clearly in Genesis 22, in verses 16 to 18, where God said, 'By myself have I sworn, saith the Lord, for because thou hast done this thing, and hast not withheld thy son, thine only son: that in blessing I will bless thee, and in multiplying I will multiply thy seed as the stars of the heaven, and as the sand which is upon the seashore; and thy seed shall possess the gate of his enemies; and in thy seed shall all the nations of the earth be blessed; because thou hast obeyed my voice.' The Apostle shows that he is referring to this promise by what he says here in verse 18: 'Who against hope believed in hope, that he might become the father of many nations; according to that which was spoken, So shall thy seed be.'

The important point for us to grasp here is that this promise was given to Abraham four hundred and thirty years before the Law was given to Moses [*see Galatians* 3: 17]. Furthermore we are reminded that the promise to Abraham was that he should be heir of the whole world and not only of the Promised Land. A careful reading of the Scriptures concerning this matter makes it quite clear that the promise to Abraham was a far greater one than merely that with respect to Canaan. Take for instance what our Lord said in the Sermon on the Mount. 'Blessed are the meek: for they shall inherit the earth' [*Matthew* 5: 5]. This can only refer to what will be true of us in the ultimate universal reign of the Lord Jesus Christ. We meet with the same truth in 1 Corinthians 6, verses 2 and 3: 'Do ye not know that the saints shall judge the world? and if the world shall be judged by you, are ye unworthy to judge the smallest matters? Know ye not that we shall judge angels? how much more things that pertain to this life?' The promise to Abraham must not therefore be limited to the Promised Land; it extends to the whole earth. It is true, of course, that the promise to the children of Abraham after the flesh was to the Promised Land, but from our very context here and from other Scriptures it is clear that we must not confine the meaning solely to that. We are dealing here with what is to be true of those who are the children of Abraham 'by faith', those who are his spiritual seed.

That brings us to the word 'seed'. This is again of crucial importance. Fortunately the Apostle has defined this for us in Galatians 3: 16, 'Now to Abraham and his seed were the promises made. He saith not, And to seeds, as of many; but as of one, And to thy seed, which is Christ.' It is there that we get the true interpretation of this word, and it is there we are given the true meaning and understanding of verses such as Genesis 17: 7-8, 'And I will establish my covenant between me and thee, and thy seed after thee in their generations for an everlasting covenant, to be a God unto thee, and thy seed after thee. And I will give unto thee, and to thy seed after thee, the land wherein thou art a stranger, all the land of Canaan, for an everlasting possession; and I will be their God.' The ultimate reference is to the Lord Jesus Christ. He is the 'Seed' and we are only the seed of Abraham by being in Christ. All the great promises that come to us, come only through our being in Him. And as we are reminded in the eighth chapter of this Epistle, in verse 17, 'because we are children, we are therefore heirs; heirs of God, and joint-heirs with Christ'. Away back in Genesis 3:15 we have the first reference to 'the seed'; then we hear nothing more for centuries until this promise is made to Abraham and his seed. The 'Seed' is Jesus Christ, who is the son of David and the son of Abraham.

What we must always bear in mind is that it is being in Christ that makes us Abraham's seed and therefore 'heirs according to the promise'. We must not confine the promise to the land of Palestine only and think that the heirs of the promise are merely the Jews who are the natural heirs of Abraham, and who are the children of Abraham only according to the flesh. What we should rejoice in is what we are told so gloriously in Ephesians 2, verses 12 and 13: 'That at that time ye were without Christ, being aliens from the commonwealth of Israel, and strangers from the covenants of promise, having no hope and without God in the world: but now in Christ Jesus ye who sometimes were afar off are made nigh by the blood of Christ.' And also the great statement in Ephesians 3, verses 5 and 6 where, in referring to the revelation which had been made known unto him concerning the mystery, the Apostle says: 'Which in other ages was not made known unto the sons of men, as it is now revealed unto his holy apostles and prophets by the Spirit; that the Gentiles should be fellow-heirs, and of the same body, and partakers of his promise in Christ by the gospel.'

This is the great and wonderful promise. It does not apply to Jews alone, or only to the land of Palestine. It applies to all the true spiritual children, 'the children of faith'. We must no longer think of these matters in terms of Jews and Gentiles, circumcision or uncircumcision, being under the Law or outside the Law. In Christ Jesus 'there is neither Gentile nor Jew, circumcision nor uncircumcision, Barbarian, Scythian, male nor female, bond nor free' [*Colossians* 3:11; *Galatians* 3:28]. Thank God, justification is by faith only and is not determined by these other considerations. The Apostle will proceed to work out this argument concerning the Law in yet greater detail.

14 *Salvation Guaranteed by Omnipotent Grace*

*

For the promise, that he should be the heir of the world, was not to Abraham, or to his seed, through the law, but through the righteousness of faith.
For if they which are of the law be heirs, faith is made void, and the promise made of none effect:
Because the law worketh wrath: for where no law is, there is no transgression.
Therefore it is of faith, that it might be by grace; to the end the promise might be sure to all the seed; not to that only which is of the law, but to that also which is of the faith of Abraham; who is the father of us all.
(As it is written, I have made thee a father of many nations,) before him whom he believed, even God, who quickeneth the dead, and calleth those things which be not as though they were.

Romans 4: 13–17

We come now to the third argument of the Apostle with regard to the question of justification by faith only. He has dealt with the argument concerning works, he has dealt with the argument concerning circumcision. Now he deals with this objection, which many Jews were bringing against the Christian faith, that it seemed to be cutting across all the teaching of the Old Testament with regard to the Law. He deals with this particular point in terms of the promise that was made to Abraham and his seed. We saw that the 'Seed' means the Lord Jesus Christ Himself and all who are in Him. We deduce that from the teaching of the third chapter of the Epistle to the Galatians where the Apostle says, 'Not as unto seeds, as of many, but to thy seed, as of one, which is Christ'. We saw furthermore, that the promise referred not only to the Hebrews' possession of the land of Palestine but to the great day which is coming, when 'the kingdoms of this world (shall) become the kingdoms of our Lord and of his Christ'. It is the promise concerning the great and glorious day when 'there shall be new heavens and a new earth wherein dwelleth righteousness', and Christ and His people shall reign in glory in this glorified world.

We come now to his precise argument. Notice the way in which he puts it. This time he does not ask a question, he makes a statement. In verse 13 there is the categorical statement that the promise was not made to Abraham through the medium of the Law, but through the medium of the righteousness of faith. Once again the Apostle is just stating what is a sheer fact of history. The history is found in those chapters of the Book of Genesis which deal with the story of Abraham; and it is important that we should go back to them. The Apostle's whole case rests upon the history. He says in effect: It is just a sheer fact of history, the history that you Jews are so fond of, and in which you make your boast. It is just a fact of history that when God made this promise to Abraham He did not do it in any sense in terms of Law; it was sheer grace; it was pure promise. He did not lay down particular conditions as to what Abraham had to do or had not to do. It was entirely a matter of promise.

I put it like that, first, because many of the authorities are agreed in saying that what is being said here is not so much a reference to the Law of Moses as law in general. They agree that the original reads like that: 'The promise that he should be the heir of the world was not to Abraham or to his seed through law.' There is no '*the* law' in the original. 'Through law.' That is right. Yet surely the Apostle is here referring more specifically to the Law through Moses. So that what he is saying is this; The promise was made by God to Abraham, not through the Law, because the Law was only given later. God gave this promise to Abraham four hundred and thirty years before He gave the Law through Moses to the Children of Israel. As the promise was given before the introduction of circumcision, so it was given before the introduction of the Law. So the promise was not made to Abraham in any sense through Law but rather, as he has already established, through what he calls 'the righteousness of faith'. It was entirely in the light of this righteousness of Abraham's, which came through faith, and not in any way because of his striving to conform to the demands of the moral law. That Law was not yet given. The distinction drawn in verse 16 between the two kinds of seed – 'that which is of the law, and that which is of faith' – confirms this interpretation that 'law' means the Law as given through Moses.

But then the Apostle has another, a second argument which he works out in verses 14 and 15. This is an argument based upon the very nature of the Law itself. That first argument was a very powerful one; history after all does count. But this is not only a matter of history. The very nature of Law itself proves that the promise was not made through the medium of Law but entirely through the medium of the righteousness of faith. What is this second argument? Once more he divides it up into the two sections, one in verse 14, and the other in verse 15; indeed both of these are divided once more into two further sub-sections. Take verse 14: 'For if they which are of the law be heirs' – well then, the first consequence would be – 'faith is made void'. What does he mean by this? He means, obviously, that if it is by the Law that the promise was made, and comes to us, well then, there is no room at all for faith. Why not? Because Law is always interested primarily in works and deeds. The Law always comes to us and says, 'If you do this', or 'You must do this, and you must not do that' – Law always has reference to our actions and conduct and behaviour. A law commands certain things, it prohibits certain other things. The principle is, that a law is always concerned about and interested in our deeds, our works, our conduct, our actions, our behaviour. The moment therefore you bring in the Law you are back on to works, and faith does not come in at all. Law is a matter of commandments, positive and negative, prohibitions, vetoes and injunctions. So the moment you bring in the Law, says Paul, faith is banished, faith is put out. Faith is something that is opposed to works.

But not only that; he says in the second half of this fourteenth verse that there is a second consequence. If you bring in the Law the 'promise also is made of none effect'. How does that happen?

[193]

If you are saying that God made the promise to Abraham on condition that he observed or kept the Law, that immediately and automatically means that the promise never could have been and never can be fulfilled. Why is that? Because, as Paul has already proved, nobody has ever been found who is capable of keeping the Law. So if God had said to Abraham, 'I am going to make a great promise to you, but it is on condition that you keep the Law', He might as well not have made the promise. No one can keep the Law. 'All have sinned and come short of the glory of God.' 'There is none righteous, no, not one.' 'By the law is the knowledge of sin.' The Law means failure. Therefore, if the promise had been made through the medium of Law, what God was giving, as it were, with His right hand, He would have been taking back with His left hand. There would have been no promise at all; it would have had no value whatsoever. That is the argument of verse 14. A double argument you see, based upon the very nature of law.

Then in verse 15 he has yet a further argument, double-edged again, in terms of another aspect of the nature of law. What is that? He says, 'because the law worketh wrath'. Now this is a most important statement. He says that what the Law does is to produce wrath; and wrath is the very opposite of the promise of blessing. Wrath means punishment. The promise offers an inheritance, and life, and joy, and glory. Wrath means punishment and suffering. So Paul argues that to speak of a promise being made through the medium of the Law is a contradiction in terms, because law always works wrath. But how does the Law work wrath? Law always leads, as he has shown so abundantly, to condemnation; and it does that, of course, because of our sinfulness. What the Law does is to show our weaknesses and sins. That was the effect of the giving of the Law. God never gave the Law in order that men might be saved by it. The business of the Law was to bring out the character of sin, that it might show 'the exceeding sinfulness of sin'. People were not clear about sin. God purposed to define it for them, and He defined it in the Law. The Law pin-points sin and therefore it aggravates it; and thereby it works wrath.

In the seventh chapter we shall find the Apostle teaching that 'law worketh wrath' in another sense, namely, that though the Law itself is holy, and good, and pure, because I am carnal and sinful it becomes death unto me. The Law in telling me not to do a thing, arouses in me, because I am sinful, an urge to do that very thing. When the Law comes to me and says, 'You must not do such and such a thing', it turns my mind on to that thing, and because my nature is sinful creates in me a desire to do it. So the very Law of God that prohibits sin ends, in a sense, by making us sin. The reason is not that there is anything wrong with the Law, but that there is something terribly wrong with us. So if the promise were in terms of the Law it would work nothing for us but wrath and condemnation.

Then the Apostle supplements that, and puts it still more clearly, by saying, 'For where no law is there is no transgression'. Now that follows from what I have been saying. He is not saying, of course, that where there is no Law there is no sin and no failure. There were sin and failure before God ever gave the Law through Moses. But what Law does is to define it, and to make it transgression. It establishes it. It codifies it. The effect of the Law is to make our guilt still more evident and obvious. The Apostle has already put that clearly in verses 19 and 20 of the third chapter in these words: 'We know that whatsoever the law saith it saith to them that are under the law; that every mouth may be stopped, and the whole world may become guilty before God. Therefore by the deeds of the law there shall no flesh be justified in his sight; for by the law is the knowledge of sin'. It should be obvious, therefore, that if the promise had been through the medium of the Law not a single person would benefit, because the Law condemns us, every one of us. It brings the knowledge of sin; it renders us all inexcusable and hopeless.

There, then, is his preliminary argument with regard to this question of the promise. The promise has not come, he says, negatively, through the medium of the Law – verses 13, 14 and 15. But in verses 16 and 17 he looks at it positively. What a change, what a difference! The negative was absolutely essential. We have got to be clear about these negatives, and so he has demolished the supposition that the promise could ever come through the medium of the Law. He has swept it out of court. But now he puts it positively, and, indeed, at the same time winds up his whole great argument on the subject of justification by faith only. What we have from verse 18 to the end of the chapter is really just a kind of sermon on the actual faith of Abraham as it showed itself in practice. The theology, as it were, finishes at the end of verse 17.

Let us look at what he says in verses 16 and 17. Here is one of these glorious, moving, resounding statements which are to be found in such profusion in the writings of this mighty Apostle. 'Therefore it is of faith, that it might be by grace; to the end that the promise might be sure to all the seed.' First, let us get our terms clear. 'Therefore', he says – for the reasons he has just been adducing, because of the whole argument that he has been working out – 'Therefore it is of faith.' What is of faith? Well, particularly the promise, the promise God made to Abraham, which promise comes to us as children of Abraham, as children of faith. Salvation – everything that is awaiting us as God's people – is of faith. The Apostle did not actually say 'it is', but the translators have rightly supplied that in italics, as also 'it might be'. What the Apostle actually said was this. Having worked out his negatives, he said, 'Therefore of faith, that by grace'.

Why must it be thus? Why must it be by faith, not by works, not by circumcision, not by law, not by actions – why must it be 'by faith' or 'of faith'? He gives a number of answers which we must consider. The first is that it must be, and it is, of faith that it might be by grace. How does that follow? What is grace? We have already seen that. He has already used this term in chapter 3 verse 24, where he says, 'Being justified freely by his grace'. Grace means 'free unmerited favour'. Grace is kindness shown to someone who does not deserve it at all, but who deserves the exact opposite. It is absolutely free, entirely unmerited on the part of the recipient. There is no need to argue about this, says the Apostle. 'Therefore' – it is clear in view of all he has been laying down.

We can sum it up like this. It has to be of faith, otherwise it cannot be by grace There are certain things that are always correlative, there are certain things that are always tied together. Here are some examples. Works and deeds are always tied to and belong to Law. That is the characteristic of Law, as we have seen – deeds, actions, conduct, behaviour. The moment you say 'Law' you think of them; or when you start speaking of actions and conduct and behaviour you automatically think of Law. But then, on the other hand, faith is the correlative of grace. The moment you mention the term grace you automatically think of faith; or if you talk about faith you automatically think of grace. This reasoning is not confined to the Apostle Paul. In the prologue to John's gospel you have exactly the same thing. 'The law', says John, 'was given by Moses, but grace and truth came through Jesus Christ'. There are contrasts – certain terms are wedded and married together. The Apostle attaches such significance to this that you will find that in the eleventh chapter of this Epistle he puts it very clearly in verse 6. He says, 'If by grace, then is it no more of works: otherwise grace is no more grace. But if it be of works, then is it no more grace; otherwise work is no more work.' If you are talking about grace, he says, well then, do not talk about work. You must not mix your terms, you must not contradict yourself. If it is by grace, then it is no more of works; otherwise grace is no more grace. But if on the other hand something is of works, well then, do not talk about grace, because if you do, you are mixing terms again, and work is no more work. You cannot mix works and grace any more than you can mix black and white. These things are eternal opposites, and if you bring works into the realm of grace, it is no more grace. Or if you bring grace into the realm of works, it is no more works. It is one or the other: these two can never be brought together.

Here, then, is Paul's argument. Under Law it is always a matter of merit and of desert. If you are under the Law and you do something, you present your bill. You say, Now I have done what you asked me to do, therefore I ask for payment. And you have a right to do so. You demand recompense. Under Law it is a matter of merit, it is a matter of man claiming a reward. But grace is entirely the free gift of God received by faith. There is no merit, no claim, no demand whatsoever. The two things are poles apart; they are eternally separated.

From this the Apostle draws certain deductions. The first is this: that the way of faith alone guarantees that it should be entirely of grace, and that therefore the glory should be altogether God's and His alone. The glory in salvation is entirely God's glory; and if you introduce anything but faith you are detracting from His glory. If you begin to talk about works, or about law, man is making a claim, and you are derogating from the glory of the grace of God. The principle of faith leads to grace; and grace is one of the manifestations of the glory of God. That, says Paul, is the way of salvation; that is how the promise came to Abraham. There is nothing for man to boast of, not even his faith. If you boast about your faith, if you boast about the fact that you have believed while someone else has not, it is no longer grace; and it is no longer to God's glory, but the credit goes to your belief. It has to be either of works or of grace; and if you claim merit even for your faith you are turning your faith into works, and you are taking from the glory of God, you are taking from the principle of grace and the freeness of God's gift. It is altogether from God; and it is of faith that it might be by grace, in order that God might have all the glory.

But the Apostle has a second argument. He says that it is this way of faith that alone guarantees the comprehensive character of the promise of salvation. When I say the 'comprehensive' character, I mean that it is the only way that guarantees the inclusion of Gentiles as well as Jews – uncircumcision as well as the circumcision. He says, 'It is all of faith that it might be by grace, to the end (with the object, that it might guarantee) the promise might be sure to all the seed: not to that only which is of the Law, but to that also which is of the faith of Abraham, who is the father of us all.' He says that salvation has to be of faith, not only because that is the only way in which grace works and in which God can have the sole glory, but also because if it were by the Law it would only be a salvation for those who are under the Law. Those who had never had the Law, and were not under it, would have no hope at all. But, he says, we have already seen and established that this is a salvation in which the uncircumcised benefit as well as the circumcision, and those who are pagans and Gentiles as well as Jews. But that is only possible on the promise of faith. If it were anything else the Gentiles would be excluded and shut out. But that is not the case; because this salvation, this promise, is not only to the seed of Abraham that was under the Law, that is, to the Jews who had been circumcised and brought up under the Law but who now have believed the Gospel and have become the true seed of Abraham. In other words he is repeating and re-enforcing the point he has already made in verse 11 in this same chapter, 'He received the sign of circumcision, a seal of the righteousness of the faith which he had being yet un-circumcised; that he might be the father of all them that believe, though they be not circumcised; that righteousness might be imputed unto them also.' Then in verse 12, 'And the father of circumcision to them who are not of the circumcision only.' What brings the blessing to them is not the fact that they have been circumcised, but that they 'walk in the steps of that faith of our father Abraham, which he had being yet uncircumcised'. What matters is not circumcision but the fact that they exercise the same faith as Abraham.

Now Paul is repeating all that here, 'to the end that the promise might be sure to all the seed; not to that only which is of the law' – not only to the physical seed of Abraham, the believers who were circumcised Jews and once under the Law, but who now have become true children of faith and therefore true children of Abraham, but also to these others who never were under the Law and who have never been circumcised, but who by faith, and having the same faith as Abraham, have become children of Abraham and of the seed of Abraham, who is the father of us all. He is the father of 'all' that believe, whether they be Jews or Gentiles, Barbarian, Scythian, bond or free, male or female. He is the father of all who are in Christ, because they are all 'of faith'. The point is that the promise was given to Abraham entirely apart from the Law. Abraham was not under the Law when the promise was given and all who are 'the children of faith' become inheritors of the promise in exactly the same way still. It is always by faith and entirely apart from the Law.

What a wonderful truth this is for us! The point is that we can come into this salvation irrespective of our antecedents. It does not matter whether you are a Jew or whether you are a Gentile. The principle is one of faith and grace, and it is still the same. We can preach this Gospel to all nations, to all people. It matters not who enters a place of worship to listen to it, whether good or bad, from a palace or from a gutter, whether highly religious or irreligious, it makes no difference. That is the glory of preaching the Gospel. Many people come to listen to the Gospel who have been brought up in a religious atmosphere, in religious homes, who have always gone to church and Sunday School, never missed meetings; yet they may be unregenerate. They need the same salvation as the man who may have come to listen, who has never been inside a House of God before. He may have come out of some moral gutter; it does not matter. It is the same way, the same Gospel for both, and both must come in in the same way. Religiosity is of no value; morality does not count; nothing matters. We are all reduced to the same level because it is 'by faith', because it is 'by grace'. This is the great missionary charter. That is why we preach the same Gospel exactly to people who have been brought up religiously and to pagans in un-evangelized countries who have never seen a Bible and who have never even heard the Name of God. It is exactly the same Gospel for all, and all who believe have to come to God through Christ in the same way. By this principle the promise is made sure 'to all the seed', whether Jews or Gentiles.

But we do not stop even there. This way of grace and of faith alone guarantees the completion of the salvation of any one of us, and all of us. 'Therefore it is of faith that it might be by grace, to the end that the promise might be sure to all the seed.' This alone makes salvation 'sure' and guarantees its completion. Salvation, thank God, is all of God; it is all of the grace of God. And it is for that reason alone that it is sure. Your ultimate salvation, and mine, in glory is guaranteed by one thing only, and that is, that it is by grace and through faith, and not by works or circumcision, or Law, or by anything in man. Our salvation is sure because it is founded on the character of God Himself, His everlasting and abounding grace. Do you realize this? If our salvation and our ultimate arrival in glory depended in any sense whatsoever upon ourselves, and upon our abilities and faculties, our powers and faithfulness or our understanding, not a single one of us would ever arrive in glory.

I can prove that. When man was perfect in Paradise he failed and fell. In Eden Adam's relationship to God was on the basis of a Covenant of Works. He was free from sin, he was perfect; he had never done anything against God, and God made with him a Covenant of Works. He said, you shall stay here, you shall have immortality, if you keep my Law. But even there in Paradise, with no sin in his being at all, man fell – even when perfect he fell. What hope would there be therefore for any one of us, imperfect as we are, with sin in our very nature, if our continuance and perseverance depended on us? If our ultimate salvation depended in any sense or in any shape or form upon anything in us, not one of us would have final salvation.

Thank God that it does not depend on us, but that 'it is of faith that it might be by grace, to the end that the promise might be sure to all the seed'. It is not in our hands, thank God. It is in His hands, and therefore it cannot fail. 'He who hath begun a good work in you will perform it until the day of Jesus Christ' [*Philippians* 1: 6]. 'I am persuaded, that neither death nor life nor angels nor principalities nor powers, nor things present nor things to come, nor height nor depth nor any other creature shall be able to separate us from the love of God which is in Christ Jesus our Lord' [*Romans* 8: 38–39]. Because of my faith? No! but because I am in His hands. Not my grasp of Him but His mighty grasp of me!

But you may say, that is only the theology of Paul. Listen then to the Lord Jesus Christ saying the same thing, 'And I give unto them eternal life, and they shall never perish, neither shall any man pluck them out of my hand. My Father which gave them me is greater than all and no man is able to pluck them out of my Father's hand' [*John* 10: 28–29]. It is impossible. It is because we are in this hand, the hand of God, the hand of Christ, that our salvation is certain and absolutely sure.

But even now the Apostle is not satisfied. He goes on to say it again, and to reinforce it, and underline it in verse 17. There is a parenthesis here; it is put in brackets at the beginning. ('As it is written, I have made thee a father of many nations.') Forget that for the moment and read the statement continuously thus: 'Therefore it is of faith that it might be by grace; to the end that the promise might be sure to all the seed; not to that only which is of the law, but to that also which is of the faith of Abraham, who is father of us all, before him whom he believed, even God ...'. What does this mean? This is the basis, the only ultimate basis of our salvation, and our hope and our assurance.

Paul here takes us back to that historic occasion when God called Abraham and said, 'Come out of your tent and stand here. Look around, look at the stars in the heavens. Can you count them? You will never succeed; they are countless, innumerable. Look at them! Abraham, I am going to make you the father of many nations, and your seed shall be as those stars in the heavens and as the sand on the seashore – innumerable'. Abraham stood there, as Paul says, 'before God'. And God looked at Abraham and said to him, 'You are to be the father of all that seed'. He is the father of all the seed 'before God' – or if you prefer it, he is the father of all the seed standing there in the presence of the God whom he had believed.

In other words, what Paul is saying is that Abraham was even then the 'father of all' in the sight of God. Of course, he was not so in actual fact. He was not the father even of Isaac at that point. Isaac had not been born, and it seemed impossible that he ever should be, because Abraham was ninety-nine years of age and Sarah was ninety – they were a childless couple. But in the sight of God he was already the father of Isaac and all the seed. That is what 'before God' means. He was the father of all the seed, father of this endless progeny, father of all the faithful, father of our Lord and Saviour Jesus Christ according to the flesh, because He came out of the loins of Abraham. God looked at Abraham and saw him in that light, even as Abraham stood there under the sky that night with the stars shining down upon him. God saw it all. He saw him as the father of the seed, the progenitor of this mighty race that was to come, and out of whom would come 'Jesus Christ, the son of David, the son of Abraham' [*Matthew* 1: 1].

How could God do this? Let us ask the question with reverence. How was it possible for God to do such a thing? How could He speak to Abraham like that, when Abraham was an old man and Sarah was ninety years of age? You do not have children at that age according to the course of nature; the thing is impossible. And yet God says it, God sees it. How is it possible? Paul gives us the answer: 'God', he says, 'who quickeneth the dead, and calleth those things which be not as though they were', which means that God could speak like that to Abraham because 'with God nothing is impossible', because God is able even 'to quicken the dead'. And He did so. He quickened Abraham, He quickened Sarah, to enable them to produce a child, a child whom they called Isaac. In a natural sense He quickened those two bodies which were 'dead' from the standpoint of producing children. But God did the same thing later on, in a picture, over the sacrifice of Isaac. That is why Abraham never faltered even when he had actually raised the knife to kill Isaac as an offering. We are told in the eleventh chapter of the Epistle to the Hebrews that he knew that, even if he slew Isaac, God had the power to raise him from the dead. He had the faith to believe that. And God actually did that in a figurative sense.

But it all looks forward to the still mightier and greater event adumbrated by what happened there to Isaac. The Son of God, the 'Seed', came into the world. But men took Him with cruel hands and condemned Him and nailed Him to a tree. He died, and they placed His dead body in a grave and rolled a stone over the entrance to the grave and sealed it. But GOD quickeneth the dead. He raised Him up from the dead and brought life and immortality to light through Him. That is why God could speak as He did to Abraham. God does not look at the difficulties. He knows His own Almighty power. He 'quickeneth the dead'. He is Omnipotent.

But secondly, 'He calleth those things which be not as though they were'. Another translation says, 'He summons the non-existing as existing'. What does this mean? It means, perhaps, that He calls them into being. There is nothing there, but God can call into being something out of nothing. God said, 'Let there be light: and there was light'. There was nothing there before, there was nothing but a void when God said, 'Let there be light'. He called it into being from nothing.

But I believe that this has another sense also, and it is equally good and equally important and equally glorious. This term to 'call' sometimes means to 'name'. 'He calleth them all by name', says Isaiah in chapter 40. He calls all by their names. God is able to do that. In other words God looked at this old man Abraham standing outside under the stars with Sarah there in the tent, and God as it were 'called' the seed into being and immediately gave them names – your name, my name. God knew the seed then and He is already using their names before they have come into being. This is because He 'sees the end from the beginning', and what He purposes is most certainly going to come to pass. That is why in the eighth chapter of this Epistle, in verse 29, Paul says, 'Whom he did foreknow, he also did predestinate to be conformed to the image of his Son. Moreover whom he did predestinate, them he also called, and whom he called, them he also justified, and whom he justified, them he also glorified.' He has already done all that. Yet you and I are still on earth; we are not glorified yet. That may be, says the Apostle, but with God things are different, He sees the end from the beginning. We are already glorified in God's sight. Indeed, in the Epistle to the Ephesians, the Apostle says that you and I are already 'seated' in the heavenly places in Christ Jesus' [*Ephesians* 2: 6]. Wherever you are seated physically at this moment, if you are in Christ I assure you that you are also seated in the heavenly places in Christ Jesus. God sees you there.

In other words the Apostle is saying that God was able in that way to look at Abraham – without an heir and without a child – and to speak like this about his being the father of so many nations, and the father of all the seed, because He is Omnipotent, and Omniscient. It was because he had understood this teaching and caught something of its spirit that the writer of the hymn was able to sing:

> *Apostles join the glorious throng*
> *And swell the loud immortal song;*
> *Prophets enraptured hear the sound*
> *And spread the Hallelujah round.*

'Victorious martyrs join their lays', he goes on to cry. Well, what do they do? 'And shout the Omnipotence of grace'. 'The Omnipotence of grace!' Death means nothing to Omnipotence. Hopelessness and despair are nothing to Omnipotence. 'God quickeneth the dead, and calleth those things which be not as though they were.' This is the charter of our salvation. If this were not true there would never have been such a thing as a Christian, not one of us would ever have been saved.

How is salvation possible? Here is the answer. 'You hath he quickened who were dead in trespasses and sins' [*Ephesians* 2: 1]. If God had not the power to quicken the dead and to give life to the lifeless we would still be in our sins and in unbelief. We do not start it. God starts it. He 'quickens the dead'. As the Apostle says, 'and he calleth those things which be not as though they were'. The Apostle says the same thing to the Corinthians: 'God hath chosen the foolish things of the world to confound the wise; and God hath chosen the weak things of the world to confound the things which are mighty; and base things of the world, and things which are despised, hath God chosen, yea, and things which are not, to bring to nought things that are; that no flesh should glory in his presence' [1 *Corinthians* 1: 27–29]. It is all of God. It is all of grace. 'It is of faith that it might be by grace, that the promise might be sure to all the seed.' Nothing but Omnipotence could ever hold and keep and guarantee the perseverance of anyone. Nothing but the same Omnipotence could ever bring any one of us unto final salvation and glory. But He can. And that is why there is hope for the vilest sinner in the world. Do not tell me about your sins. I am talking about the Omnipotence of grace. Your vileness makes no difference. There is as much hope for the vilest as for the best and the purest. Still more wonderful, nothing can stop this process, nothing can frustrate it. What God has planned and purposed He will carry out. The 'fulness of the Gentiles' will come in, 'all Israel shall be saved', and the work will be finally completed. The promise is 'sure' to all the seed. It is guaranteed because God 'quickeneth the dead and calleth into being things which have no being'. It is sure to all the seed because of the Omnipotence of grace. Thank God it is of faith and not of works, not of Law, not of circumcision, not of anything in man: but all of grace – all of God.

> *A debtor to mercy alone,*
> *Of Covenant mercy I sing;*
> *Nor fear, with Thy righteousness on,*
> *My person and off'rings to bring.*
> *The terrors of law and of God*
> *With me can have nothing to do;*
> *My Saviour's obedience and blood*
> *Hide all my transgressions from view.*
>
> *The work which His goodness began,*
> *The arm of His strength will complete;*
> *His promise is Yea and Amen,*
> *And never was forfeited yet.*
> *Things future, nor things that are now,*
> *Not all things below or above,*
> *Can make Him His purpose forego,*
> *Or sever my soul from His love.*
>
> *My name from the palms of His hands*
> *Eternity will not erase;*
> *Impressed on His heart it remains*
> *In marks of indelible grace.*
> *Yes, I to the end shall endure,*
> *As sure as the earnest is given;*
> *More happy, but not more secure,*
> *The glorified spirits in heaven.*

'It is of faith that it might be by grace, that the promise might be sure to all the seed.' Thank God!

15 *The Nature of Faith*

*

Who against hope believed in hope, that he might become the father of many nations, according to that which was spoken, So shall thy seed be.   Romans 4: 18

With verses 16 and 17 in this fourth chapter we have reached the point at which the Apostle has finally dealt with all the arguments against the doctrine of justification by faith only, and has met every conceivable objection to it. He has been patient; he has taken his time; he has given full weight to everything that can be said against the doctrine, and having considered all these he says, 'Therefore it is of faith that it might be by grace (of grace), to the end that the promise might be sure to all the seed; not to that which is of the law only, but to that also which is of the faith of Abraham, who is the father of us all; before him whom he believed, even God, who quickeneth the dead, and calleth those things which be not as though they were.'

However, the Apostle seems to feel that he cannot leave it at that. It is not that he is going to argue any further, but that this case of Abraham is such a big one, such an important one, that it provides a perfect illustration in this whole matter of justification by faith. He seems to be saying, 'I am trying to show that justification is by faith only; and if any of you are in trouble as to what faith means, or as to how justification comes to us by faith, there is a perfect illustration of it in the case of Abraham. We have looked at it in theory, let us now look at it in practice. Do you know what faith is? Do you know the characteristics of faith? Let us look at Abraham whom I have been using as an argument. Abraham was justified by faith. Abraham believed

God and it was counted unto him for righteousness. Let us see exactly what that means.'

There is no clearer or more dramatic statement as to the nature of faith anywhere in the Scripture than that which we have in these verses. All we have to do, therefore, is to follow the Apostle as he gives us the details and shows us their importance, and thereby introduces us to the great subject of faith. This will serve two purposes. The Apostle's ultimate object, as we shall see, is to show the truth concerning justification, as he says in verse 23 and 24. 'Now it was not written for his sake alone that it was imputed to him; but for us also, to whom it shall be imputed, if we believe on Him that raised up Jesus our Lord from the dead.' That is his real object. But, at the same time, what the Apostle says here about the faith of Abraham is always true of faith, faith in every application. What he says about faith is not only true for justification but also for living, for battling, for surmounting obstacles – faith in the whole range of its great activities. So that as we are looking at justification by faith we shall be learning something about faith itself and the things which always characterize it. This is one of the greatest definitions of faith found anywhere in the whole of the Scripture, even bearing in mind the great eleventh chapter of the Epistle to the Hebrews. All the great elements in faith are found here in short compass.

The first thing Paul does is to remind us that Abraham became the father of many nations: 'Who against hope believed in hope that he might become the father of many nations; according to that which was spoken, so shall thy seed be.' Here is the starting-point, this astounding thing that is true in the history of Abraham – that this one man became the father of many nations. We are dealing with history. This is not theory, this is historical truth, historical fact. It is the record that you can read in the Old Testament, the great story of the origin of the Children of Israel. That is why the psalmists and the prophets so frequently took the Children of Israel back to the story. Look again, they keep on saying, at the rock from which you have been hewn, look to Abraham, your father: you are the Children of Abraham,

Abraham's seed. That is the great fact which he was concerned to emphasize.

The second thing I note is that the Apostle says that this became true of Abraham, as the result of his faith, through his faith alone. 'Who, against hope believed in hope, that he might become the father of many nations.' That is how it has come to pass. It is through the medium of his faith, the instrumentality of his faith, that all this has become true of Abraham.

Let us then look at it like this. What was it exactly that Abraham's faith enabled him to do? The Apostle gives five answers to the question. First, it enabled him to believe God's word of promise, that staggering word of promise that God made to Abraham. What was this? It is all summarized for us by the Apostle in one phrase: 'So shall thy seed be.' You notice how he puts it in the eighteenth verse: 'Who against hope believed in hope that he might become the father of many nations; according to that which was spoken' (and he sums up everything that God said to Abraham in just that one phrase), 'So shall thy seed be.' It is one of the most amazing and astounding things that God has ever said to man. It means in the first place that Abraham was to have a very large and numerous progeny. You remember how God used two illustrations when He told him this. He said, 'As the sand by the seashore is innumerable, and you cannot count it, so shall thy seed be.' Or 'as the stars, if thou be able to count them'. Try to realize the staggering character of this. Here is a man who is drawing near to a hundred years of age, and his wife is over ninety. They have no child. Yet God makes this astounding statement to him about his natural progeny. Faith, I say, enabled Abraham to believe that.

But that does not exhaust this little word 'So' – 'So shall thy seed be.' It includes that but it does not stop at that. The second thing it means is this. When God spoke thus to Abraham He was at the same time speaking to him about another Seed, not only his own natural descendants; He was speaking to him of one in particular. You remember the argument of the Apostle Paul in the Epistle to the Galatians in chapter 3, verse 16 to which we referred earlier. He says, 'Now to Abraham and his seed were the promises made. He saith not, And to seeds, as of many; but as of one, And to thy Seed, which is Christ.' We must include that. I have already made that clear when dealing with the first part of this fourth chapter, but I must remind you of it again. The statement, the promise, that was made to Abraham was not simply about his natural seed and progeny. God definitely made to Abraham this promise concerning the Lord Jesus Christ. He told Abraham that out of his loins, his descendants, was going to come the great Saviour, the Messiah, the Deliverer of His people. You recall how our Lord Himself makes that perfectly clear when He said to the Jews, 'Your father Abraham rejoiced to see my day: and he saw it and was glad'. The Apostle Paul includes that here.

It is a serious misunderstanding of God's promise to Abraham to confine it to his natural seed, and to the land of Israel. The astounding thing is that God there revealed to Abraham the whole plan and way of salvation through Jesus Christ our Lord. Abraham did not see it very clearly, but he did see it. Abraham was given to see, away back at that point, that salvation was not by works, not by anything a man does; but by an act of God. God was going to save by sending His Son, who after the flesh was to be the seed of Abraham. So in this word 'So' we have included not only the Lord Jesus Christ but the way of salvation through His death, through His blood, through His crucifixion. God revealed to Abraham that He was going to 'set him forth as a propitiation for sin'. He repeated it again, in a sense, in the incident connected with God's command to Abraham to sacrifice Isaac. But God revealed it to Abraham, and Abraham saw it – 'So shall thy seed be.'

But it has a third element in it, something the Apostle has kept on repeating in this chapter, that the Gentiles also are to come into this salvation. 'Not to that only which is of the law, but to that also which is of the faith of our father Abraham, who is the father of us all.' So that when God said to him, 'So shall thy seed be', He was saying, as the quotation reminds us, that Abraham was going to be the father of many nations in a spiritual sense. He is the father of the Jews only in the natural sense. He is not the natural father of these Gentile nations, but he is their spiritual father, he is 'the father of many nations'.

The history of the Christian Church has verified all that and proved and substantiated it. 'Many shall come from the east and the west (and from all directions) and shall sit down with Abraham, Isaac and Jacob in the kingdom of heaven' [*Matthew* 8:11]. From all tribes and nations and languages they shall come and shall all be the seed of Abraham, children of Abraham. Why? Because they are children of faith. Abraham is the father of all who are justified by faith. Therefore this word 'So' includes all that. The first thing that Abraham's faith enabled him to do was to believe this staggering promise in all the fullness that I have just been describing to you.

But, secondly, it enabled him to believe it on the bare Word of God and on nothing else whatsoever. Abraham had nothing to go upon when he believed this, except the mere statement of God. There he was, as we were reminded in the seventeenth verse, standing before God with the stars looking down upon him, standing there in his solitariness, and God made this tremendous statement to him, the God 'who quickeneth the dead and calleth those things which be not as though they were'. God made the statement, and Abraham, on that alone, believed. There was nothing but the bare word of God. That is always true of faith, and it is one of its most marvellous characteristics. There is always this naked element in faith. It does not ask for proofs, it does not seek them; in a sense it does not need them. Faith is content with the bare Word of God, because He is God. 'Abraham believed God, and it was counted to him for righteousness.'

But I must elaborate that in a third point. Abraham's faith enabled him to believe this staggering promise merely on the Word of God, and also in spite of all appearances to the contrary. This has to be added because it is a part of the story, 'Who against hope believed in hope'. What that means is that there really was no hope whatsoever for this thing to happen, speaking in a natural sense; everything was against it. Consider the facts. One was Abraham's own body now dead when he was about an hundred years old, and secondly, the deadness of Sarah's womb. Where was there any conceivable hope that Abraham and Sarah might have a child? There was none. It was impossible. Everything was against it – the course of nature, the course of life, everything. It was a completely hopeless situation; there was not a glimmer of hope in any respect. 'Against hope.' How then did Abraham believe? He believed in the hope that God laid before him. That is what this statement means. It does not just mean 'Who against hope believed hopefully'. It means, 'Who against hope believed in this hope that God was outlining to him, this future that He was painting before him'. That is the hope. The hope of the coming of the Son of God in the flesh, the hope of salvation, the hope of deliverance, the hope of the coming in of the Gentiles – that is the hope. It is the great hope that runs right through the Old Testament. What we are told is that Abraham believed in this hope, this promise, in spite of everything. Though everything was against it, and every reasonable argument was opposed to it, though all common sense was dead against it, and the whole story of the human race seemed to ridicule it, still Abraham believed it – he 'against hope believed in hope'. That, again, is another very important aspect of faith, a real element in faith wherever you get it, wherever it manifests itself.

But even that does not exhaust the achievements of faith. Abraham's faith enabled him to have an assurance with respect to all this. That is the message of verse 21: 'And being fully persuaded that what he (God) had promised he was able also to perform.' He was fully persuaded of it. Or if you prefer another translation, 'He was strongly convinced of it'. Are you somewhat surprised at this statement? We must realize that faith, true faith, always has in it this element of assurance, of certainty, and of confidence. This needs to be emphasized at the present time. Faith is not mere hopefulness; faith is fully persuaded, faith is assured, faith is certain. Faith is not just 'whistling in the dark' to keep up one's courage. True faith is 'fully persuaded'.

As this is so important I must produce some further statements from Scripture to substantiate this point. It is not only here that we have this statement about faith. Take, for instance, the classic statement of it in the Epistle to the Hebrews in the first verse of the eleventh chapter. Faith we are told, 'is the substance of things hoped for, the evidence of things not seen'. That means that faith is the substantiating of the thing we hope for, it is the evidence for it. There is an evidential value and element in faith; it is 'the evidence of things that we do not see'. Faith, if you like, is a kind of title-deed, and there is certainty in a title-deed. In other words, we must not think of faith as something vague and uncertain, indefinite and nebulous. No, says this man in writing to the Hebrews; faith is that which substantiates. But he repeats that in the thirteenth verse of that same chapter. He says, 'These all died in faith, not having received the promises, but having seen them afar off, and were persuaded of them and embraced them.' All this means that there is this element of certainty and of assurance in faith. You have it here in Romans 4, and again in the Epistle to the Hebrews. This is important for the reason that it is this that differentiates faith from a mere intellectual belief. It is this which differentiates faith from what is called 'believism' or 'fideism'.

You may have heard of the heresy called Sandemanianism that troubled the Church in the eighteenth century. What is Sandemanianism? It is a teaching which declares that as long as you say that 'Jesus is Lord', that as long as you say that you believe, you are saved. It excludes all feeling and all assurance. But that is not right; that is heresy. A man who does truly believe, a man who is regenerate, certainly does say that he believes; but merely to say that you believe these things is not faith. Faith includes this other element of certainty, of assurance, of confidence. Faith knows! There is this element of knowledge which we must never take out of faith: 'Being fully persuaded.'

That was Abraham's faith, he was 'fully persuaded', and that is why he did what he did and acted as he did. He was certain of the promise. It is important for us to keep this ever before our minds. If we do not we shall be opening the door to what is so often to be seen, namely, people who are urged and over-persuaded, in emotional circumstances, to say that they believe and accept the Gospel, and who are then told that they are Christians. They regard themselves, and are regarded by others, as Christians, but may be found in a few months' time denying it all, and saying that there is nothing in it. They maintain that they were just psychologically affected for the time being, and that they now have 'no use for it' at all. What is the explanation of that? It is that they never had true faith. They said they believed, but that is not faith; that can be nothing but mere intellectual assent. There is nothing to prevent a man from saying that. If he is persuaded by the argument he will say, 'Very well, I believe it'. But he does not feel anything. Faith is bigger than that; it includes the sensibilities, it takes in the heart, it takes in the whole man. He is 'fully persuaded' – this is a very real and essential element in faith. Faith is not just 'hoping against hope' in the usually accepted meaning of that phrase; it is being fully persuaded; it is 'embracing the promise' because you are 'fully persuaded'.

That brings us to the last element in faith, or the fifth thing which Abraham's faith enabled him to do. That is, that in the light of all this he acted upon what he believed; he believed God's Word and he acted upon it. It is very interesting to notice how the record tells us, back in the Book of Genesis in chapter 17 and the fifth verse, one of the things which Abraham did. There you will read that God said to Abraham, 'Neither shall thy name any more be called Abram, but thy name shall be Abraham; for a father of many nations have I made thee.' The meaning of the words there is important. Abram means 'high father'; Abraham means, 'the father of many nations'. From now on, said God, I am not going to call you Abram any longer, I am going to call you Abraham. And from that moment Abram called himself Abraham. He was now known as Abraham; he let everybody know that he had a new name. He said to the people, as it were, 'Call me Abraham. God has told me that I am Abraham, therefore do not call me Abram any longer.' He acted on it in that and in other respects. In other words – to complete the quotation of Hebrews 11:13 – 'These all died in faith, not having received the promises, but having seen them afar off, and were persuaded of them and embraced them, and confessed that they were strangers and pilgrims on the earth.' That is stated in the context of what we are told about Abraham. Abraham believed all this, and his whole life henceforward was lived in this persuasion, on this statement of God. He became a 'stranger and a pilgrim'. He began 'looking for a City which hath foundations, whose builder and maker is God'. He kept his eye on this Messiah that was to come; and whatever happened to him he held on to that great promise. He acted on what he had believed, and on this promise of which he had become 'fully assured'. Those are the five things which Abraham's faith enabled him to do.

But still we have not exhausted what the Apostle tells us. The next big matter that he puts before us is to tell us how Abraham's faith enabled him to do those five things. What is it about faith, what was it in Abraham's faith that enabled him in this way to accept that staggering promise simply on the bare Word of God? And to become absolutely sure of it, and to act on it, and to risk his everything upon it? How does faith do this? The Apostle's answer is that faith is something that makes a man strong. There it is in verse 20: 'He staggered not at the promise of God through unbelief.' 'He', says the Authorized Version, 'was strong in faith, giving God the glory.' A better translation is, 'Was made strong by faith', or 'was strengthened by faith' or 'in his faith'. In any case the statement is that faith enables us by making us strong, by putting vigour and power and strength into our whole life, into our thinking and all our activities.

Observe the way in which the Apostle puts this. He is so concerned about this point that he first puts it negatively, and then positively. Negatively he puts it in two ways. He says in verse 19, 'And being not weak in faith he considered not his own body now dead when he was about an hundred years old, neither yet the deadness of Sarah's womb'. How was he strong, how was he made strong? Well he was delivered from being weak; he was 'not weak'. But here, again, the translation is important. In the Revised Version the translation is different. The Authorized Version says, '. . . and being not weak in faith he considered not his own body'. The word 'not' is omitted in the Revised Version, which has, 'without being weakened in faith he considered his own body'. The Revised Standard Version agrees with the Revised Version, and undoubtedly it is right. The four oldest manuscripts of the New Testament do not have that negative. They put the statement in the positive form. They all say that he did consider his body, but that he was not weakened in faith when he considered his own body and the deadness of Sarah's womb.

Why do I trouble to make that point? For the reason that it brings out another glorious element and aspect of faith. Let me show what I mean. The AV might well give us the impression that 'being not weak in faith' he 'considered not' his own body; in other words, did not think of it for a moment, neither did he consider Sarah's condition. But if you read the history of the book of Genesis you will find that that is not true. Abraham did consider it, he spoke to himself about it. He said, 'Shall I indeed at my age be the father of a son, and shall Sarah at her age bear a son?' He did consider it, and therefore it is important that we should be quite clear about this. We could, of course, interpret this Authorized translation, 'Being not weak in faith he considered not his own body now dead', as meaning that he did not keep on considering it and thereby become weak. But even that would not be good enough; it is actually this, 'Without being weakened in faith he did consider his own body'.

That brings out the vital element in faith, that it is not something that refuses to face facts. There are some people who think of faith in that way, and the result is that the man of the world says, 'What you Christians call faith I call escapism'. That is what the clever men of the world say about Christians. They say that Christian people are not realists, that they meet together in their buildings and pull down the blinds and shut out the world and its problems, and then persuade themselves of certain things. They say it is all wishful thinking and escapism, that such people do not face the facts of life but run away from them. One man reads a novel, these others believe the Christian message, they say, but it is all escapism.

Here we have the answer to that. Abraham faced the facts, he reminded himself of his own age, as the Apostle tells us here;

[216]

and also of Sarah's age. He looked at the facts as they were, at their very worst; and yet, though he did that, he was not at all weakened in his faith. Why? This is the important point. Abraham looked at the facts but he did not stop there. He did not just go on looking at the facts and the difficulties and the obstacles. He looked at them, but having looked at them he looked at something else, he looked at Someone else. The trouble with unbelief is that it only looks at the difficulties. We have a perfect illustration of that in the famous incident of Peter walking upon the water. As long as he looked at the Lord Jesus Christ he could walk on the waves, but when he began to look at the waves, and 'saw them boisterous', he began to sink. Because he was looking at the difficulties only, he 'considered' them in the sense that he considered them only and considered nothing else. That is unbelief. Faith does not turn its back upon problems, it surmounts them. It looks at them, straight in the face, and then rises above them.

Let me put it like this. There are some people who think that, because they are assailed by doubts, they have no faith. That is a complete fallacy. To be entirely free from doubts does not always signify faith, it may mean presumption or the kind of psychological state that the cults often produce. There is a sense in which we can define faith as that which enables a man to overcome his doubts and to answer them. Some of the greatest saints that the Church has ever known have testified to the fact that they have been attacked and assailed by doubts to the end of their lives. But they were not weakened, they did not give in; they mastered their doubts, they conquered them, they overcame them. This is a most important aspect of faith; it considers the difficulties but it overcomes them. Though it considers the difficulties it is not weakened, it still remains strong.

Let us now look at the other negative. It is that Abraham did not stagger at the promise of God through unbelief. What is the difference between this and being weak? What does the Scripture mean by this 'staggering'? We discover the answer by realizing in experience that unbelief attacks us along two lines. We have already described the way in which it says, Look at the facts, look at the difficulties, look at yourself, look at your weakness, look at your age, look at this and that. But when you overcome that it takes up the second line and says, 'But look at the greatness of the promise'. 'If it were some ordinary promise,' it says, 'indeed even if it were a remarkable promise you might believe it. But look at what God is promising you.' 'Look at it,' said the devil to Abraham, 'look at what God is actually promising you. I will accept what you have said about yourself, but look at this – that your seed is going to be like the sand on the sea-shore innumerable, like the stars in the heaven, beyond computation. The thing is impossible, it is too good to be true, it cannot be true.' The greatness of the promise has often caused us to stagger.

What is the meaning of this word 'to stagger'? It is a very interesting word. In its origin it means 'to discriminate' and 'to judge' and 'to estimate'. But then it goes beyond that; it means that a man begins to argue with himself and to be at variance with himself. There is that within him which says, 'Believe that'. 'Ah but,' says another voice, 'wait a minute.' And the argument begins and the man is at variance with himself. Faith says, 'Believe it', and then reason comes in and asks, 'Can you believe that? It is too good to be true, it is too big, it is too vast.' And there you have the man arguing with himself, at variance with himself. The result is that instead of walking he is staggering, he is going backwards and forwards, and from side to side. He is staggering. He believes and he doesn't believe. 'I believe, help Thou mine unbelief.' That is staggering. Or he is like the man that James describes, who is 'unstable in all his ways'. The man who lacks faith, says James, is like 'a wave of the sea driven with the wind and tossed'. There is no stability, he is double-minded, staggering about, wavering, hesitating. What we are told here by the Apostle about Abraham's faith is that it was so great that he did not stagger. It was not only 'not weak', he did not stagger either. He held firm, he remained erect, upright, and he went on walking steadily with a firm step. He did not stagger at the greatness of the promise.

Let us summarize the Apostle's teaching concerning Faith.

Faith – this amazing thing – enabled Abraham and all others who have it truly, to do certain things. It does so by making us strong. It prevents our being weak, it prevents our staggering. Do not forget the negatives, they are tremendously important in the daily life and walk and fight of the Christian. The devil would persuade you that, because doubts come to you, you have never had faith. The devil will see to it that doubts will come. They are what Paul calls in Ephesians 6 the 'fiery darts' that he throws at us. But if you hold up the shield of faith they will all be quenched. Do not confuse temptation with sin. Do not confuse doubts that are hurled at you by the devil with unbelief. The question is, what do you do with the doubts? They will come to you as they came to Abraham. Abraham considered the problem but, though he considered it, he was not weak, he was not weakened, and though he looked at the staggering promise he did not stagger. Thank God for these negatives.

16 Faith Glorifying God

*

Who against hope believed in hope, that he might become the father of many nations; according to that which was spoken, So shall thy seed be.

And being not weak in faith, he considered not his own body, now dead, when he was about an hundred years old, neither yet the deadness of Sarah's womb:

He staggered not at the promise of God through unbelief, but was strong in faith, giving glory to God.

And being fully persuaded that what he had promised he was able also to perform.

And therefore it was imputed to him for righteousness.

Romans 4: 18–22

So far we have been looking at what I have described as the negative work of faith. Do not despise that, but rather thank God for it. But after all it is only negative. We can now go on to consider the positive, which obviously is the most important thing of all, and which is really the thing that explains the negative. It is because of the positive that you can have the two negatives. What is the positive? It is found in the phrase, 'He was strong in faith, giving glory to God'. We must be clear about the translation here. A better translation than 'was strong in faith' is, 'was made strong'. Abraham did not give way to weakness, he did not stagger, but rather was 'made strong' – made strong, either in faith, or else made strong by faith. I believe that both are true. He was made strong in his faith, but also he was made strong by his faith. This is an interesting and indeed fascinating point. It is a kind of circle, and it is very difficult to decide which to put first. In a sense it is like the old question of the hen and the egg. Faith makes us strong, and because we are strong we have more faith.

can happen. But God is Omnipotent, nothing is too hard for the Lord. "With God nothing shall be impossible." ' The one thing that mattered with Abraham was that God had spoken, that God had made a promise; and because it was God who had spoken, and because it was God who had made the promise Abraham says, 'Nothing else need be considered at all. I am wasting my time in putting up these reasonings and impossibilities. The one thing that matters is that it is God who has spoken.' 'He gave glory to God.'

Nothing is more important for us than to bear all that in mind, and especially if we look at it in the negative way. There is nothing so insulting to God as not to believe Him. That is the terrible thing about unbelief, it is insulting to God. What a wonderful way this is of looking at faith and defining faith. Faith is that which always glorifies God. Faith is to believe God simply and solely because He is God. Nothing glorifies God more than this; nothing is so insulting to God as not to believe His word.

That is the great lesson here; and you will find that the men who have glorified God most of all in this world have been the great 'men of faith'. You will also find that no body of men, perhaps, has been called upon to endure so many trials and difficulties and temptations as these selfsame men of faith. Why? Obviously for the reason that it is in the midst of their trials and their testings and their problems that their faith has stood out most gloriously. Or to put it in other words, it is just when everything is going against them 'to drive them to despair' on the natural level, that they glorify God most of all, because in spite of all these things they still go on believing, they are unshaken, they do not stagger, they do not fall through unbelief. So the severer the test the more they give glory to God. The more difficult the situation becomes the more they go on looking to Him, and the greater is the extent to which they are giving glory to God.

This then is the summary of the teaching at this point, that faith is ultimately that which gives glory to God by seeing the truth about Him and trusting to Him utterly and absolutely at all costs. That is faith. And that, according to the Apostle, is faith in its very essence. That was the faith of Abraham. That is the thing Paul is concerned about. He picks that out and uses it as an illustration, because in this one man and what he did we see perfectly delineated the main elements and characteristics of faith.

At this point, it seems to me that it is good for us to consider certain difficulties or problems. Were I to leave the matter without further enlargement I am certain that a number of people would not only be somewhat confused, but might even be discouraged. I must therefore make it clear that our passage obviously teaches that there are degrees of faith. The very terms used themselves suggest that. The term 'strong' and the term 'weak' are indicative of the fact that there are degrees of faith, or, if you like, degrees in faith. The Scriptures put before us these big, outstanding examples of faith. That is the method which is characteristic of Scriptural teaching. Almost invariably it picks out the striking and notable illustrations, as Paul does here in the case of Abraham. No man has glorified God more than Abraham, and that is why he is picked out here by the Apostle.

The biblical method is to put before us faith as it really is in its essence, as it always ought to be. The Scripture does that, not only with faith, but with many other aspects of the Christian life. Let me give a negative example of this. Take the case of Ananias and Sapphira. These two people were struck dead because they had lied to the Holy Ghost. But it does not follow from that that everybody who lies to the Holy Ghost is immediately going to be struck dead. That does not happen. But the case of Ananias and Sapphira is put before us that we may see the thing in its essence, and that we may learn our lesson, and be warned. The Flood is another example of the same thing. Again, those 'cities of the plain' lived as they did, giving no heed to the warnings of Lot, and the result was the destruction of Sodom and Gomorrah. These are outstanding illustrations to teach the principle of a final judgment to come.

I suggest that it is exactly the same here with regard to faith. Abraham's case shows faith at its best, faith as it ought to be. The Apostle says it was 'strong faith', or that 'he was strong in

The statement is that he 'was made strong in his faith'. What was the secret of Abraham's strength? According to the Apostle, it was that he gave glory to God. That is the answer, that is the secret of a strong faith. Indeed I will go further and say that that is of the very essence of faith. Faith, ultimately, is that which gives glory to God. In other words, as we give glory to God we shall be made strong ourselves, and our faith will be strong. And that undoubtedly – as the Apostle shows us here clearly, and the author of the Epistle to the Hebrews does in very much the same way in the eleventh chapter – that was undoubtedly the whole secret of Abraham and his remarkable faith. Abraham, instead of looking only at the difficulties in terms of his own body and the age of Sarah, instead of staggering at the greatness of the promise, Abraham, instead of stumbling at those two things, looked to God and looked at God. That is the real secret of faith. The main explanation of the troubles and difficulties which most of us experience in our lives is that, instead of keeping our eyes steadfastly on God, we look at ourselves and our weaknesses and the staggering greatness of the life to which we have been called. We look at these things and we become weak and begin to stagger. Abraham did not stagger for the reason that he gave glory to God. He kept his eyes on God, and he looked to God.

But we must analyse this a little further. What does it mean exactly to say that he gave glory to God? It means that Abraham considered God, he considered who God is and what God is. That is how he gave glory to God. It does not mean primarily anything that Abraham said or anything that Abraham did. That followed. Abraham glorified God by just realizing who and what God is. In other words, he contemplated and meditated upon all the glorious attributes of God. That is how one glorifies God. We glorify God by realizing something of the truth about Him, and worshipping Him because of that, and committing ourselves to Him in the light of that.

Abraham considered the Eternity of God – that God is. Though God had not yet defined it fully at this point as He did later to Moses, Abraham knew something about the fact that God is Jehovah, I Am that I Am, the self-existent and eternal God.

He meditated on that and he considered it, and dwelt upon it. He also thought about and reminded himself of the majesty of God. There is nothing that is so glorious about the being of God as his majesty. Read the Scriptures and you will find that these men of God, these great men of faith, are constantly celebrating this – the majesty of God and the glory of God. In many ways the glory of God is the ultimate attribute of God. God is full of glory, ineffable glory, beyond our comprehension, beyond our imagination. He dwells in a light that is unapproachable, 'pavilioned in splendour and girded with praise'.

> *Immortal, invisible, God only wise,*
> *In light inaccessible hid from our eyes,*
> *Most blessed, most glorious, the Ancient of Days,*
> *Almighty, Victorious, Thy great Name we praise.*

Abraham thought of all this. Then he reminded himself of another attribute of God – His Omnipresence. God is everywhere, there is no place in the whole cosmos where God is not. Think of the many places in the Scripture where that is celebrated. Look at it in Psalm 139: 'If I ascend up into heaven, thou art there: if I make my bed in hell, behold, thou art there.' 'Whither shall I go from thy spirit? or whither shall I flee from thy presence?' It is impossible. God is everywhere, filling the whole universe. Abraham thought about that and meditated on that. Then the Omniscience of God. God knows everything. There is nothing that God does not know. He knows the end from the beginning. All things are always present before His sight and His scan. He knows all, and nothing can happen anywhere, or ever has happened, but that God not only knows it, but has known it beforehand. His Omniscience! His foreknowledge! His complete knowledge without gap or blemish or any defect whatsoever! Everything is known to Him.

Then His Omnipotence. There is no limit to His power – none whatsoever. Indeed, you remember, it is in connection with Abraham that the statement is made, the question is put, 'Is anything too hard for the Lord?' Is there anything that God cannot do? And the answer is, 'Nothing'. 'With God nothing shall be impossible.' 'With God all things are possible.' There is nothing that God cannot do, there is nothing that can withstand Him. His power is absolute, it is eternal, it is all-mighty. There is in no sense any limit whatsoever to it. Abraham thought about that.

Then he thought of His righteousness, His justice, His truth, His holiness, His unchangeability, His everlasting and eternal consistency. Those are the chief attributes of the being and the character of God. What the Apostle is saying here is that what Abraham did was to look at God, and he looked at these attributes of God, and he went on looking at them. That is how he gave glory to God.

Then, having looked at them, he deduced certain things from them. It is not difficult to follow him in imagination as he did so. We can hear him saying to himself, 'Well, God has made this extraordinary statement to me, God has made this amazing promise, that I, at this age, nearly a hundred, and Sarah in her condition, are going to bear a child who is going to be my heir, who is going to be my seed, and out of whom, and through whom all the nations of the earth are going to be blessed. God has said that. It is amazing, it is astounding. Yes, but having looked at God and His eternal attributes and characteristics, and having contemplated them and having worshipped, I am able to deduce this, that because God is who and what He is, He never makes a promise lightly or loosely, still less thoughtlessly.'

That is a tremendous thing. We all make promises but, alas, we do not always keep them. The reason is that we make them without thinking out fully what we are saying. We are in a happy mood so we promise to do this or that. We had not thought it out, we had not considered the possibilities, the difficulties, the repercussions of what might happen. We make our promises lightly and thoughtlessly, and then we do not keep them, and there is trouble. But that is never true of God. Because God is who and what He is, He never makes a promise without seeing all from beginning to end, every factor and conceivable circumstance and situation. He knows exactly what He is doing; He never promises lightly or loosely, or thoughtlessly.

Secondly, Abraham knew that God does not change His mind. And this, because He is God, because He is what and who He is. God, we are told, is 'the Father of lights with whom there is no variableness, neither shadow of turning' [*James* 1: 17] – always everlastingly the same. What God has promised therefore, He will most surely perform. The best statement of this in the Scripture, surely, is in Paul's Epistle to Titus. In the second verse of the first chapter he speaks of 'God who cannot lie'. God who cannot lie, never contradicts Himself, never goes back from what He has said, never changes His mind! His eternal righteousness and uprightness and truthfulness make that impossible. Abraham deduced that. 'The promise', he must have reasoned with himself, 'is sure because God knows what He is doing, and more than that, God will never go back on it. God does not change His mind, He does not change His point of view or His purpose.' And, over and above all this, are God's ability and eternal power which enable Him to carry out all that He has purposed – 'And being fully persuaded that what God had promised He was able also to perform.' Or as Toplady put it:

> *The work which His goodness began,*
> *The arm of His strength will complete;*
> *His promise is Yea and Amen,*
> *And never was forfeited yet.*

There, I imagine, are the three main deductions; and being clear about them, Abraham was in a position to say to himself that because these things were true nothing else mattered at all. Yes, he did consider his own body, and he considered the deadness of Sarah's womb. He knew that what was promised was contrary to nature, and that from the human standpoint the thing was a sheer impossibility; but the moment those thoughts came to him he answered them by saying, 'I am aware of all that and know that it is true; but God knew all that before He made the promise. God was aware that I am nearly a hundred, God knows all about Sarah and her age and condition. There is no point in looking at these things. God knows all about them, yet in the full light of that knowledge He has said this. I cannot see how it can happen. But God is Omnipotent, nothing is too hard for the Lord. "With God nothing shall be impossible." ' The one thing that mattered with Abraham was that God had spoken, that God had made a promise; and because it was God who had spoken, and because it was God who had made the promise Abraham says, 'Nothing else need be considered at all. I am wasting my time in putting up these reasonings and impossibilities. The one thing that matters is that it is God who has spoken.' 'He gave glory to God.'

Nothing is more important for us than to bear all that in mind, and especially if we look at it in the negative way. There is nothing so insulting to God as not to believe Him. That is the terrible thing about unbelief, it is insulting to God. What a wonderful way this is of looking at faith and defining faith. Faith is that which always glorifies God. Faith is to believe God simply and solely because He is God. Nothing glorifies God more than this; nothing is so insulting to God as not to believe His word.

That is the great lesson here; and you will find that the men who have glorified God most of all in this world have been the great 'men of faith'. You will also find that no body of men, perhaps, has been called upon to endure so many trials and difficulties and temptations as these selfsame men of faith. Why? Obviously for the reason that it is in the midst of their trials and their testings and their problems that their faith has stood out most gloriously. Or to put it in other words, it is just when everything is going against them 'to drive them to despair' on the natural level, that they glorify God most of all, because in spite of all these things they still go on believing, they are unshaken, they do not stagger, they do not fall through unbelief. So the severer the test the more they give glory to God. The more difficult the situation becomes the more they go on looking to Him, and the greater is the extent to which they are giving glory to God.

This then is the summary of the teaching at this point, that faith is ultimately that which gives glory to God by seeing the truth about Him and trusting to Him utterly and absolutely at all costs. That is faith. And that, according to the Apostle, is faith in its very essence. That was the faith of Abraham. That is the thing Paul is concerned about. He picks that out and uses it as an illustration, because in this one man and what he did we see perfectly delineated the main elements and characteristics of faith.

At this point, it seems to me that it is good for us to consider certain difficulties or problems. Were I to leave the matter without further enlargement I am certain that a number of people would not only be somewhat confused, but might even be discouraged. I must therefore make it clear that our passage obviously teaches that there are degrees of faith. The very terms used themselves suggest that. The term 'strong' and the term 'weak' are indicative of the fact that there are degrees of faith, or, if you like, degrees in faith. The Scriptures put before us these big, outstanding examples of faith. That is the method which is characteristic of Scriptural teaching. Almost invariably it picks out the striking and notable illustrations, as Paul does here in the case of Abraham. No man has glorified God more than Abraham, and that is why he is picked out here by the Apostle.

The biblical method is to put before us faith as it really is in its essence, as it always ought to be. The Scripture does that, not only with faith, but with many other aspects of the Christian life. Let me give a negative example of this. Take the case of Ananias and Sapphira. These two people were struck dead because they had lied to the Holy Ghost. But it does not follow from that that everybody who lies to the Holy Ghost is immediately going to be struck dead. That does not happen. But the case of Ananias and Sapphira is put before us that we may see the thing in its essence, and that we may learn our lesson, and be warned. The Flood is another example of the same thing. Again, those 'cities of the plain' lived as they did, giving no heed to the warnings of Lot, and the result was the destruction of Sodom and Gomorrah. These are outstanding illustrations to teach the principle of a final judgment to come.

I suggest that it is exactly the same here with regard to faith. Abraham's case shows faith at its best, faith as it ought to be. The Apostle says it was 'strong faith', or that 'he was strong in

[226]

faith'. But that leads us to see that there are degrees of faith or variations in faith. Let me adduce some other Scriptural quotations to establish the point I am making. You remember what our Lord said to Peter on that famous occasion when the walking on the water took place. What our Lord said to him was, 'O thou of little faith'. He did not say that Peter had no faith at all; He charges him with 'little faith'. But 'little faith' suggests that there is the possibility of 'more faith', and still more, and an abundance of faith. Or take another example. You remember how the disciples were in the boat with our Lord. He was tired and went to the stern of the vessel and fell asleep. Suddenly a storm arose and the water began to come into the boat and they thought they were going to drown. The terrified disciples awoke Him and said, 'Master, carest thou not that we perish?' And our Lord, rebuking them, said, 'Where is your faith?' Again there is a suggestion of a limitation. You get the same idea in the case of the devil-possessed boy at the foot of the Mount of Transfiguration, when the distracted father cried out, 'Lord, I believe, help thou mine unbelief'. He had faith, he had belief, and yet he is aware of its weakness. He asks for help and strength.

In addition to these practical examples there is explicit teaching by our Lord. Take, for instance, Matthew 17: 20; 'If you have faith like a grain of mustard seed, you shall say unto this mountain, Remove hence into yonder place, and it shall remove, and nothing shall be impossible unto you.' If you have 'faith like a grain of mustard seed'. It is the smallest of all seeds. You can have that amount of faith, and you can have more – again the suggestion of degrees of faith. Or take the case of the Syro-Phoenician woman who persisted in holding on, though our Lord was, as it were, discouraging her, and trying and testing her. In the end our Lord turned to her and said, 'Woman, great is thy faith'. Take one other case, that of the centurion who sent the message to our Lord about his servant who was sick, and said that our Lord need not come to his house but had only to 'speak the word'. And our Lord said, 'I have not found so great faith, no, not in Israel'. Great faith, strong faith! Then there is the phrase in Hebrews 10: 22, 'Let us draw near with a true heart in full assurance of faith.' You can go to God in faith but it is not of necessity 'full assurance of faith'. You can have just enough faith to take you to God at all; but how different is that from a full assurance of faith, and a 'holy boldness'.

It is important that we should recognize these distinctions which are drawn in the Scriptures themselves. I can put this in the form of a number of principles. First, there is such a thing as weak faith. But, secondly, let us remember that a weak faith is, nevertheless, faith. It is very difficult to know how to put this; but the very fact that you say it is a weak faith is a statement to the effect that it is, after all, faith. 'But', you say, 'if a man has any faith at all in God it must be an absolute faith.' That is true, in the sense that a young sapling has the essence of the oak-tree in it but is certainly not as strong. So our faith may be weak, and yet be a real faith. You cannot call it anything else. It is not unbelief. If it is only like the glimmer of a taper's light, it is light; so it is faith though it may be a very weak faith. It is, if you like, the difference between a child and a grown man. You cannot say that a child, a babe, has no strength at all. He has a certain amount of strength, but his strength is very small when you compare it with the strength of a man, or when you compare it with the strength of an athlete, or that of a man who has taken some special exercises. Though the child does not seem to have any strength at all when you contrast it with this great man and his powerful muscles, nevertheless you must grant that the child has strength – he is able to move his limbs, he is able to do certain things. He has a strength though it is not very much strength.

The third principle is that there are two factors, two main factors certainly, which determine the strength of our faith. The first is our knowledge of God. That is the most important factor in faith always – our knowledge of God. It was Abraham's knowledge of God that made him the man he was, it was also the thing that made his faith great.

The second element is our application of what we know. That is most important also. 'If ye know these things,' said our Lord, 'happy are ye if ye do them.' That can be applied to faith. A mere theoretical knowledge that never ventures out upon what it knows and believes will never be a strong faith. So that in addition to our knowledge there must be the application of the knowledge. The disciples in the boat during the storm were failing to apply their faith and that is why our Lord put His question to them in that particular form. He said, 'Where is your faith?' You have faith, but where is it? Why do you not apply it to this situation. What have you been doing with your faith? Have you left it at home? Why isn't it here? Why isn't it being applied at this point? You have faith, but why are you not applying it to this very situation in which you find yourselves? The trouble with the disciples was that they did not use the faith they had; they did not think. They were looking at the waves and the water coming into the boat. They were baling it out, but still more was coming in, and they said, 'We are undone, we are going to drown; let us see if He can save us'. He says, 'Where is your faith'? In addition to our knowledge of God there is this vital and important element of the application of what we know.

There is one other aspect of this matter which I must mention, because of the difficulties which it causes to so many, and that is the difference between faith and foolhardiness. There are many who are very unhappy concerning this question of faith because of their failure to draw that distinction. We can perhaps illustrate what we mean by dealing with the particular question of 'faith-healing'. There are two passages of the Scripture concerning this matter which cause a great deal of confusion and a great deal of unhappiness. The first is the well-known statement in James, chapter 5, verses 13 and following: 'Is any among you afflicted? Let him pray. Is any merry? Let him sing psalms. Is any sick among you? Let him call for the elders of the Church and let them pray over him, anointing him with oil in the Name of the Lord: And the prayer of faith shall save the sick, and the Lord shall raise him up; and if he have committed sins they shall be forgiven him.' The other statement is in the Gospel according to Mark, chapter 11, verses 20–24. It is in connection with the incident of the cursing of the barren fig tree. 'Peter calling to remembrance saith unto him, Master, behold, the fig tree which thou cursedst is withered away. And Jesus answering saith unto him, Have faith in God. For verily I say unto you, that whosoever shall say unto this mountain, Be thou removed, and be thou cast into the sea, and shall not doubt in his heart, but shall believe that those things which he saith shall come to pass, he shall have whatsoever he saith. Therefore I say unto you, What things soever ye desire, when ye pray, believe that ye receive them, and ye shall have them.'

There are many people who are in great trouble because of these two passages. Their story generally is that either they themselves were taken ill, or some loved one, and they went to these two passages and, believing them, they put them into operation. They prayed this 'prayer of faith' and they really believed that 'what things soever ye desire, when ye pray, believe that ye receive them, and ye shall have them'. They not only prayed to God for healing, but in accordance with the teaching they had received they even went so far as to thank God for having done it already. That is their understanding of these statements of Scripture. You believe that you have had what you asked for, you say that it must have happened already, therefore you no longer ask; you thank God that He has already done it. But unfortunately the healing does not take place, and they are greatly perplexed. The most notable example of this that I have ever encountered, either in personal experience or in my reading, is a case found in the *Life of Andrew Murray* of South Africa. He held the view that Christians should never resort to doctors or to means. He taught that for years, and for years had practised it. There came a time when he was going out on a preaching tour. He had a nephew who was most anxious to go with him, but the poor fellow suffered from tuberculosis of the lungs. Clearly he was not in a fit condition to go. So they talked about this and Andrew Murray said to him, 'You believe that God can heal you, do you not?' The nephew said, 'Yes.' 'Well,' said Andrew Murray, 'let us go to God in faith believing.' So they quoted these passages, and they prayed to God for healing and ended by thanking God for the healing which they knew had already taken place. They 'took it by faith'. That was how they interpreted these verses. So they went off on their tour, confident and assured that the young man was totally healed and that all would be well. But in three weeks he was dead.

There are many such illustrations and examples. We are not at the moment discussing faith-healing as such. The same is true with respect to many other matters – praying for fine weather, or praying for some post, or praying for something to happen in your own life or experience, praying that some success may come to your children. People are constantly in trouble about these things. I suggest that there are two main causes. The first is – and this comes out clearly in the faith of Abraham – that they misunderstand what God's Word promises. Now Abraham, on the contrary, was perfectly clear about that. Abraham knew that God had spoken, that God had made that particular specific promise. There was no question about it and Abraham believed it. But with regard to these friends there is confusion in their minds as to what God has said. There are some who teach that it is never God's will that any one of His children should be ill. But that is unscriptural. And if they believe that and act upon it they are bound to get into trouble. If it is never God's will that any of His children should be ill, then it must be God's will always that we be healed and that we be well. They act on that, and pray on the strength of that belief, so when healing does not take place they are in trouble. They are in trouble because their theology is wrong.

God has not promised that His people are always to be well. There is teaching in the Scripture quite plainly that God may use an illness to chastise us and to punish us for the good of our souls. 'Many are weak and sickly among you', said the Apostle Paul to the Corinthians, because of their sinful life [1 *Corinthians* 11: 30]. God chastises sometimes through illness. That does not mean that every illness is chastisement. But it may be so. I am simply countering the argument which says that it is never God's will that His children be ill, and that it is always His will that they be well. I say that that is unscriptural, and consequently people who hold that view are sure to get into trouble when they try to exercise faith in that way.

Some again are guilty of misunderstanding the character of

faith. They seem to regard faith as something that you and I can 'go in for', to use the common phrase. In other words, you read a book on these matters, or you hear an address or a sermon, and you say, 'Ah, I am going in for that, I would like to do that.' But you cannot do that with faith. You cannot decide to 'go in' for faith. You can 'go in' for cults, and people do go in for cults; but you cannot do that with faith, for the reason that faith is what it is. It is very dangerous to think that you can 'go in' for faith. 'Isn't this marvellous!' says someone. 'Look at these people, listen to this man's story: "a thousand miles of miracles",' or something equally wonderful. So they decide to go in for it. But it does not seem to work in their case. Why not? Because they have misunderstood the meaning of faith. You cannot take up faith as you like and when you choose. You cannot take up faith, as it were, in cold blood, and decide that you are going to be 'a man of faith.'

Still less is it true to say of faith – 'Faith? Why, there is no difficulty about faith. We all have faith. When you sit down on a chair you are exercising faith that the chair is going to hold you. When you go for a ride in a train or in a bus you are exercising faith.' The argument is that we all have faith, and that all we need to do is to exercise that faith that is innate in human nature, in the matter of believing God. But that is what I call applying 'the law of mathematical probability'. When I sit on a chair I do so because I am acting on the principle that the chances are that it is not going to break down at the moment. It may at some other moment. That is the law of mathematical probability. When I go in a train or ride in a bus I am doing exactly the same thing. I am not exercising faith in the bus or in the bus driver. I am simply resting in the knowledge – and generally unconsciously – that nine hundred and ninety-nine times out of a thousand, probably much more than that, it is going to be safe enough. That is not faith. That is natural; and faith is not natural. Faith is spiritual, it is the gift of God. It is only Christian people who have faith. You cannot have faith and not be a Christian. It is impossible. Faith is not something natural in man.

Another negative way of putting it is to say that faith is not just persuading ourselves after the manner of Couéism and auto-suggestion, or arguing desperately that we really do believe. Saying, 'I believe this, I am going to believe this', is not faith. Look again at Mark 11: 22–24. This is the statement that is so much misinterpreted. 'Therefore I say unto you, what things soever ye desire, when ye pray, believe that ye have received them, and ye shall have them.' A common interpretation of these words is something like this. I want something and I begin to pray for it. I persuade myself that I do really believe that I shall receive it, that I must believe so. Many go so far as to say that having made your request known to God, you should then stop asking, believe that you have had it, and thank God for it. They say that it must happen. But it does not happen always. Why not? Because in many cases the poor soul did not truly believe that he would receive it, but was trying to persuade himself that he would receive it. What a different thing that is! 'Believe', in our Lord's statement, means certainty and assurance and the confidence that results from that. And we cannot command that at will.

What does this amount to positively? We can put it like this. Faith is something that is inwrought, it is something that is given. I believe that as God spoke to Abraham He was giving him the faith to believe the promise. It was nothing natural in Abraham that responded to God. Faith is given, faith is inwrought in us, and therefore it is something which always leads to quiet confidence in God and a quiet resting upon God. There is no strain, there is no tension where there is faith. Faith, as we have seen previously, always has this element of assurance and of confidence in it. 'Being fully persuaded' in his own mind, we are told. That is the thing that characterized Abraham. Abraham was certain, he was sure. This element is always present in faith. If there is strain or tension, or if you are just trying, or having to keep yourself to it and trying to persuade yourself, you can be quite sure that it is not faith. Faith is the substance of things hoped for, the evidence of things not seen. The great characteristic of these wonderful heroes of the faith was that they had that certainty. There was this profound assurance based upon their deep knowledge of God.

In other words, and to give a positive interpretation of that passage in Mark 11 which begins with the statement, 'Have faith in God', there is no question but that Hudson Taylor's translation of it is the right one, and the true one. Hudson Taylor used to say that you should translate it, not as 'Have faith in God', but 'Hold on to the faithfulness of God'. The reference is to God. Faith is holding on to the faithfulness of God, and as long as you do that you cannot go wrong. Faith does not look at the difficulties. Faith does not even look at itself. I go further. Faith is never interested in itself and never talks about itself. That to me is a very good test. I always distrust people who talk about their faith. That is the characteristic of the cults. They always direct attention to themselves and to what they are doing or have done. You have to be 'thinking positively', or you have to be doing this, that or the other. The emphasis is always upon self. But faith does not look at itself or at the person who is exercising it. Faith looks at God, holds on to the faithfulness of God. The big thing about faith is not what I am doing, but God's faithfulness. Abraham 'gave glory to God'. Faith is interested in God only, and it talks about God and it praises God and it extols the virtues of God. The measure of the strength of a man's faith, always, is ultimately the measure of his knowledge of God. There is no more important principle and vital principle than that.

Faith always glorifies God. There is none of the excitement that is ever present in the cults, and in other teachings that are not always known as cults, but which really belong to them. There is nothing hectic about faith, nothing excitable. The great characteristic of Abraham, that man of God, that great gentleman, that man who went on quietly whatever was happening, was that he was 'a friend of God'. He knew God so well that he became more and more like God. There was something of the mark of eternity upon him. When a man is a friend of God, he is a man of great faith, strong faith; he is not weak and he does not stagger. It is nothing in the man himself; it is his knowledge of God and of the attributes of God. He knows God so well that he can rest on that knowledge. And it is the prayers of such a man that are answered.

It is clearly therefore not something that you can take up. If you want to be a man of faith, if you want to be a man of strong faith, you must realize that it will always be the result of your becoming a certain type of person. You cannot have strong faith without holiness and without obedience to God. If you are anxious to know how to have a strong faith, here is the method. It means thorough and deep knowledge of the Bible and of God through it; not suddenly taking up an idea and deciding to 'go in' for faith. If you want to have strong faith, read your Bible; go through it from beginning to end. Concentrate on the revelation that God has given of Himself and of His character. Keep your eye especially also on prophecy, and then watch His promises being fulfilled. That is the way to develop strong faith – be grounded in all this. Then read the historical portions of the Bible, and the stories of the great heroes. That is why the author of the Epistle to the Hebrews gives that gallery of portraits of these great saints in his eleventh chapter. He says, Look at these men, who were men like yourselves. What was their secret? It was that they knew God, they gave glory to God and relied utterly upon Him and His Word. Turn that over in your mind, keep on speaking to yourself about it; meditate upon it. That is the way to develop strong faith. It is generally a process, and it normally takes time, unless you have been given it suddenly for some specific purpose by God. Above all, it means a knowledge of God personally; praying, spending time in His presence, waiting upon Him.

Then, finally, you apply all that in practice to particular cases as they arise in your own life and experience. 'He staggered not, but gave glory to God.' That is the secret of faith. It is our ignorance of God that constitutes our main trouble. So do not think too much about your little faith; think more about God. Get to know God, realize the truth about Him, and as you do so you will find, to your surprise perhaps, that your faith is becoming strong, and you will be amazed at yourself. May God enable us all to do so by His grace!

17 Raised for our Justification

*

> *Now it was not written for his sake alone that it was imputed to him;*
> *but for us also, to whom it shall be imputed, if we believe on him that raised up Jesus our Lord from the dead;*
> *who was delivered for our offences, and was raised again for our justification.*
>
> Romans 4: 23–25

Having worked through the Apostle's great and masterly analysis of faith we must now remind ourselves that the Apostle was not only interested in describing and defining faith in and of itself. What he is particularly concerned about is 'justification' by faith. He has taken up the illustration of Abraham's faith, not only to illustrate that faith in and of itself, but particularly to show us that Abraham was justified by faith, and that 'his faith was counted or reckoned unto him for righteousness'. That is how he puts it in the twenty-second verse. Abraham is the first person in whose case this great doctrine of justification by faith is declared and emphasized in an explicit manner; and we have already seen in the earlier parts of the chapter the importance of realizing that.

Having dealt with that, the Apostle goes on in verses 23 to 25 to say one of the most important things that any human being can ever consider. Martin Luther says of these verses something like this: 'In these verses the whole of Christianity is comprehended'; and he is undoubtedly right. This is one of Paul's tremendous statements about justification. Of course, it is not the only one; we have already found others in earlier parts of the Epistle. Here, he is winding up his mighty argument about justification by faith, and he puts it in this glowing climax:

[236]

'Now', he says, 'it was not written for his sake alone that it was imputed to him; but for us also, to whom it shall be imputed if we believe on Him that raised up Jesus our Lord from the dead.' He is saying in effect: I am quoting this faith of Abraham not only to emphasize Abraham's faith, and not only even to emphasize the fact that Abraham was justified by faith; I am doing that, but my real purpose is not simply to say things about Abraham. The case of Abraham is the case of everybody who is in Christ. The case of Abraham is just the most outstanding and dramatic example and illustration of God's method of righteousness, of God's way of salvation, of God's whole process of justification by faith.

The statement about Abraham, therefore, must not be confined to Abraham. What was true of Abraham is true of every man who has ever been, or ever will be, reconciled to God. This is God's only way of justifying man, this is God's way of reconciling men unto Himself. There is no other. So he tells us not to look at Abraham and regard his case as something exceptional or strange or odd. 'It was not written for his sake alone' but for us also, for everybody who believes in the same way as Abraham believed. If we believe as Abraham believed, we shall be justified as Abraham was justified. Having given us a piece of history, Paul returns to that great theme and makes one of these profound statements with regard to the whole method of justification by faith only.

What is this faith that justifies? That is the question. Or if you prefer it in a different form, How can a man be just with God? That was Job's ancient question [9: 2]. It is the greatest question a man can ever face – How can a man be right with God? How can a man know that his sins are forgiven? How can one approach God in prayer with confidence? How can one face death without fear? How can one think of the judgement without despair and alarm? These are the questions that are comprehended in this one great question, How can a man be just with God? This is, as Luther constantly emphasized, the crucial question. This really is the essence of Christianity, so that it is not surprising that Luther speaks as he does. It was his re-discovery of this truth that led to the Protestant Reformation. This is essential Protestantism, as it is Evangelical Christianity in its very essence. These verses are obviously of supreme importance.

What is this faith that justifies? Here are the Apostle's answers. First, it is a faith that believes in God and glorifies God. Notice how he repeats that. He says, 'It is written for us also, to whom it shall be imputed if we believe on him that raised up Jesus our Lord from the dead.' This faith of which he is speaking is a faith in God, and it is always a faith that glorifies God. It is a faith that believes His Word. It is a faith which is concerned above all else to please God and to glorify His great and holy Name.

I sometimes have a fear that there is much today that passes as faith which never mentions the Name of God at all. I am thinking of those who only speak about the Lord Jesus Christ. They always pray to the Lord Jesus Christ, and always speak about Him, and never refer to God the Father. Yet you notice that in the Apostle's great definition of this faith that justifies he puts it in terms of believing on God. These things are subtle, and the devil is not troubled at all as to what we believe as long as he can confuse us. So it comes to pass that some people put the whole of their emphasis on God and do not see the need of the Lord Jesus Christ at all, while others are led to put the whole of their emphasis upon the Lord Jesus Christ to the exclusion of the Father. It is tragic to observe the constant tendency to do violence to the great doctrine of the Trinity. In the same way the Holy Spirit is either neglected, or, at the other extreme, the whole emphasis is put upon Him. Thus we tend to go astray. We must always keep these things in the order in which they are found in the Scriptures. There everything starts with God, everything must end with God. All the work of the Lord Jesus Christ is designed to bring us to God, to reconcile us to God. It is God who sent Him to do that work, therefore it must all centre ultimately upon God Himself. This is the starting point of true faith. This is the starting point of all Christianity. It does not start with me and my subjective states and feelings, or with anything that may happen to me, primarily; it does not start even with the Son of God Himself, nor the Holy Spirit, but always with God the

Father. 'Believe on him that raised up Jesus our Lord from the dead.'

That is the starting point. But the Apostle proceeds in the second place to define the matter yet more closely; this faith believes in God particularly in terms of the resurrection of the Lord Jesus Christ. He narrows it down to that because he is really concerned here about the way in which a man is reconciled to God. 'It shall be reckoned to us also if we believe on Him that raised up Jesus our Lord from the dead.' Faith is a belief in God, but not only a belief in God in general. There are people who believe in God in general, but that does not make them Christians. An orthodox Jew, or a Mohammedan, is not a Christian for that very reason. The Christian's faith, justifying faith, is a faith that believes in God in a particular manner, in terms of the fact that He raised up the Lord Jesus Christ from the dead.

What the Apostle means by that is that God has said something special and peculiar in the resurrection. We remember that Abraham was justified in this way, that God made a particular statement to him. Abraham had already believed in God in general, but there came a day when God said something special and peculiar to Abraham; and Abraham believed that. That is the thing that justified him. It was that that was 'reckoned to him for righteousness'. In exactly the same way, argues the Apostle, God has said something peculiar and special in raising His Son, the Lord Jesus Christ, from the dead; and justifying faith is faith that believes that. So it is not a mere general belief in God; it is this peculiar belief in the word of God that comes to us through the resurrection.

The obvious implication of this is the all-importance of believing in the fact of the resurrection. Is it not extraordinary how anyone can ever wander away from that? There are those who teach, and claim to be teachers of Christian doctrine, who do not believe in the literal physical resurrection of the Lord Jesus Christ from the dead. But according to the Apostle here, and not only here, you cannot have true Christian faith unless you believe in the fact of the literal physical resurrection of the Lord Jesus Christ from the dead. This faith is a faith 'in Him that raised up

Jesus our Lord from the dead'. It is not a faith which merely believes that Jesus, who was crucified and died and was buried, is still existing in the spiritual realm. That is not what Paul is saying. He is not teaching merely the persistence of the life of our Lord beyond the veil. No, it is more particular, it is a faith based on the fact of the literal bodily resurrection of our Lord. You remember how in the great fifteenth chapter of the First Epistle to the Corinthians the Apostle argues this out at great length. 'If there be no resurrection of the dead, then is Christ not risen. And if Christ be not risen, then is our preaching vain, and your faith is also vain.' Also, 'ye are yet in your sins'. That is what he is saying here. The fact of the resurrection is basic and central and vital to Christianity. It is not a matter about which there can be any discussion. It is crucial; there would never have been a Christian faith or a Christian Church without it. The Apostle puts it here at the very centre. In the tenth chapter of this Epistle we shall find him saying the same thing yet again, 'If thou shalt confess with thy mouth the Lord Jesus, and shalt believe in thine heart that God hath raised Him from the dead thou shalt be saved'. We see then that this man, this Christian, this justified person, this man to whom righteousness is imputed, is a man who believes in God. He also believes, particularly, in what God has said to him in the resurrection of Jesus Christ.

That brings us to the third point: What does he believe that God has said in the resurrection of Jesus Christ? This is a crucial question. The Apostle answers the question saying, 'Christ was delivered for our offences and was raised again for our justification'. Let us analyse this. What does God say in raising the Lord Jesus from the dead? The first thing he says is that Jesus is the Lord. You notice the terms: 'If we believe on Him that raised up Jesus our Lord' – not 'our Saviour', but 'our Lord' – 'Jesus our Lord'. He is asserting that the resurrection is a proclamation of the fact that Jesus is the Lord! In other words, when God raised Him from the dead He was making a proclamation, and the proclamation was, 'This is My only begotten Son'. The Apostle has already said this, of course, but he repeats it. These things must be repeated because we are all so liable to go astray.

We think we know a thing, the next moment we deny it. The Apostle said all this in the third and fourth verses of the first chapter in introducing his Gospel, saying, 'Concerning his Son Jesus Christ our Lord, which was made of the seed of David according to the flesh; and declared to be the Son of God with power, according to the spirit of holiness, by the resurrection from the dead.' Here, he is just saying it all over again. And we must be clear about this. It is the resurrection that finally establishes the fact that Jesus is God, that Jesus is the Son of God, the Eternal Son of God. It is the final proof of the doctrine of the Person of Christ, the two natures in the One Person. That is the first great thing God says in the resurrection.

Who is a Christian? What is true of the man who is reconciled to God and justified by faith? He is at any rate a man who believes that Jesus of Nazareth is the Son of God. He believes it partly in the light of the resurrection. He is clear about this, and must be. You cannot be a Christian unless you are clear about the Person of our Lord, and believe that He is the Lord of Glory, the Eternal Son of God, one in substance with the Father. This involves the whole marvel and mystery of the incarnation.

The Apostle then goes on to two other things. The next is that this selfsame Jesus was 'delivered for our offences'. What a statement! We must examine it carefully and in detail. You notice that he does not merely say that 'Jesus died'. It is a fact that Jesus died, but that is not the way in which the Christian puts what he believes. The vital question is, What is your view of that death? It is regrettable that the Revised Standard Version translates it, 'was put to death' – 'Who was put to death for our trespasses.' But Paul did not write that He was put to death for our offences or trespasses. That is quite true, but the Apostle says more than that. The translation 'delivered' is right. He was 'delivered up for our offences'. It is the same word that we shall find later in the eighth chapter in verse 32: 'He that spared not His own Son but delivered Him up for us all.' Now the Revised Standard Version does not say 'put to death for us all' there; it says, 'but gave Him up for us all'; it is therefore inconsistent with itself. Why take anything from this great word 'delivered'? I am afraid that it is, once more, because of what it means – that He the Son of God really was delivered up to death. By whom? That verse in the eighth chapter tells us, 'He (God) that spared not His own Son but delivered Him up for us all' – it was God the Father Who delivered Him up. And that is what the Apostle is saying here in the fourth chapter, 'Christ was delivered up for our offences', and it was God the Father who delivered Him up for our offences. Let us note this. It is not merely that the Lord Jesus Christ died but that He was given over to death, He was handed over to death.

The next word is the word 'for' – 'delivered for our offences'. It means 'on account of' our offences. 'For' is a very strong word, a most important word in this whole matter of the atonement. It was on account of our offences that God delivered up His only begotten Son to death.

Then comes the word 'offences'. It means transgressions, violations of law, deliberate rebellion and disobedience, trespass, transgression. The Apostle is narrowing down his definition. We begin with belief in God, but we particularly believe in what God is declaring and is doing in the resurrection. And what He is doing there is to say that Jesus of Nazareth is His only begotten Son. He is raising Him from the dead and proclaiming Him to be His Son. But that immediately raises this question: If Jesus is the Son of God, why did He ever die? Why did the Son of God die on the Cross? Could He not have avoided that? The answer is, says the Apostle, that God sent Him to the Cross on account of our offences. We who believe in Him know that He has died for our sins, that He was delivered up for our transgressions, for our trespasses.

This is, once more, the great classic doctrine of the atonement. We have already had it in the third chapter in verses 24, 25. 'Being justified freely by His grace through the redemption which is in Christ Jesus, whom God hath set forth to be a propitiation through faith in His blood, to declare His righteousness for the remission of sins that are past, through the forbearance of God.' The Apostle comes back to it again; and any true Christian must always do the same, for it is here that he sees the way in which God has forgiven him and saved him and reconciled him unto Himself. God has delivered up His own Son for our sins. Paul says it again in 2 Corinthians 5: 21, 'He hath made Him to be sin for us, who knew no sin, that we might be made the righteousness of God in Him.' But the prophet Isaiah had already said it; it is there in Isaiah 53: 'God hath laid on Him the iniquity of us all'; 'It pleased the Lord to bruise him.'

'Delivered up for our offences.' What does it mean? That He was delivered up to the punishment that the guilt of our offences deserves. God has taken our offences and put them on Him; and He has punished them in Him. 'Ah but', you may say, 'it was men who crucified Christ.' They were only the instruments. As Peter states in his sermon on the Day of Pentecost, as recorded in Acts 2: 23, though it was done by the cruel hands of men and the rulers of the Jews, it was 'according to the determinate counsel and foreknowledge of God'. It was God who sent Christ to the Cross. That is why our Lord Himself said that He must go there. 'He set His face steadfastly to go to Jerusalem.' Nobody and nothing could dissuade Him. It was the only way. It was God who delivered Him up, laid on Him our sins, and thereby made Him to be sin for us. All those terms mean exactly the same thing. Our Lord volunteered to do this, saying, 'Here am I, send me.' He submitted Himself willingly, voluntarily. There is a sense, therefore, in which we can say that He took our sins upon Himself. But the Apostle here puts it the other way round and emphasizes the other aspect. God laid them upon Him as the Judge Eternal, and dealt with them there once and for ever. This is what the Christian believes, and he does so because it is proclaimed in the resurrection. The Son of God died because it was the way, the only way, to deal with sins. And God has dealt with our sins there. 'God was in Christ reconciling the world unto Himself, not imputing their trespasses unto them.'

The next step is this last one: 'and was raised again for our justification'. What is the meaning of this? You will notice that in the next chapter, in the ninth verse, the Apostle says, 'Much more then, being now justified by His blood'. Is he contradicting himself? Elsewhere we are told that we are justified by the death of

Christ; here we are told that we are justified by the resurrection. Is there a contradiction? Patently there is not. You cannot separate the death and the resurrection. Some people foolishly do so, and even go so far as to say that in Corinth Paul only preached the death of Christ, and did not preach the resurrection. Their argument is that he says, 'I determined not to know anything among you save Jesus Christ and Him crucified'. But that whole Epistle is full of the Resurrection. The Apostle himself reminds them in the fifteenth chapter that he preached the death and the resurrection [1 *Corinthians* 15: 1–4]. Of course! You cannot separate these things, they belong together; but it is helpful to differentiate the various aspects for the sake of intellectual clarity.

The resurrection is the proclamation of the fact that God is fully and completely satisfied with the work that His Son did upon the Cross. You remember how our Lord on the Cross cried, 'It is finished'. He knew that it was finished, and the people heard Him saying 'It is finished'. But He died, and His body was put in a grave; and the people thought that 'it was finished' in another sense. Even some of His followers thought that, and said, 'Ah, it is the end.' 'We trusted that it had been He which should have redeemed Israel [*Luke* 24: 21], the one who was going to deliver us and bring in the Kingdom, but it is finished, He is dead, He is buried'. But He arose from the grave; 'God raised Him from the dead', and in raising Him from the dead God was making a tremendous proclamation. It is that His Son has borne the full punishment of our sins, that He is fully satisfied, that His Law is fully and completely vindicated. If God had not raised Him from the grave we might draw the conclusion that our Lord was not able to bear the punishment of the guilt of our sins, that it was too much for Him, and that His death was the end. But He was raised from the dead; and in raising Him up God was proclaiming that His Son had completed the work, that full expiation has been made, that He is propitiated and completely satisfied. The resurrection declares that, and it is in that sense that He is 'risen again for our justification'. It is there we see it clearly. The work was done on the Cross, but here is the proclamation that it is enough.

[244]

Beyond that, Scripture declares that our Lord, having risen from the dead, and having appeared for forty days to chosen witnesses, ascended into heaven; as it is put in Hebrews 4: 14, 'He has passed through the heavens'. That is a reference to the Old Testament ceremonial. The High Priest once a year entered into the Holiest of all with the blood of the sacrificed animal, to represent the people and to make atonement for their sins. He would sprinkle the blood on the mercy seat. The people were all waiting outside, and the question for them was, 'Is God going to accept this offering, this sacrifice? Will He accept this blood of atonement?' And they would wait and listen. Suddenly they would hear the tinkling of the bells on the hem of the High Priest's robe, and they knew then that he was coming out alive and that all was well, that his offering had been accepted. Christ is our great High Priest. He has entered into heaven, offering His own blood; and there He remains, and the fact that He remains there is a proof that God has fully accepted Him and His offering on our behalf. There 'He ever liveth to make intercession for us'. There He is, ever proclaiming that He has borne the guilt and its punishment. His very presence there makes intercession for us.

But more than that. Having gone in, He has received on our behalf, and as our representative, all the great and rich gifts that God has for His people. Every grace we receive and possess is from Christ. You remember how John puts it in the prologue of his Gospel: 'Of His fullness have all we received and grace for grace.' All the gifts of God for His people are in Christ. He has entered and received them all for us, and we receive them from Him. The resurrection proclaims all this.

This then is the statement that the resurrection makes, it proclaims that Jesus Christ is the Son of God; that He died, and had to die, to make atonement for our sins; that, furthermore, He has risen and taken His seat at the right hand of God the Father in the glory. In raising Him up God is making this great proclamation. It is another way of saying 'that God was in Christ reconciling the world unto himself'. This is God's way of saving us: and this is what the Christian, therefore, believes. He believes that the only way of salvation is the way that God has provided;

that He sent His Son, His only begotten Son, from heaven to earth as Jesus of Nazareth; that He has put Him under the Law; that the Son kept the Law perfectly; that God has laid our sins and our guilt upon Him and has punished it and dealt with it there once and for ever; and that God is fully satisfied.

That is the faith, says the Apostle in effect, about which I am speaking. As Abraham of old believed what God had said to him, you and I must believe this, for this is what God is saying in the resurrection. This is the special, particular Christian faith. This is the thing that makes a man a Christian. Not only belief in God, not merely living a good life and trying to follow Christ. It is to see that your entire salvation is in Jesus Christ, and Him crucified and risen again from the dead, and to believe that, and to trust to that alone. That is what is 'counted to us for righteousness'. Or to use the language that the Apostle uses elsewhere, the Christian believes that God has imputed (reckoned) his sins to Jesus Christ, and that God has also reckoned the righteousness of Jesus Christ to him. Justification is the declaration of God Himself from the throne of glory that all who believe in Christ in this way are freely forgiven, that all their sins are blotted out. More, that He clothes them with the righteousness of Jesus Christ His Son. God has declared in the resurrection that any man who believes in that way in the Lord Jesus Christ is just and righteous in His sight. That is 'justification by faith'. It is legal, it is forensic; it is the declaration of God to us, as we are in our sins, as we have already been told in the fifth verse of this chapter. 'To him that worketh not but believeth on Him that justifieth the ungodly, his faith is counted for righteousness'. The Christian is a man who believes what God tells him in bringing Christ from the dead. He believes that as he looks to, and trusts in Christ only for his salvation, that he stands before God fully and freely forgiven, that in Christ he is righteous, and indeed a child of God.

Let me put it, finally, in a more direct and practical manner. I do this because the Apostle has brought in this case of Abraham; and I bring in the case of Abraham in order to show what all this means in detail and in practice. The faith of Abraham, as we have seen, enabled him to do the following things. He believed the promise of God; he did so solely and entirely on the Word of God; he believed it in spite of everything to the contrary. He was confident and assured of it, being 'fully persuaded that what He had promised He was able also to perform'. He therefore acted on it. Now Christian faith is always like that and must be like that. I have reminded you that there is such a thing as a weak faith and a strong faith, but these elements must be there, otherwise it is not Christian faith at all. So it comes to this – the Christian believer, the Christian man, is a man who rests quietly and assuredly on this Word, this promise of God, as Abraham did of old. To Abraham was made the staggering promise that through his seed the nations of the world should be blessed, and from him should come the Messiah. And he believed it. You and I have got to believe something that is equally staggering, that Christ was delivered for *our* offences, and was raised again for *our* justification. The Christian is a man who rests upon this Word of God that comes to him through the resurrection of Jesus Christ, and all that that includes. It is all there – the incarnation, life, obedience, death, burial, rising again, ascension.

Obviously, the believer is a man who ceases to justify, or to try to justify himself by his works or by anything else. Would you know for certain whether you have justifying faith? Here is the way to find the answer: are you looking in any sense to yourself? Are you in any sense relying even to the slightest extent upon any good you have ever done, or anything you have ever been? Are you even relying upon your own faith? Do you think that it is your belief that saves you? Is it that? Is that your righteousness? If it is, you are not saved, you are not a Christian, because the Christian is a man who looks only and entirely to the righteousness of Jesus Christ. His entire righteousness is in Christ. Christian faith is a faith that looks only to the Lord Jesus Christ and to nothing and to nobody else.

Let me emphasize the matter by putting it like this: the Christian is a man who like Abraham of old believes the Word of God in spite of everything that he knows to be true about himself. Now you remember what we are told about Abraham? 'Being not weak in faith, he considered his own body now dead when he was about an hundred years old, and the deadness of Sarah's womb.' Abraham believed what God said to him in spite of the fact that he knew that he was ninety-nine years old, and in spite of the fact that he knew that Sarah's womb was dead, and that in a natural sense she could not possibly have a child. What is justifying faith? It is the faith that believes what God says in Christ in spite of all I know about myself, my past sins, my present sinfulness, in spite of the fact that I know that I still have an evil nature within me which makes me say with Paul, 'In me, that is, in my flesh, dwelleth no good thing'. Justifying faith is that which enables a man to believe the Word of God in spite of all that, to believe the Word of God in spite of knowing his own weakness, his own proneness to fall, his own proneness to fail – that is justifying faith.

We must always remember this analogy of Abraham. How helpful and encouraging it is! Abraham's faith was a faith that held on to the Word of God, and gave glory to God, in spite of all he knew to be true about himself. Your faith and mine must be the same. It is of no use saying, 'I would indeed like to believe that, but I have been a terrible sinner.' It you say that, and if you bring that 'but' in, you are not a Christian at all. The Christian is a man who says, 'Yes, alas, it is true; I have been vile and horrible and a desperate sinner, yet I believe I stand righteous in the presence of God in Christ.' He can face his past, he can look into himself and see the vileness, the pollution, of sin still remaining, and when the devil says, 'Do you think you have a right to say that you are a Christian?', he says, 'Yes, I do. In spite of the fact that all this is true of me, I know I am righteous in Christ.' He does not look at himself to find justification, he looks entirely out to Christ and all that he is in Christ. He believes this Word about the resurrection, the proclamation of God in raising Christ from the dead. He looks to that in spite of all. If you cannot do that you have not got justifying faith. Faith is this confident protest against every voice that assails us from within and from hell. It stands with Paul in chapter 8 and says, 'Who shall lay anything to the charge of God's elect? It is God that justifieth.' Who is he that condemneth in the light of that? There is no one, there is nothing. It is in spite of what we know about ourselves, of what the Law knows about us, of what hell knows about us. So stop talking about your past sins, stop talking about your present sinfulness. In this matter of justification you must not mention them. You just stand as you are in the righteousness of Jesus Christ, and in Him believe the staggering Word of God about yourself.

That is the final word – Abraham did not stagger at the greatness of the promise. The devil will come to you, and voices within you will say, 'How can I possibly say a thing like that? Look at this life which I am entering as seen in the Sermon on the Mount, the lives of the saints, and the life of Jesus Christ. I am so weak, I am constantly falling – how can I?' You must just say, 'I believe this word of the resurrection, I believe the old word spoken unto Abraham. That man was dead, as it were, physically, and so was Sarah's womb. But God told him that they would have a child. He believed God, and I believe God. I believe that though I am weak and helpless and hopeless and vile and without strength, I believe this God of the resurrection, this God who can "bring to life" the things that are not, "who quickeneth the dead and calleth those things which be not as though they were". I believe He can call into life within me a new man and a new nature and give me strength and power.' That is Christian faith. That is justifying faith. It is faith that enables the believer to dare to believe on the bare word of God, that one day he will be 'faultless and blameless, without spot or wrinkle or any such thing'. Through this faith he can believe 'that he which hath begun a good work in us will perform it until the day of Jesus Christ' [*Philippians* 1: 6], and can stand confidently and defy everybody and everything. Possessing it he no longer fears death and the grave. Indeed, he no longer fears the final judgement because he knows that he has 'passed from judgement into life' in Christ Jesus.

This sounds as if the believer were boasting; but it is extreme humility, because he looks out of himself altogether, and entirely unto the Lord Jesus Christ. It is that faith by which the believer rests upon the word, the proclamation, the declaration of God when He raised Jesus our Lord from the dead. Like Abraham, you must never look at yourself again, and at all that is so true of you. You are justified in spite of all that; it is what God has done in Christ. Look to that, rest on that, be confident in that. Hold up your head with boldness; yea, I say it with reverence, go even into the presence of God with 'holy boldness' and in 'the full assurance of faith'; not boldness in yourself, but in your Mediator, in your great High Priest, in the One whom God raised from the dead in order to let you know that your sins were dealt with at the Cross once and for ever, and that He looks upon you as His dear child.

> *Bold shall I stand in Thy great day;*
> *For who aught to my charge shall lay?*
> *Fully through Thee absolved I am*
> *From sin and fear, from guilt and shame.*

ZINZENDORF
[Translated by John Wesley]

> *The terrors of law and of God*
> *With me can have nothing to do;*
> *My Saviour's obedience and blood*
> *Hide all my transgressions from view.*

TOPLADY

Notes